Camping Alaska

A Comprehensive Guide to the State's Best Campgrounds

Second Edition

Montana Hodges

FALCONGUIDES

ESSEX, CONNECTICUT

FALCONGUIDES®

An imprint of Globe Pequot, the trade division of The Rowman & Littlefield Publishing Group, Inc.
4501 Forbes Blvd., Ste. 200
Lanham, MD 20706
www.rowman.com
Falcon and FalconGuides are registered trademarks and Make Adventure Your Story is a trademark of The Rowman & Littlefield Publishing Group, Inc.

Distributed by NATIONAL BOOK NETWORK

Photos by Montana Hodges
Maps by Trailhead Graphics

British Library Cataloguing in Publication Information available

Library of Congress Cataloging-in-Publication Data available

ISBN 978-1-4930-5479-4 (paper : alk. paper)
ISBN 978-1-4930-5480-0 (electronic)

∞™ The paper used in this publication meets the minimum requirements of American National Standard for Information Sciences—Permanence of Paper for Printed Library Materials, ANSI/NISO Z39.48-1992.

The author and The Rowman & Littlefield Publishing Group, Inc. assume no liability for accidents happening to, or injuries sustained by, readers who engage in the activities described in this book.

Contents

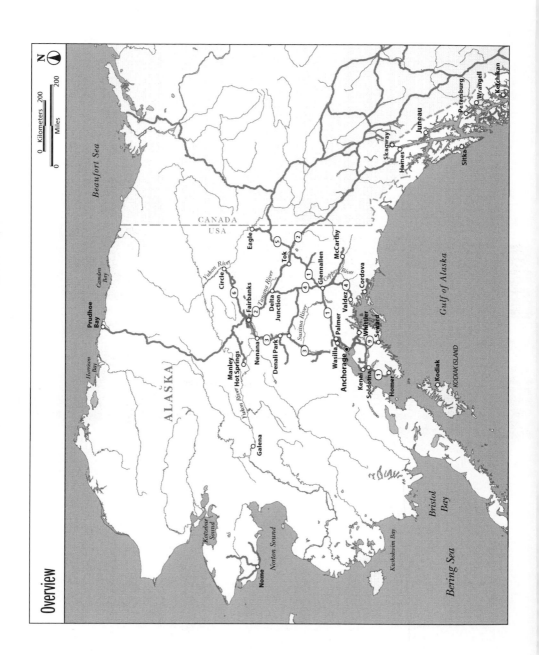

Overview

Acknowledgments

Camping Alaska could not have been completed without the help of the many public and private land managers who took time out of their busy summer schedules to offer advice, information, and enthusiasm for this project. A special thanks to the real heroes of Alaskan camping, the hundreds of camp hosts scattered across the state who personally maintain these amazing campgrounds, many of whom are volunteers.

Introduction

Alaska is a magnet for campers. It is a state so large that it could engulf Texas twice—and then some. The epic proportions of wilderness stretch over 600,000 square miles. It is by far the biggest state, home to fifty mountain ranges, millions of lakes, thousands of islands, the continent's highest mountain and densest population of glaciers, and the nation's largest national park. Of this unsurpassed bounty, less than 1 percent is privately owned.

There is some dispute over when the first humans crossed an ice bridge from Siberia into the far northwestern tip of North America. One thing is for sure—the original Native Americans have thrived in every region of Alaska for more than 10,000 years. Life in this state is rough, the climate can be unforgiving, and the people have to work hard. Despite all this, even the first residents to call Alaska home knew this land was full of greatness. In fact, the name *Alaska* is derived from the Aleut word *Alyeska,* meaning "great land." You don't have to look far within this state to realize the title is well earned.

Getting to Alaska itself is a journey. This forty-ninth state is located outside the contiguous United States or "lower 48" as locals call it. To the east Alaska is bordered by equally remote regions of western Canada. To the south lies the Pacific Ocean. The Alaska Peninsula and Aleutian chain comprise more than 1,000 miles of islands that divide the Pacific from the Bering Sea above. Both the Bering and Chukchi Sea separate Alaska from Russia. The Arctic Ocean finally encloses the package along the cold northern border.

Washington State is the closest US kin to Alaska. Even from Washington it is a 2,000-mile drive or 500-mile ferry ride north just to reach the state line. This has never dissuaded those drawn to Alaska. Much like the campers of today, pioneers have been pulled to this land since the first European contact in the eighteenth century. Some places here have been ruled by five nations under four flags. Many newcomers looked upon this Great Land for opportunities to exploit it. Alaska has experienced fur crazes, epic gold rushes, and recently an oil boom. Combined with fishing and logging, these are still a large part of the economy. Each industry brought, and continues to bring, a new wave of frontiersmen. This led to the state's unofficial slogan, "the Last Frontier."

Some people are drawn to Alaska on a more emotional level. Romantic characterizations of a raw unspoiled land on the cusp of the Last Frontier draw campers in like migratory birds. Many famous naturalists have written about the features that surround the very campgrounds you will visit. They saw unrivaled nature, solitude, and beauty. Luckily, much of Alaska has been protected. National forests, parks, and preserves have been set aside along with state lands to ensure that Alaska remains the Great Land.

It will require research and soul searching to decide where you will take your camping journey within the state. The land, people, and wildlife are diverse. Whether you are a beginner or a grizzled sourdough, there will be a campground to impress you. Alaska is full of new experiences for most people. It is a land with midnight sun, moose wandering business districts, roadside glaciers, bomber-size mosquitoes, and national parks without roads. Air traffic can be diverted due to active volcanoes spurting ashes into the sky. Caribou herds can bottleneck the highways.

There are around 300 campgrounds within the road systems of Alaska from the Arctic Ocean to Kodiak Island, spanning landscapes from temperate rain forests to tundra. These are located throughout dozens of ecosystems, climates, and ranges of wildlife. Still, with the exception of a couple of special blessings in the bush, campgrounds in Alaska are limited to a few ribbons that follow the major highways.

Southeastern Alaska is the closest link to mainland United States and is also known as the Inside Passage or Panhandle. Here hundreds of mountainous islands are woven between the west coast of Canada's British Columbia and the Pacific Ocean. This land is home to flourishing populations of black and brown bears, bald eagles, and sea life including humpback whales. You will find lively small towns and misty fishing ports, mild climate, and a whole lot of rain. Dripping in moss and sprouting mushrooms, much of the nation's largest temperate rain forest is located in Alaska's southeast. Campers can travel here by plane or boat. Many use the Alaska Marine Highway, a state-operated public ferry system, sailing from Washington and Canada to twenty-eight Alaskan ports.

South-central Alaska is home to most of the state's population. Anchorage is Alaska's largest city and hosts excellent museums and trails. South of Anchorage, the Kenai Peninsula is the poster child of Alaskan camping. A third of the state's campgrounds are located on this 170-mile-long stretch of land. On "the Kenai," salmon runs are famous, campgrounds are top-rate, and the tourists are everywhere. If the Kenai is too busy, take the Richardson Highway to the high-alpine campgrounds of Alaska's "Little Switzerland." This beautiful region of jagged peaks and steep canyon waterfalls has glaciers that nearly touch the highway. From there it's not far to the rugged back roads of 13.2-million-acre Wrangell–St. Elias National Park, the largest national park in the country.

In the heart of the state is interior Alaska, a wide-open land of rolling tundra and braided river valleys. Most classic Alaskan big game calls the interior home. Keep an eye out for caribou, moose, grizzly bears, and wolves. In the interior you will also find world-renowned Denali National Park, the breathtaking home to Denali. The mountain is the highest on the continent and tallest base-to-top mountain in the world. Alaska's second largest city, Fairbanks, is also in the interior on the edge of the Arctic gateway.

North of the interior is the land of the never-ending summer sun, arctic creatures, and native villages. The Elliott, Steese, and Dalton Highways all fork off into remote regions of this lunar landscape known as the far north. Camping along these roads is extremely primitive. At one point on the Dalton Highway, there is a 240-mile stretch of gravel road without services. This is the price you pay to cross the Arctic Circle. The several-day trip up the Dalton ends at the eyesore of an industrial oil camp known as Deadhorse. From there it is just a couple of short miles to Prudhoe Bay and the Arctic Ocean, but the road is sealed. You will have to park your valiant vehicle after it has made it this far and book a tour through the oilfields. But don't worry: They allow time for you to jump in the frigid waters and join the "polar bear" club!

All of these roads combined, from the southeast to the Arctic, pass through very little of Alaska. The land beyond the road—or the bush, as you will come to know it—is accessible only by plane, boat, or dogsled. Camping in these areas is for experienced and seasoned backcountry campers only. However, if you would like to get a taste of the bush, book a flight to Nome and rent a car. You can touch the Bering Sea then drive 40 miles into the bush and find the Salmon Lake Campground. This well-maintained surprise is operated by the Bureau of Land Management and has authentic lakeside campsites.

Camping Alaska may lead you in many directions and could be the journey of a lifetime. So pack your tent or RV or throw your backpack in a car or on a plane, and do as all pioneers have done before you in this Great Land—go "North to the Future!"

A hiker surveys the options in Denali National Park.

How to Use This Guide

Camping Alaska is a guide to the public and private campgrounds of the state of Alaska. These roadside campgrounds are accessible by car, RVs, and campers. The campgrounds are divided by highways. Side roads are located in conjunction with corresponding highways. Not every campground in the state was included in this book. Some campgrounds were excluded due to accessibility issues, inadequate supervision, hazards, or primitive facilities.

Understanding the Sites

Campgrounds are organized into sections based on the access highway. Descriptions of each site are given under the following categories.

Location: This is an overview of the general location. Many of the sites are listed by their milepost number. It may seem awkward at first to use mileposts, but eventually you will find this system of directions very effective in travel and well used throughout the state. Campgrounds in this book are divided along highways and listed in sequential order from the beginning of the highway (mile 0) to its end. For example, the Seward Highway runs from the city of Seward (mile 0) north to the city of Anchorage (mile 127). Thus, if a campground is located at mile 23 of the Seward Highway, then it is 23 miles north of Seward. Some campgrounds are grouped by city and don't use milepost numbers.

GPS: Global positioning system coordinates are provided for each campground. These measurements were taken at the entrance to each campground and are accurate to around 30 feet. The GPS unit derives coordinate positions from satellites. These can be listed in degrees, minutes, and seconds, or the more common method of decimal minutes. Units can be adjusted accordingly. Descriptions in this book are written in decimal minutes, also known as simply "GPS." If you need to program your unit to this system, refer to your owner's manual. You do not need a GPS unit to visit or locate any of these campgrounds. Coordinates were included to simply assist you in locating a campground or plotting it on a map.

Season: Mother Nature controls camping in Alaska. Most campgrounds are open from Memorial Day through Labor Day. RV parks may stay open later in the season, but not by much. Public campgrounds open when the snow has melted and they've had a chance to clean up. They close when the snow pushes campers out. To simplify the process, many government agencies use an extra-late opening date (Memorial Day weekend) and an early closure (Labor Day). Sometimes they lock the gates immediately. Other times they may leave them open. Some gates remain open to unofficial camping year-round but are not maintained. Some campgrounds are maintained and open for business all year. Very few campgrounds follow exact and consistent season dates. Private parks are more reliable but still depend on weather. Conditions beyond snowfall can affect the season as well. Inadequate staff, construction, and the vagaries of nature can all be factors. It is important to check with the land manager for the status of a campground before you journey in.

Sites and Maximum length: Campsites are listed as basic, RV, tent, or walk-in tent. Basic sites are suitable for tents or RVs and include a table and fire pit. An RV site is restricted to RVs or campers. "Maximum length" of an RV or camper for each campground is also listed in feet, as is information on utility hookups. Full hookups include at a minimum water, sewer, and electricity. Sites might also have luxuries like cable or satellite television, but those details are not listed. Partial hookups include any one or two of water, electricity, and sewage. RV sites may not include tables and fire pits. Tent sites are any sites that accept tents only and may not have tables or fire pits. Walk-in tent sites that are included are within an established roadside campground a short walk from the parking area (up to 1,000 feet). Backpacking sites are not listed in this book.

Facilities: The list of facilities includes all amenities to date and is subject to change. Campgrounds are constantly upgrading or downsizing their facilities. WiFi is becoming quite popular. Telephones are slowly being removed from campgrounds as cell phone reception improves. If you are interested in a specific amenity, call ahead and double-check its status.

Descriptions of water quality are also included. Most government campgrounds are very efficient at posting signs noting changes in water quality. Unfortunately, this quality changes often. Always be prepared with a water purifier, tablets, or camp stove, even in private campgrounds. Restrooms are categorized as flush, vault, pit, or portable toilets.

Fee per night: Probably nothing at campgrounds varies quite as often as the camp fees. Certain areas, such as the Anchorage vicinity, see prices rise annually. Fees listed in this book are from the 2021 season. Exact prices are not given. The system is designed to relay a price range for each campground. Many factors could increase the cost of your stay. Extra fees are sometimes imposed for large groups, multiple vehicles, pets, and extra amenities. The fees listed here are for a single campsite for a single night and a single vehicle with up to two people.

The price range is as follows:

$	=	Less than $20
$$	=	$20-30
$$$	=	$31-40
$$$$	=	$41-50
$$$$$	=	$51 and higher

Maximum stay and reservations: Most government campgrounds have a maximum stay. This can range from as little as twenty-four hours to as much as thirty days. Maximum stays may change with the season. Luckily, many campsites in Alaska can be reserved. Check the amenities chart at the beginning of each chapter to find out if a particular campground accepts reservations.

Management: Campgrounds are either public or private—and there's a big difference between the two. Public campgrounds are open to the public but still subject to rules. They are managed by a variety of government bureaus. Sometimes the maintenance of public campgrounds is contracted to private companies. Campgrounds do not always have a host. Most often the hosts at public campgrounds are volunteers. These gracious people receive very little money for their time and volunteer their time for the love of the outdoors. So stop by, say hello, and thank these lovely folks.

Private campgrounds, particularly in Alaska, are often run by the owner or by hosts who live on site. The rules and regulations can vary greatly since this is private property. Private campgrounds often don't like it when you roll in at midnight or just show up early Sunday morning. Especially for the smaller operations, you will want to call in advance and check with the managers as to the appropriate etiquette on the property. Never trespass behind closed gates or assume it is acceptable to enter the grounds and start setting up camp without checking in with someone first.

Many public campgrounds are hosted by volunteers.

Contact information is given for each campground. This crucial section is essential to your journey. Whenever possible, the telephone number and website have been listed for each campground. Often the appropriate contact is not physically at the campground. Always contact them in advance.

Finding the campground: Directions to each campground are given to use in conjunction with maps. If a campground is located within a few miles of a city or town, written descriptions are given in relation to the city; otherwise they refer to the access milepost number (for more on mileposts in Alaska, refer to "Location").

About the campground: The conditions of each campground are highly subject to change. Brief descriptions of the area, geography, aesthetics, and activities are also included. This is a rough overview of the campground and does not include all features or activities.

Camping Alaska Amenities Charts

Key:

N	=	None
Y	=	Yes
F	=	Flush toilets (Toilets)
NF	=	Non-flushing toilets (Toilets)
H	=	Hiking (Recreation)
F	=	Fishing (Recreation)
C	=	Cycling (Recreation)
S	=	Swimming (Recreation)
BL	=	Boat launch (Recreation)
W	=	Water (Hookups)
E	=	Electric (Hookups)
S	=	Sewer (Hookups)
C	=	Cable (Hookups)
T	=	Tent sites only (Max RV Length)

All RV lengths are in feet.

"Total Sites" with a plus (+) means more open camping. For example, "50+" means that there are 50 official campsites and an open area for tents, overflow, et cetera.

Planning Your Trip

Where to go: Given Alaska's limited amenities and remote roads, researching your destinations in advance is mandatory. Alaska may fit on a standard map, but you'll have to pay attention to the scale. It is not physically possible to see every site in Alaska in one vacation, so review your options. On the plus side, there aren't a lot of roads here, so your choices within regions are simplified. Focus on the areas you would like to visit and research the details. Take into account the specific features you're looking for at a campground—restroom facilities, potable water, or views, for instance. Certain areas are more developed. The Kenai Peninsula is one of the most traveled regions, with plenty of rest stops and well-developed campgrounds. More remote areas, such as Prince of Wales Island and the Dalton Highway, are more difficult and time consuming to access and have fewer modern amenities. Whatever direction you take your journey, always do your research ahead of time—and try not to get overwhelmed by the size of Alaska. Stop and smell the wild roses.

Although some campgrounds may leave their gates open for campers in fall, the sites are often not maintained in the off-season.

When to go: All regions have their merits and challenges. Climate varies from warm, dry days and nights of never-ending sun to wet misty rain forest. Camping seasons, however, are relatively similar across the state.

Conditions are also unpredictable. It could be a beautiful sunny day in the southeast in May and a cold wet day in Fairbanks in July. So relying on anything you've heard about the climate of a region is, well, unreliable. Take into account the things you would like to see. Salmon runs, festivals, holidays, geologic features, fall colors, ferry schedules, airline ticket prices, and campground season dates can all influence your decision. Most campgrounds are open June through August, which is the warmest time of the year for Alaska. It's also the most crowded.

What to Bring

Cell phones in Alaska: You will probably be surprised at how well your cell phone works in Alaska. At the Riley Creek Campground in Denali National Park, many phones can pick up full reception. Most places without physical phone lines rely on mobile numbers. Check with your provider before you leave home to ensure that Alaska is included in your plan and that your phone will work within the state. Public phones are slowly disappearing from campgrounds. Be prepared anyway; for every spot that you can pick up a signal, there are hundreds of miles of road where you cannot.

Water: Water quality and availability could change at any time. Carry a purifier, tablets, or a camp stove as a backup plan. If you are traveling by RV or car, take a few gallons along for the ride. Often stores close early or take Sundays off, so don't rely on being able to buy water, especially in smaller towns. Always have your backup ready and never assume that a natural body of water is safe for drinking. The waters may look like the cleanest you've ever seen, but even Alaska has *Giardia lamblia*.

Mosquito repellent and head net: It's an alien! It's a beekeeper! No, it's just a camper in a head net! Comedy aside, the simple gesture of packing a head net can be the key to ensuring an enjoyable time in outdoor Alaska. Don't worry—you won't be the only one. Everyone has heard of the state's bomber-size mosquitoes, and they are a force to be reckoned with. Pack your bug spray and some bite gel to soothe your stings. Keep these with you at any time during the season. It would be a shame to let pesky insects drive you indoors.

Clothing: In a land with such unpredictable and quickly changing weather, layers are the way to go. Backpackers will already be familiar with layering principles. Layering allows you to be prepared for all sorts of weather and keeps things lightweight. Synthetic fibers are a must. Cotton does not insulate. For your base layer, choose a long-sleeved synthetic shirt and pants. On top of this you can add a fleece and a warm vest. The outer layer should be a waterproof shell. If the weather is chilly, you can always add thermals under your base, along with gloves and a hat. Bring both a warm waterproof hat and a sun hat. Don't forget sunblock and lip balm.

Secure footwear is best for campgrounds. Wandering around the wilderness with open toes could cause any number of problems—not to mention how happy the mosquitoes will be to see your toes. Depending on your activity, you may want hiking boots, running shoes, or something in between. And make sure that those shoes are waterproof. You can choose a sealed leather boot or one lined in a waterproof breathable material (such as Gore-Tex). Many visitors to the wetter areas will carry rubber rain boots (the preferred footwear of locals and fishermen within the state). Always be prepared for wet ground. And that brings me to a crucial topic—bring plenty of socks. Wool socks are best, because they still insulate even if they get wet.

Survival gear: Unless you're on foot, you cannot carry too much stuff in Alaska. Bring the essential survival gear. Pack a water purifier, compass, emergency blanket, pocketknife, waterproof matches, stove, first-aid kit, and safety whistle. If you are traveling by car, a full-size spare should be mandatory, along with flares, a gas can, and a shovel. If you are traveling the Dalton Highway or other remote roads, two full-size spares are recommended. Above all, do not forget your maps.

Maps: Rough maps are included in this book. These maps are meant to serve as an overview of campground locations. You will need to purchase more specific ones for each area you visit. You can purchase maps from the Forest Service, state parks, or Bureau of Land Management. If you are in Anchorage, you can purchase maps at the US Geological Survey office on University Avenue.

Safety

Wildlife: Alaska is home to both black and brown bears, and it's almost certain that you'll come into sight of one. Many of these bears are acclimated to human interaction, especially around fishing holes. Bear attacks are rare, and fatal bear attacks are especially rare. In the history of Denali National Park, there has never been a fatal bear attack.

Bears are curious creatures; they are attracted to odors, especially of food. Eliminate odors as much as possible. Bears also don't like surprises. Exercise caution and common sense. Most encounters can be avoided with the proper precautions. Always make your presence known, and never put yourself in a position where you could surprise a bear. Make lots of noise. Use your voice, probably the most effective bear repellent out there. The saying "Hey bear" must be chanted thousands of times a day in Alaska as hikers slither through the bush. Use it!

People often seem comfortable walking within a few yards of a moose to snap a photo, but this is extremely dangerous. Moose, especially cows with calves, are known to charge. Encounters with these big-legged stampeders can be fatal. Never approach a moose. If you come across one on a trail or at a campground, give way to the beast and change your course.

The biggest threat between wildlife and humans is the threat to wildlife by humans. Remember that the animals you come across are working for their survival. Do not interfere with what they are doing or distract them when taking photos. Do not stalk them. Think about purchasing a telephoto lens before you travel to Alaska if you'd like to catch wildlife up close and personal. Probably the biggest wildlife hazard to humans is the possibility of a caribou or moose crossing a highway, or plain old mosquitoes driving you crazy. So pack bug spray, practice your call of "Hey bear," and watch out for moose crossings.

Daylight: There is a common misconception among travelers to Alaska that during summer, they will be experiencing twenty-four hours of daylight wherever they are within the state. This is entirely possible if you are driving above the Arctic Circle (some campers do!). Most people will not travel farther north than Fairbanks. The amount of daylight you will have depends on what latitude you are at. (Latitudes are the fictional lines we use to measure our distance on Earth either north or south from the equator.) The amount of daylight increases with the latitude as you move north. The Summer Solstice is on June 21, which is the longest day of the year. At this time Fairbanks experiences more than twenty-two hours with the sun above the horizon. Anchorage averages nineteen hours of daylight during summer (and less than six in winter!). When the daylight does fade, the night skies are not dark—more

A bear cub takes a break on a fish pass.

like twilight. The farther south you go, the darker the night will be. In southeastern Alaska it will be fully dark for a brief time at night. During summer it does not get dark enough to view the aurora borealis (northern lights), and often not even a star. Spring and fall campers may be able to view the aurora, however.

Campers, especially tenters, are susceptible to the effects of extended daylight. Even seasoned Alaskans keep a late schedule in summer. You will find that most people lose sleep during this time. Businesses have extended hours to accommodate the liveliness of summer nights. Fishermen cast lines into the wee hours of the morning, and Fairbanks has Midnight Baseball. Insomnia can be common. Sometimes it's hard to tell how late it is when you're rolling in to set up camp; just remember that others may not be so susceptible to the light and would like to sleep in peace. Mind the quiet hours. Wherever you go, wear a watch and keep track of the time. You may

Alaskans really do play sports at midnight, including the famous game of Midnight Baseball held on the longest day of the year in Fairbanks.

not feel tired, but if you have been driving for eight hours it's time to stop and let your body rest.

Road conditions: Many Alaskans will tell you there are two seasons in Alaska: winter and construction. With only a few short weeks of summer, crews scramble to make road improvements. They often work twenty-four hours a day. Drive cautiously near roadwork signs; whatever the hour, odds are someone is out there working hard.

Checking in with land managers: It is crucial to check in with a land manager as to the status of each campground and all facilities before you visit.

Hypothermia: It is entirely possible to get hypothermia during an Alaskan summer. Most often this is a result of wet clothing. Car campers shouldn't have as much a challenge in staying dry and warm as backpackers. The most important thing to remember is that it can rain anywhere in Alaska, even if there was beautiful weather a few minutes before. Weather patterns can move very quickly across the state, and hypothermia can occur when it is not "freezing" out. Refer to "Clothing" for details on layering. A waterproof shell (for you and your tent) is essential.

Zero Impact

Probably the most valuable thing for humans and nature is observing a zero-impact backcountry ethic. Exercise these simple rules and you'll get along fine in any campground in Alaska. The following is a simplified version pertaining to campgrounds.

Plan ahead and prepare: Research your campground and its regulations. Purchase the maps, permits, and supplies you need for each campground. In case of emergency, pack survival gear (for details, refer to "What to Bring").

Minimize impact: Camp within the designated camping areas on durable surfaces. Use the established sites and do not stray out of established tent pads and parking spaces. The same goes for footpaths or hiking trails. Even if a footpath is wet or muddy, walk through it. Stepping off the trail damages the surrounding vegetation and widens your impact. Use the designated fire pits. If the area is open to fires, use a pit that has already been established. Collect dead wood and keep your fire small.

Dispose of your waste: Dispose of all your trash properly. If there are no garbage cans at the campground, pack out your waste with you. The same goes for any garbage you may have found left by others. Bring sealed containers and bags for packing all materials out. Never leave behind or bury anything. Do not put garbage in vault toilets. Remove all unburned materials from your fire ring.

Leave what you find: Collecting materials of any kind at most campgrounds is illegal. Always check the regulations before you collect firewood.

Respect wildlife: Never disturb or inhibit an animal you encounter. Observe these creatures from a distance; do not stalk them for photos. Do not interfere with their activities. *Never* feed the animals.

Respect neighbors: Keep your camp quiet. Given the lengthy days, it can be difficult in Alaska to mind quiet hours. The best way to handle this is to always keep things quiet. Keep your voices low and leave stereos at home. Enjoy the soft sounds of nature and minimize the effect of your presence.

Food storage: Bears dictate food storage. Knowing how to properly store your food is essential in Alaska. Never leave food or an ice chest out in the open at a campground. Flavored drinks, food wrappers, cookware, utensils, and garbage should all be sealed away immediately after the meal is over. If you are without a vehicle, be sure to use a bear-proof container and store it accordingly.

Map Legend

State Highway	———————①———————
Other Road	———————————————
Four–Wheel–Drive Road	= = = = = = = = = = = = =
Railroad	+–+–+–+–+–+–+–+–+–+–+–+
Trail	– – – – – – – – – – –
Point of Interest	▪
Small State Park, Wilderness, or Natural Area	▲
Pass	) (
Mountain, Peak, or Butte	▲ *Mount Alice*
River, Stream, or Creek	∼∼∼∼∼∼∼
Reservoir or Lake	
Glacier	
Waterfall	≈
International Boundary	CANADA
State/Province Boundary	BRITISH COLUMBIA
National Park, National Forest, Large State Park, or Other Federal Area	

The Kenai Peninsula

Impressively developed for being wild, and impressively wild for being developed, the Kenai Peninsula is often referred to as Alaska's playground. Perhaps there is no more suitable title for this camper's paradise. On "the Kenai" you'll find world-renowned outdoor opportunities, top-rate amenities, clean public rest stops, and warm roadhouse meals. The easily traveled peninsula is home to grizzly bears and glacier-side campgrounds, not to mention paved roads and hot showers.

Located just half an hour's drive south of Anchorage, connected by a thin isthmus, the 150-mile-long and 70-mile-wide Kenai Peninsula is otherwise surrounded by water. To the north Turnagain Arm separates the Kenai from Anchorage and Girdwood. To the west the Cook Inlet divides it from the Aleutian Range. The Gulf of Alaska surrounds the south and east portions. Along with hundreds of miles of seashore, the peninsula supports impressive peaks. The Kenai Mountains stretch as far south as Seldovia and up to the northern end of the peninsula.

From the sea to the mountains and back to the sea again—wherever you cross the Kenai, the landscape is diverse. Many travelers find their classic desired Alaskan scenery here, from glacial cruises past icebergs to high mountains and tundra. From salmon streams through marshes to turbulent beaches, the Kenai is home to just about every Alaskan ecosystem. Even better for the outdoor adventurer, the weather on the Kenai is mild; the southern longitude combines with moderating ocean winds to create a temperate environment and Alaska's well-known year-round gem.

The diversity of land leads to a diversity of habitats and habitants. Marshlands provide homes to scores of migrant birds, seals rest on the ice, goats seek sanctity in the high peaks, brown bears eat berries on mountain tundra, fish and fishermen work the streams together. Whether you're out to spy a moose or a sea otter, whales or bald eagles, the wildlife of the Kenai, like much of Alaska, offers a great deal of possibilities. During a few months of the year, though, one particular wildlife opportunity seems

◀ *There are many towering spruce trees in Southeast Alaska.*

to overshadow all others. World-class fishing, particularly for salmon, draws a strong influx of travelers to the Kenai, and campgrounds become crowded. Whether you're viewing the wildlife or the people (although they may often seem synonymous), keep the binoculars handy.

The eastern portion of the Kenai is mountainous. The dramatic drive down the Seward Highway crests over high mountain passes and dips down into glacial valleys and bays. The road to Portage offers access to stunning Glacier Bay National Park. Many continue the drive into Whittier through the longest tunnel in North America, a one-lane 2.5-mile thrill ride down slippery train tracks under a grand mountain. Back on the Seward Highway, the road continues south, passing the entrance to Kenai Fjords National Park, humbling Exit Glacier, and the rest of the Harding Icefields. This highway ends at Seward Municipal Campgrounds. Here you can nestle up both your camp and fishing pole to Resurrection Bay while watching boats and cruise ships sail by.

The Sterling Highway leads to the west coast, passing through the heart of the Kenai Mountains, and the unforgettable aqua hues of the glacial meltwaters of Kenai Lake and River. Record salmon nearing a hundred pounds are snagged on the Kenai River, the epicenter of Alaskan angling. The shoulder-to-shoulder combat fishing of the Kenai and Russian River confluence is a classic Alaskan scene.

The northern edge of the Pacific Ring of Fire meets the west coast of the Kenai across the Cook Inlet from the Aleutian Range. Active volcanoes occasionally spurt ashes toward the Kenai. Even when the mountains are sleeping, the snowcapped beauty of the peaks never disappoints an onlooker. There are four active volcanoes visible with the naked eye from the Sterling Highway. As the Sterling follows the coast south, eagles become the "Alaskan seagulls," easily viewable on beaches, circling clammers and anglers. The Sterling Highway ends in the fabulously cultured city of Homer, home to famous halibut fishing and water taxis to Kachemak Bay State Park. Where the road ends, the camping stories begin. Once a less regulated base camp for fishermen, camping on the Homer Spit is legendary. Wherever you end up on this Alaskan playground, you will be surrounded by adventuresome choices, and choice campgrounds.

◀ *Makenna White and her father, Kelly White, display a day's catch from the Russian River Ferry during the mid-July salmon run.*

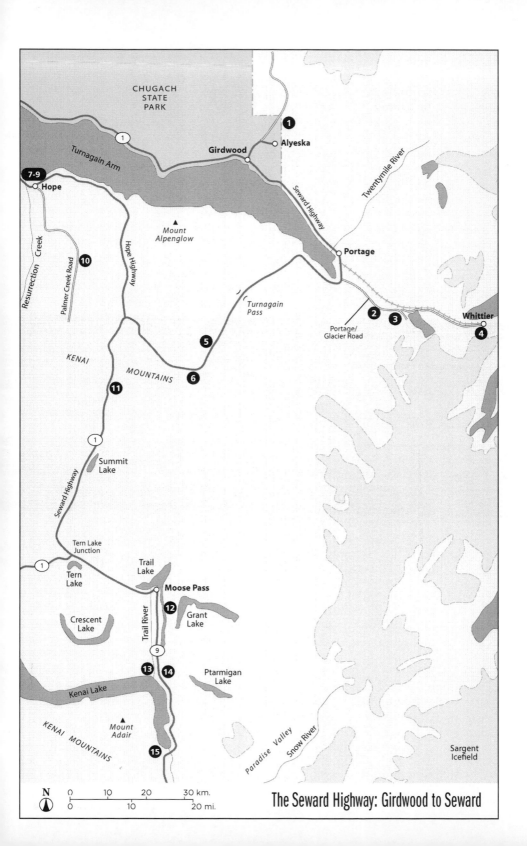

CHUGACH
STATE
PARK

①

Turnagain Arm

① Girdwood
Alyeska

⑦-⑨
Hope

Seward Highway

Twentymile River

Resurrection Creek

Palmer Creek Road

⑩

Hope Highway

Mount
Alpenglow

Portage

KENAI

Turnagain
Pass

Portage/
Glacier Road

② ③

Whittier

④

⑤

MOUNTAINS

⑥

⑪

① Seward Highway

Summit
Lake

Tern Lake
Junction

Trail
Lake

① Tern
Lake

Moose Pass

⑫

Crescent
Lake

Trail River

Grant
Lake

⑨

⑬ ⑭

Ptarmigan
Lake

Kenai Lake

KENAI MOUNTAINS

Mount
Adair

⑮

Paradise Valley

Snow River

Sargent
Icefield

N

0   10   20   30 km.

0   10   20 mi.

The Seward Highway: Girdwood to Seward

The Seward Highway: Girdwood to Seward

The Seward Highway: Girdwood to Seward	Hookup Sites	Total Sites	Max. RV Length	Hookups	Toilets	Showers	Drinking Water	Fires	Dump Station	Recreation	Fee	Reservations
1 Crow Creek Mine	0	20	Any	N	NF	N	N	Y	N/A	N	$$-$$$	N
2 Black Bear Campground	0	12	25	N	NF	N	Y	Y	N	H	$	N
3 Williwaw Campground	0	60	Any	N	NF	N	Y	Y	N	HF	$	Y
4 Whittier Creekside Campground	0	35	Any	N	NF	N	Y	Y	N	N	$-$$	N
5 Bertha Creek Campground	0	12	30	N	NF	N	Y	Y	N	HF	$	N
6 Granite Creek Campground	0	19	30	N	NF	N	Y	Y	N	F	$	Y
7 Coldwater Lodge	13	20+	40	WES	F	Y	Y	Y	Y	N	$-$$$$	Y
8 Seaview Cafe	17	23+	Any	E	NF	N	Y	Y	N	F	$-$$$	Y
9 Porcupine Campground	0	24	30	N	NF	N	Y	Y	N	HF	$	N
10 Coeur D'Alene Campground	0	6	T	N	NF	N	N	Y	N	H	Free	N
11 Tenderfoot Creek Campground	0	27	35	N	NF	N	Y	Y	N	FBL	$	N
12 Moose Pass RV Park	15	30	35	E	NF	N	N	Y	N		$$	N
13 Trail River Campground	0	91	Any	N	NF	N	Y	Y	N	F	$	Y
14 Ptarmigan Creek Campground	0	16	35	N	NF	N	Y	Y	N	HF	$	Y
15 Primrose Landing Campground	0	10	25	N	N	N	Y	Y	N	HFBL	$	N

1 Crow Creek Mine

Location: In Girdwood
GPS: N 60° 59.970' / W 149° 04.999'
Season: Mid-May through mid-September
Sites: 20 primitive sites
Maximum length: Any
Facilities: Some fire rings and tables, portable toilets
Fee per night: $$-$$$
Maximum stay: None
Management: Crow Creek Mine, (907) 229-3105, www.crowcreekgoldmine.com

Finding the campground: From mile 90 of the Seward Highway, turn north onto Alyeska Road. Drive 1.9 miles and turn left onto Crow Creek Road—the road with possibly the most potholes in Alaska. Drive 3.1 miles and turn right at the sign for the Crow Creek Mine. The camping area is on your left just before the mine.

About the campground: The Crow Creek Mine began operation in 1898 and not much has changed since then. Original buildings and mining equipment still dot the grounds, and the dedicated owners do a good job keeping things authentic here, complete with roaming chickens.

Today locals and tourists alike come to try their luck at gold panning (tools supplied). With gold still to be found in Crow Creek, who knows if you'll go home with the next nugget! The camping is in a circular gravel parking lot under the forest canopy. Your money gets you a parking spot for your tent or rig and a place for an open fire. The grounds are primitive, but the area is the closest official campground to downtown Girdwood, home of the Alyeska Resort.

2 Black Bear Campground

Location: Near mile 78 of the Seward Highway
GPS: N 60° 47.336' / W 148° 53.350'
Season: Mid-May through September
Sites: 12 basic sites
Maximum length: 25 feet
Facilities: Tables, fire pits, potable water, vault toilets, hiking access
Fee per night: $
Maximum stay: 14 days
Management: USDA Forest Service, Chugach National Forest, Glacier Ranger District, (907) 783-3242, www.fs.fed.us/r10/chugach
Finding the campground: From mile 78.9 of the Seward Highway, drive east on Portage Glacier Road for 3.6 miles to the campground on your right.
About the campground: This rugged campground isn't as manicured as nearby Williwaw, and also doesn't take reservations. The sites are only a couple of dollars less than those at Williwaw and are designed more with the tenter in mind. Each campsite is well separated from neighbors, with additional privacy from dividing brush and thick shady spruce—which unfortunately masks views of the surrounding mountains. The sites include the same nearly new facilities, and the standard table and fire pit, but with a little less traffic. Nearby Portage Creek is popular with rafters.

3 Williwaw Campground

Location: Near mile 78 of the Seward Highway
GPS: N 60° 47.168' / W 148° 52.537'
Season: Mid-May through late September
Sites: 60 basic sites
Maximum length: Any
Facilities: Tables, fire pits, potable water, vault toilets, hiking/fishing/river access

Fee per night: $

Maximum stay: 14 days

Management: USDA Forest Service, Chugach National Forest, Glacier Ranger District, (907) 783-3242, www.fs.fed.us/r10/chugach; reservations at www.recreation.gov, (877) 444-6777

Finding the campground: From mile 78.9 of the Seward Highway, drive east on Portage Glacier Road for 4.1 miles to the campground on your right.

About the campground: This star of a public campground is a favorite for many visitors along Portage Glacier Road. Located on wooded grounds, nestled between lengthy mountain and glacier views, the spacious campsites and clean facilities support Williwaw's reputation. The sites are nestled off a wide paved road, well developed, and separated by thick brush, offering a feeling of privacy that does not interfere with the towering views. Several of the sites are pull-thru-style and can hold larger rigs. Popular area activities include fishing Williwaw ponds or visiting the fish-viewing platform, where from late July through early September salmon can be seen traveling up the creek to spawn. The campground gets very busy during the season, and reservations are accepted. This is also the last campground in the Glacier Ranger District to lock its gates in September, so if you're traveling late in the season, check out Williwaw.

4 Whittier Creekside Campground

Location: In Whittier

GPS: N 60° 46.303' / W 148° 41.348'

Season: May through mid-October

Sites: 50 basic sites

Maximum length: Any

Facilities: Tables, some fire rings, covered picnic area, portable toilets, playground

Fee per night: $–$$

Maximum stay: None

Management: Whittier Parking and Camping, (907) 472-2670

Finding the campground: As you enter town after the tunnel, turn right onto Whittier Street. Cross the Whittier Creek Bridge and the railroad tracks (watch for trains); drive 0.1 mile and turn right at the sign for the campground.

About the campground: Whittier was named for a poet, and poetry seems easily inspired with one look around the area. However, the Whittier Creekside Campground resembles something of an industrial parking lot. The towering mountainsides, rushing waterfalls, and a misty ocean port offer scenery to compensate for what the development lacks. You'll have to look beyond the portable toilets, rocky road, dumpsters, parked heavy machinery, and potholes of this campground. All sites are side-by-side back-ins, some with tables and fire pits. The creekside sites are an excellent choice; some have mountain, creek, and harbor views. For a more basic option, the City of Whittier also offers a place to pitch a tent or park in the gravel parking lot down by the water.

5 Bertha Creek Campground

Location: Near mile 65 of the Seward Highway
GPS: N 60° 45.075' / W 149° 15.251'
Season: Mid-May through September
Sites: 12 basic sites
Maximum length: 30 feet
Facilities: Tables, fire pits, potable water, vault toilets
Fee per night: $
Maximum stay: 14 days
Management: USDA Forest Service, Chugach National Forest, Glacier Ranger District, (907) 783-3242, www.fs.fed.us/r10/chugach
Finding the campground: This campground is located on the west side of the Seward Highway at mile 65.4.
About the campground: Located at a fairly high elevation on Turnagain Pass, this small campground can get chilly even during the warmest months; luckily, free firewood is often provided. The campsites sit off a gravel loop, surrounded by cottonwoods, providing both shade and the sweet sound of quaking leaves in the often breezy grounds. Surprisingly, the sound of Bertha Creek is more prominent than the sound of the highway for some sites. This campground tends to be low-key, as it is lacking a major component—fishing in this area is nonexistent. This can sometimes be a relief for the weary camper. Unless a rafting party is on the grounds preparing to float nearby Sixmile Creek, Bertha Creek is rather quiet. Keep an eye out for mountain goats in the high-mountain backdrop.

6 Granite Creek Campground

Location: Near mile 62 of the Seward Highway
GPS: N 60° 43.266' / W 149° 17.634'
Season: Mid-May through September
Sites: 19 basic sites
Maximum length: 30 feet
Facilities: Tables, fire pits, potable water, vault toilets, fishing access
Fee per night: $
Maximum stay: 14 days
Management: USDA Forest Service, Chugach National Forest, Glacier Ranger District, (907) 783-3242, www.fs.fed.us/r10/chugach; reservations at www.recreation.gov, (877) 444-6777
Finding the campground: From mile 62.9 of the Seward Highway, turn south at the sign for Granite Creek Campground and drive 0.2 mile.
About the campground: Similar to Bertha Creek Campground, this spacious campground is directly off the blazing Seward Highway. There are nineteen well-spaced basic sites within a shaded stand of spruce trees. Some crisp and cool sites are right next to the rushing creek. There isn't a lot of fishing in the area, but whitewater rafting of Sixmile Creek beckons some. Elevation is still relatively high, so bring the cool-weather bag. Backpackers will be happy to find bear lockers.

7 Coldwater Lodge

Location: In Hope
GPS: N 60° 55.160' / W 149° 37.188'
Season: May through September
Sites: 13 full-hookup RV sites, open tent camping
Maximum length: 40 feet
Facilities: Communal picnic table and fire pit, showers, laundry, WiFi, small store
Fee per night: $–$$$$
Maximum stay: None
Management: Coldwater Lodge, (907) 782-3223, creekbendco.com
Finding the campground: From mile 56.7 of the Seward Highway, take the Hope Highway 16 miles northwest and look for this campground on the north side of the road at 19742 Hope Highway.
About the campground: The Coldwater Lodge RV park is also part of the Creekbend Café. Along with the small campground, the property has well priced cabins, a café, store, laundry and showers. They have live music every weekend and gather quite a following of return guests.

8 Seaview Cafe

Location: In Hope
GPS: N 60° 55.233' / W 149° 38.656'
Season: Mid-May through mid-September
Sites: 17 partial-hookup RV sites, 6 dry RV sites, open tent camping
Maximum length: Any
Facilities: Communal fire pits, potable water, portable toilets, fishing/river access, cafe
Fee per night: $–$$$
Maximum stay: None
Management: Seaview Cafe, Bar and RV Park, (907) 782-3300, seaviewcafealaska.com
Finding the campground: From mile 56.7 of the Seward Highway, take the Hope Highway northwest for 16.9 miles and follow the signs toward Main Street/Old Town Hope. Turn left onto Main Street and drive 0.1 mile to the Seaview Café, Bar and RV Park.
About the campground: Resurrection Creek meets Turnagain Arm in front of the Seaview Cafe, and the camping area buddies up to all the action. During summer the grounds fill regularly on weekends and during salmon runs. In mid-July a run of pink salmon comes through Resurrection Creek and anglers take advantage of the direct fishing access, making the otherwise sleepy Seaview busy. Camping is in a very basic open lot with eight pull-thrus and an open area on the creek for tent camping. True to its name, there are uninterrupted views from the shore of Turnagain Arm, unless you count your neighbors in the open lot. Although it may look like a ghost town, the Seaview Cafe is often a lively joint. A weekend bluegrass show at this roadhouse-on-the-sea is a real treat. The Seaview has been around since the original gold rush, relics and antiques decorate the walls, and many regulars are reminiscent of times past as well.

9 Porcupine Campground

Location: In Hope
GPS: N 60° 55.794' / W 149° 39.692'
Season: Mid-May through September
Sites: 34 basic sites
Maximum length: 30 feet
Facilities: Tables, fire pits, potable water, vault toilets, hiking/fishing access
Fee per night: $
Maximum stay: 14 days
Management: USDA Forest Service, Seward Ranger District, (907) 224-3374, www.fs.fed.us/r10/chugach; reservations at www.recreation.gov, (877) 444-6777
Finding the campground: From mile 56.7 of the Seward Highway, take the Hope Highway northwest to its dead end at mile 18.
About the campground: Turnagain Arm never fails to impress the eyes, and this popular campground nudges the scenic shores. Only a couple of campsites directly overlook the water, but several day-use sites are waterside as well. Camping is located off a paved loop; the lower sites are separated by birch with views of the water and the Chugach Range. The upper sites are located in an impressive cottonwood forest and are sheltered from the waterfront wind. Accommodating hosts can send you to nearby gold panning areas and trails. From the campground, the Hope Point and Gull Rock trails lead to overlooks; both are 5-mile hikes. This is the nicest campground in Hope; even for RVers, sacrificing the hookups for a fire overlooking Turnagain Arm can be a real opportunity to enjoy powerful views.

10 Coeur D'Alene Campground

Location: About 9 miles southeast of Hope
GPS: N 60° 50.989' / W 149° 32.036'
Season: Mid-June through September
Sites: 6 tent sites
Maximum length: N/A
Facilities: Some tables, fire pits, pit toilets
Fee per night: Free
Maximum stay: 14 days
Management: USDA Forest Service, Seward Ranger District, (907) 224-3374, www.fs.fed.us/r10/chugach
Finding the campground: From mile 56.7 of the Seward Highway, take the Hope Highway northwest for 16 miles and turn south onto Palmer Creek Road. Drive 0.5 mile to a Y in the road and stay left, following the sign to the Coeur D'Alene Campground. Continue for 6.8 miles up a winding, narrow gravel road to the campground on your left. Due to avalanches, this road is often closed until mid-June, creating a short camping season.
About the campground: If you're looking for the off-the-beaten path of the already less traveled road, the Coeur D'Alene is for you. This primitive alpine valley campground has six walk-in tent

sites, some located directly on the creek. All are within earshot of your neighbor. Palmer Creek Road is a rough road, and this campground offers the same rugged charm for hikers and gold prospectors. The facilities are not so well maintained. A dark pit toilet is reminiscent of the time before the now standard airy vault. This campground is popular for that reason, leaving behind the punctilious manner of hosted grounds to offer good old-fashioned free tent camping, true to the Alaskan spirit of little regulation.

11   Tenderfoot Creek Campground

Location: Near mile 46 of the Seward Highway
GPS: N 60° 38.214' / W 149° 29.833'
Season: Mid-May through September
Sites: 35 basic sites
Maximum length: 35 feet
Facilities: Tables, fire pits, potable water, vault toilets, fishing/lake access, boat launch
Fee per night: $
Maximum stay: 14 days
Management: USDA Forest Service, Seward Ranger District, (907) 224-3374, www.fs.fed.us/r10/ chugach; reservations at www.recreation.gov, (877) 444-6777
Finding the campground: From mile 46 of the Seward Highway just north of the Summit Lake Lodge and south of Colorado Creek, drive east onto the gravel road at the sign for Tenderfoot Creek Campground. The road dead-ends into the campground entrance 0.5 mile down the road.
About the campground: Wedged among a mountain base, Summit Lake, and a small creek, this campground has a comely atmosphere that balances out its location near the highway. Tenderfoot Creek has twenty-seven well-dispersed sites, all with a fire pit and table, several of which are pull-thrus. Many sites are located lakefront or creekside, and slightly shaded by spruce. Fish and Game keeps Summit Lake stocked with Dolly Varden, and the boat launch offers easy access. This campground has the potential to fill all season, so reservations are recommended.

12   Moose Pass RV Park

Location: Mile 29 of the Seward Highway
GPS: 60° 29.174' / W 149° 22.232'
Season: Mid-May through late September
Sites: 15 partial-hookup RV sites, 15 basic sites
Maximum length: 35 feet
Facilities: Some picnic tables and fire pits, pit toilets
Fee per night: $$
Maximum stay: None
Management: Moose Pass RV Park, (907) 288-5682, moosepasscampground.com
Finding the campground: Moose Pass RV Park is located on the east side of the Seward Highway at mile 29 at 34984 Seward Highway.

About the campground: This RV park is really more of an open gravel lot and even allows tenting. About half of the sites have electric-only hookups. Other than outhouses, there aren't many amenities at Moose Pass. Nevertheless, this is a good place to stop for a night if you want to avoid the crowds of Seward. It's usually open through September. You won't find an owner or a host on site; pay at the self-service check-in station. Be on your best food-cautious behavior at this campground—the campground is surrounded by woods and there are a lot of bears in the area!

13 Trail River Campground

Location: Near mile 24 of the Seward Highway
GPS: N 60° 24.874' / W 149° 22.916'
Season: Mid-May through September
Sites: 91 basic sites
Maximum length: Any
Facilities: Tables, fire pits, picnic area, potable water, vault toilets, fishing/lake access, volleyball, horseshoes
Fee per night: $
Maximum stay: 14 days
Management: USDA Forest Service, Seward Ranger District, (907) 224-3374, www.fs.fed.us/r10/ chugach; reservations at www.recreation.gov, (877) 444-6777
Finding the campground: From mile 24.2 of the Seward Highway, turn west onto the gravel road at the sign for the Trail River Campground. Drive 1.1 miles to the campground entrance.
About the campground: This campground is divided into four sections between the Trail River and the distinctively bright turquoise Kenai Lake. All of the sites offer the best of a government campground, with well-maintained and fairly new facilities. It doesn't matter if you don't snag a lakefront site here, since there is a beautiful new day-use area on the water with ten fire pits and tables—an attractive choice for lunching. This clean-cut campground is complete with volleyball and horseshoes, creating a less rustic camping choice, popular with families. Fishing for Dolly Varden and rainbow trout is popular in Kenai Lake, as well as boating and just soaking up the prevailing lake scenery. When the fishing season dies down in August, these grounds become a popular berry-picking spot. Although this is officially hosted May through September, the gates at this campground stay open until the snow is too deep to drive in the wooded area.

14 Ptarmigan Creek Campground

Location: Near mile 23 of the Seward Highway
GPS: N 60° 24.350' / W 149° 21.810'
Season: Mid-May through September
Sites: 16 basic sites
Maximum length: 35 feet
Facilities: Tables, fire pits, potable water, vault toilets, hiking/fishing access
Fee per night: $

Maximum stay: 14 days

Management: USDA Forest Service, Seward Ranger District, (907) 224-3374, www.fs.fed.us/
r10/chugach; reservations at www.recreation.gov, (877) 444-6777

Finding the campground: This campground is located on the east side of the Seward Highway at
mile 23.3.

About the campground: Known and loved for good Dolly Varden fishing, the Ptarmigan Creek
Campground is located across the highway from the Trail River Campground. Much like its neighbor, these grounds have well-spaced sites located under the shade of spruce and in the shadow
of mountains, some with the comforting sound of the creek. There are only a couple of pull-thrus
here, so if you're in a long RV you will want to call ahead and see if you can reserve a larger site.
A short stroll will take you to the fish-viewing platform, a must-see during the spawning season. If
you're determined to find peaceful private angling, hit the 3.5-mile access trail to Ptarmigan Lake,
also known for good Dolly Varden fishing. If you haven't yet seen a ptarmigan—Alaska's chicken-
like state bird—check with the hosts for sightings!

15 Primrose Landing Campground

Location: Near mile 16 of the Seward Highway

GPS: N 60° 20.439' / W 149° 22.104'

Season: Mid-May through September

Sites: 10 basic sites, open overflow area

Maximum length: 25 feet

Facilities: Tables, fire pits, potable water, vault toilets, hiking/creek/lake/fishing access,
boat launch

Fee per night: $

Maximum stay: 14 days

Management: USDA Forest Service, Seward Ranger District, (907) 224-3374, www.fs.fed.us/r10/
chugach

Finding the campground: From mile 16.9 of the Seward Highway, drive west on the access road
at the sign for the Primrose Campground. Continue 1.1 miles to the campground.

About the campground: This small, popular campground is situated right on Kenai Lake, Primrose Creek, and the trail to Lost Lake, creating an excellent choice for those seeking a pragmatic
stay close to the water. The sites are small and basic with a table and fire pit. The camping area
is nicely tucked away from the road and noise of the creek can be heard from almost every site.
Since Kenai Lake is home to a surplus of fish, and hike-in Lost Lake is stocked with rainbows, the
fishing here is popular and the grounds fill up quickly with hikers and anglers on a first-come, first-
served basis.

Seward

Seward

	Hookup Sites	Total Sites	Max. RV Length	Hookups	Toilets	Showers	Drinking Water	Fires	Dump Station	Recreation	Fee	Reservations
16 Exit Glacier Campground	0	12	T	N	NF	N	Y	Y	N	H	Free	N
17 Bear Creek RV Park	89	89	Any	WESC	F	Y	Y	Y	Y	N	$$$–$$$$	Y
18 Stoney Creek RV Park	80	80	Any	WESC	F	Y	Y	Y	Y	N	$$$–$$$$$	Y
19 Seward KOA Journey	60	70	65	WESC	F	Y	Y	Y	Y	Y	$$$–$$$$$	Y
20 JJK Campsites	25	31	Any	E	F	N	Y	Y	N	N	$	N
21 Spring Creek Campground	0	30+	Any	N	NF	N	N	Y	N	F	$–$$	N
22 Forest Acres Campground	0	40	35	N	F	N	Y	Y	N	N	$–$$	N
23 Williams Park	0	32	20	N	NF	N	Y	Y	N	HCF	$	N
24 Seward Municipal Campgrounds	100	422	Any	WE	F	N	Y	Y	Y	HCF	$–$$$$$	N
25 Miller's Landing	30	50	40	E	F	Y	Y	Y	Y	HBF	$$$–$$$$$	Y

16 Exit Glacier Campground

Location: Near Seward
GPS: N 60° 11.468' / W 149° 37.094'
Season: May through late September
Sites: 12 tent sites
Maximum length: N/A
Facilities: Covered communal picnic area with food storage and fire pit, vault toilets, potable water, hiking access
Fee per night: Free
Maximum stay: 14 days
Management: Kenai Fjords National Park, (907) 224-7500, www.nps.gov/kefj
Finding the campground: From mile 3.7 of the Seward Highway, turn west onto Exit Glacier Road. Drive 8.1 miles to the campground on your left. The low-profile sign is easy to miss in the lush forest, so drive slowly.
About the campground: The drive out to the Exit Glacier is a must, whether or not you stay at the campground. The paved road takes you through a sweeping, breathtaking glacial valley, following the shallow braided channels of the Resurrection River. In fall deciduous trees create a spectacular display. Just before the campground, turnouts offer brilliant photographic opportunities with

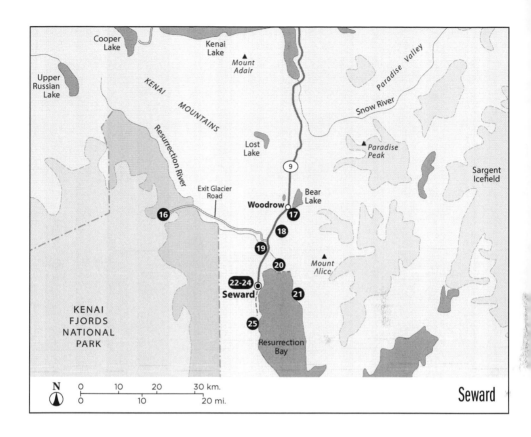

Seward

Note: Seward sites 1–15 can be found on page 4.

It is important to remember that Alaska is an immense state, both beautiful and potentially dangerous. So always keep a sense of location of where you are, and ultimately, where you need to be at the forefront of your thought.

valley and glacier backdrops. Just past the campground, at the road's end, is the visitor center for Kenai Fjords National Park and a short 0.5-mile hike to Exit Glacier.

Exit Glacier Campground is well suited for backpackers or as a base camp for those looking to get off the road. The campground has twelve walk-in tent sites and is an excellent example of the low-impact campgrounds many national parks are supporting. Activities are based around a communal covered picnic area with tables, large walk-in food storage, and a fire pit with tree-stump stools. Since bears are prevalent, the shareable area is designed to keep food and fires away from individual sites, lessening the impact area of campers and the draw for bears. The facilities are new right down to the impressively clean vault toilets. You can't actually see the glacier from campsites, since the grounds are so lush. The greenery provides privacy for each tent. Exit Glacier does occasionally peek over the treetops from some areas of the grounds. You can hear the roar of the river from some sites, and a small footpath connects campers directly to the river valley.

Seward's Waterfront Campground.

17 Bear Creek RV Park

Location: Near Seward
GPS: N 60° 11.068' / W 149° 22.350'
Season: May through October, monthly October through April
Sites: 78 full-hookup RV sites, 11 partial-hookup RV sites
Maximum length: Any
Facilities: Tables, communal fire pit, potable water, flush toilets, showers, dump station, laundry, WiFi, grocery store, game room, bar, shuttle
Fee per night: $$$–$$$$
Maximum stay: None
Management: Bear Creek RV Park, (907) 224-5725, (877) 924-5725, www.bearcreekrv.com
Finding the campground: From mile 6.6 of the Seward Highway, turn east onto Bear Lake Road. Drive 0.3 mile and turn right onto Lincoln Avenue. The campground is located at the intersection of Bear Lake Road and Lincoln Avenue at 33508 Lincoln Avenue.
About the campground: This unpretentious full-service RV park has 78 full-hookup sites and 11 partial hookups. The side-by-side spaces are located closely together in an open gravel lot. Bear Creek RV Park is far enough off the highway that traffic is light, but it gets busy when the salmon are running in Resurrection Bay. The campground is surrounded by views of mountains and the neighboring mobile-home park. Helpful staff can organize various charters within the Seward area.

18 Stoney Creek RV Park

Location: Near Seward
GPS: N 60° 10. 836' / W 149° 22.706'
Season: Mid-May through mid-September
Sites: 67 full-hookup RV sites, 13 partial-hookup RV sites
Maximum length: Any
Facilities: Tables, some fire pits, potable water, flush toilets, showers, laundry, creek access, WiFi, shuttle
Fee per night: $$$$$
Maximum stay: None
Management: Stoney Creek RV Park, (877) 437-6366, May 15–September 15 (907) 224-6465, off-season (907) 235-8741, www.stoneycreekrvpark.com
Finding the campground: From mile 6.6 of the Seward Highway, turn east onto Stoney Creek Avenue. Drive 0.2 mile and turn right onto Bruno Road. Drive another 0.2 mile on the winding road and turn left onto Winterset (Trail) Road. Drive 0.3 mile and turn left onto Leslie Place; continue for 0.1 mile to the Stoney Creek RV Park.
About the campground: Advertised as Seward's "only luxury RV park," Stoney Creek is the most developed full-amenities park to be found in the area. Located a few miles out of town off the quiet back roads of a residential neighborhood, the wooded grounds lack the pulse of Seward and the bay. They are also out of walking proximity to downtown attractions. Most guests who choose to stay at Stoney Creek don't mind the trade-off of urban proximity for the handsome mountain

setting, creekside sites, fire pits, and a more exclusive group of fellow campers. Each oversize gravel site is 30 feet wide, well-manicured, and has a lawn. Half of the sites are pull-thrus suitable for rigs of any size.

19 Seward KOA Journey

Location: In Seward
GPS: N 60° 9.500' / W 149° 26.309'
Season: April 15–Sept 30
Sites: 38 full hookups, 24 partial hookups, 9 tent sites
Maximum length: 65 feet
Facilities: Tables, fire pits, potable water, flush toilets, showers, WiFi, laundry, dump station, playground, dog park, miniature golf, shuttle
Fee per night: $$$$$
Maximum stay: None
Management: Seward KOA Journey, (907) 224-4887, https://koa.com/campgrounds/seward/
Finding the campground: From downtown Seward drive north on the Seward Highway for 3 miles and turn left (west) onto Herman Leirer Road (Exit Glacier Road). Drive one mile to the KOA on the right at 31702 Herman Leirer Road. Pond RV Park and Campground is just north of Seward on the west side of the Seward Highway at mile 3.
About the campground: This fairly new KOA is a welcome addition to Seward, where campgrounds are consistently full throughout the summer. You will find the basic attributes of any KOA plus more, like a dog park and shuttle service. The sites are in an open gravel lot.

20 JJK Campsites

Location: In Seward
GPS: N 60° 7.892' / W 149° 22.805'
Season: Late May through September
Sites: 25 partial hookups, 6 dry RV sites
Maximum length: Any
Facilities: Tables, fire pits, potable water, portable toilets
Fee per night: $$
Maximum stay: None
Management: JJK Campsites, (907) 230-0890
Finding the campground: From downtown Seward take the Seward Highway north 3 miles and turn east onto Nash Road, drive 1.5 miles to the campground on the right.
About the campground: This basic gravel lot is right along the water and has an attendant on site. The partial hookups are electric only and serve mostly anglers.

21 Spring Creek Campground

Location: In Seward
GPS: N 60° 05.353' / W 149° 21.376'
Season: Mid-April through October
Sites: 30 primitive sites
Maximum length: Any
Facilities: Some tables and fire pits, portable toilets, beach/fishing access
Fee per night: $–$$
Maximum stay: 14 days
Management: Seward Parks and Recreation Department, (907) 224-4055, www.cityofseward .net/parksrec
Finding the campground: From mile 3.2 of the Seward Highway, just north of Seward, turn east onto Nash Road. Drive 5.2 miles and turn right onto the unlabeled gravel road at the sign for Spring Creek Campground. Continue 0.1 mile to the beachside sites.
About the campground: You might expect the Spring Creek Campground to be a low-key place to camp—it lies across the bay from the bustling action of Seward—but on any summer weekend, or even most weekdays during high season, this spot is still busy. Spring Creek is much more rustic than the other city-operated campgrounds. Primitive campsites with makeshift fire rings are spread out along a waterfront gravel lot. Lucky tenters get an opportunity to camp outside the gravel in the soft grasses along the shore. A permit is required to tent out of the lot; inquire with the city of Seward before you cross the line!

22 Forest Acres Campground

Location: In Seward
GPS: N 60° 8.097' / W 149° 26.122'
Season: May through late September
Sites: 40 basic sites
Maximum length: 35 feet
Facilities: Tables, fire pits, potable water, flush toilets, playground
Fee per night: $–$$
Maximum stay: 14 days
Management: Seward Parks and Recreation Department, (907) 224-4055, www.cityofseward .net/parksrec
Finding the campground: At mile 2.5 of the Seward Highway, about 0.3 mile south of the airport road, turn west onto Hemlock Street. Drive 0.1 mile to Forest Acres Park campground is on your left.
About the campground: This aptly named campground is located in a forested park navigable by a narrow winding road. All the sites are earthen, separated by towering trees and lush foliage. The basic campsites are located throughout forested grounds and include one block of flush toilets and a small playground. This is an excellent choice in the Seward area if you're looking for a public campground seemingly out of the downtown atmosphere.

23 Williams Park

Location: In Seward
GPS: N 60° 06.572' / W 149° 26.181'
Season: Mid-April through late September
Sites: 32 tent sites
Maximum length: Tents only
Facilities: Tables, fire pits, portable toilets
Fee per night: $
Maximum stay: 14 days
Management: Seward Parks and Recreation Department, (907) 224-4055, www.cityofseward
.net/parksrec
Finding the campground: Williams Park is located across the street from Seward Municipal
Campgrounds. To reach the campground from the Seward Highway, drive south into town and fol-
low the highway as it becomes 3rd Avenue. Pass the Harbormaster Building and Van Buren Street,
then turn left onto Ballaine Boulevard. The camping area is on your right.
About the campground: This small basic campground is located across from the Seward Municipal
Campgrounds tent area, about midway along the Seward Municipal Campgrounds span. It consists of
32 tightly packed sites accessed by a narrow loop road. Williams Park is intended for tents, although
small RVs and campers are allowed. Some of the sites are separated by small trees and others are
completely exposed. If you'd like to be away from gusty wind, this is a good option. Most sites don't
have views of water, but mountain views, including Mount Marathon, are still present.

24 Seward Municipal Campgrounds

Location: In Seward
GPS: N 60° 06.488' / W 149° 26.087'
Season: Year-round
Sites: 100 partial-hookup RV sites, 300 basic sites, 22 tent sites
Maximum length: Any
Facilities: Some tables and fire pits, covered picnic area, potable water, flush toilets, dump sta-
tion, hiking/fishing/beach/cycling access, skate park, volleyball
Fee per night: $–$$$$$
Maximum stay: 14 days
Management: Seward Parks and Recreation Department, (907) 224-4055, www.cityofseward
.net/parksrec
Finding the campground: To reach the waterfront camping area from the Seward Highway, drive
south into town and follow the highway as it becomes 3rd Avenue. Pass the Harbormaster Building
and Van Buren Street, then turn left onto Ballaine Boulevard. The camping area is on your left.
About the campground: Located along Resurrection Bay, sprawling along the coastline of downtown, Seward Municipal Campgrounds hosts hundreds of campsites in lots along the shore
labeled from north to south: Alice Campground, Marathon RV Parking, Obihiro Campground, Resurrection Campground, Godwin Campground, Otter Beach Campground, and Iditarod Campground.

The city of Seward uniquely caters to the thousands of campers who make their town a destination every year by setting aside its most beautiful waterfront property for the public to enjoy. Campers are offered the opportunity to set up shop directly next to the water and watch sea life, fishing boats, and cruise ships drift by—all within walking distance of the museums, Alaska SeaLife Center, stores, and charter services. A paved bicycle path and picnic areas also line the coast, so true to the campground's theme the coast belongs to everyone in this city, whether or not you snag a beachfront site. Inland views also draw attention, with towering mountains rising steeply behind the city. From your campsite you likely can look up directly at the unmistakable Mount Marathon, identifiable by the deeply etched trail carved up its side. Once a year on the Fourth of July, endurance athletes come to Seward to run straight up the trail (reaching an elevation of over 3,000 feet) in the annual Mount Marathon Race.

The park's camping areas are divided into the loosely defined sections listed above. Several information boards, located with payment drop-boxes, will help you find the right area and numbered site for your setup. In the cramped twenty-two-site tent area, you'll find a fire pit and table at each small basic site. Most tent sites are earthen and located under the shade of humble trees. Campsites with the most spectacular views sit out in the open panorama. Unfortunately for tenters, winds can be gusty along the waterfront. If you are without a four-season tent, consider bringing extra stakes and possibly a tarp for a shield on those rainy days. The RV sections are all similar: open gravel lots with parking-lot-style side-by-side spaces, a line of which peer directly over stunning Resurrection Bay. There are some fire pits and some tables throughout the RV sections. About a hundred of the RV sites offer water and electric hookups.

The campground has three blocks of basic public restrooms with flush toilets. The Harbormaster Building has a dump and water-fill station, along with pay showers. Another free city-operated dump station is located across the street from the Williams Park campground. During the season it is possible for the entire park to fill. The campground is operated from mid-April through October; a small dry portion stays open year-round (small nightly fee).

25 Miller's Landing

Location: 3 miles south of Seward
GPS: N 60° 04.241' / W 149° 26.148'
Season: Mid-May through mid-September
Sites: 30 partial-hookup RV sites, 20 tent sites
Maximum length: 40 feet
Facilities: Tables, fire pits, grills, potable water, flush toilets, showers, laundry, fishing/beach access, charters, small store, WiFi
Fee per night: $$$–$$$$$
Maximum stay: None
Management: Miller's Landing, (907) 224-5739, (866) 541-5739, www.millerslandingak.com
Finding the campground: Follow the Seward Highway to its end at the southern tip of Seward. Take the small gravel Lowell Point Road south along the bay, over two one-lane bridges, 3 miles to the campground.
About the campground: This secluded end-of-the-gravel-road RV park and campground has an amazing waterfront location. The views of Resurrection Bay combined with the calm isolation of

being away from the city can't be beat. Staying at this campground might remind you of a classic summer camp. Miller's Landing advertises as a "One Stop Shop" and hosts both a rustic wilderness atmosphere and links to more activities than you could probably even attempt in one summer. The charters and equipment rentals are a main draw for many: kayaks and canoes line the shore, and lessons and tours can be organized. You can also choose to fish from shore or just soak in the lovely views. The owners will give you fishing advice for a nickel—and it's guaranteed effective or your money back.

The camping area is divided into two sections. Those traveling by RV have a chance to park their rig directly along the water, in the open gravel lot facing Resurrection Bay. The RV sites are electric-only hookups, but there is a dump station on site. The earthen tent grounds are tucked away from the water among old-growth spruce trees. Several wooden outbuildings offer a lot of charm and show the pride of ownership.

The Sterling Highway: Tern Lake Junction to Soldotna

	Hookup Sites	Total Sites	Max. RV Length	Hookups	Toilets	Showers	Drinking Water	Fires	Dump Station	Recreation	Fee	Reservations
26 Quartz Creek Campground	0	45	Any	N	F & NF	N	Y	Y	N	HFBL	$-$$	Y
27 Crescent Creek Campground	0	9	25	N	NF	N	Y	Y	N	HF	$-$$	N
28 Kenai Princess RV Park	40	40	40	WESC	F	Y	Y	N	Y	N	$$$$-$$$$$	Y
29 Kenai Riverside Campground and RV Park	18	28+	Any	WE	F & NF	Y	Y	Y	Y	F	$$-$$$$	Y
30 Cooper Creek Campground	0	29	35	N	N	N	Y	Y	N	F	$	Y
31 Russian River Campground	0	83	40	N	F & NF	N	Y	Y	Y	HF	$$-$$$	Y
32 Russian River Ferry	0	70	Any	N	NF	N	Y	N	N	HFBL	$$	N
33 Hidden Lake Campground	0	54	40	N	NF	N	Y	Y	Y	HFBL	$	N
34 Upper Skilak Lake Campground	0	25	35	N	NF	N	Y	Y	N	HFBL	$	N
35 Lower Ohmer Lake Campground	0	3	25	N	N	N	N	Y	N	F	Free	N
36 Engineer Lake Campground	0	4	25	N	N	N	N	Y	N	FBL	Free	N
37 Lower Skilak Lake Campground	0	14	25	N	NF	N	Y	Y	N	FBL	Free	N
38 Jean Lake Campground	0	3	20	N	N	N	N	Y	N	F	Free	N
39 Kelly Lake Campground	0	3	Any	N	NF	N	Y	Y	N	HFBL	Free	N
40 Peterson Lake Campground	0	3	Any	N	NF	N	Y	Y	N	FBL	Free	N
41 Watson Lake Campground	0	3	Any	N	NF	N	Y	Y	M	FBL	Free	N
42 Bing's Landing Campground	0	36	Any	N	NF	N	Y	Y	N	HFBL	$-$$	N
43 Real Alaskan Cabins and RV Park	34	34	40	WES	F	Y	Y	Y	N	N	$$$	Y
44 Bing Brown's RV Park and Motel	26	26+	50	WES	F	Y	Y	Y	Y	N	$$-$$$	Y
45 Moose River RV Park	4	4	45	WESC	F	Y	Y	Y	N	N	$$-$$$$$	Y
46 Izaak Walton Campground	0	31	25	N	NF	N	Y	Y	N	FBL	$	Y
47 Jana House Hostel and RV Park	10	10+	Any	WES	F	Y	Y	N	N	N	$$-$$$	Y
48 Dolly Varden Lake Campground	0	12	25	N	NF	N	Y	Y	N	FBL	Free	N
49 Rainbow Lake Campground	0	3	25	N	NF	N	Y	Y	N	FBL	Free	N
50 Swanson River Campground	0	4	25	N	NF	N	Y	Y	N	FBL	Free	N
51 Alaska Canoe & Campground	24	24+	35	WESC	F	Y	Y	Y	Y	N	$$-$$$	Y
52 Morgan's Landing Campground	0	41	Any	N	NF	N	Y	Y	N	F	$	N
53 Cast Away Riverside RV Park	10	13	Any	E	F	Y	Y	Y	Y	N	$$$	Y
54 Funny River Campground	0	6	20	N	NF	N	N	Y	N	F	$	N
55 Diamond M Ranch	40	40+	Any	WESC	F	Y	Y	Y	Y	N	$$-$$$$	Y

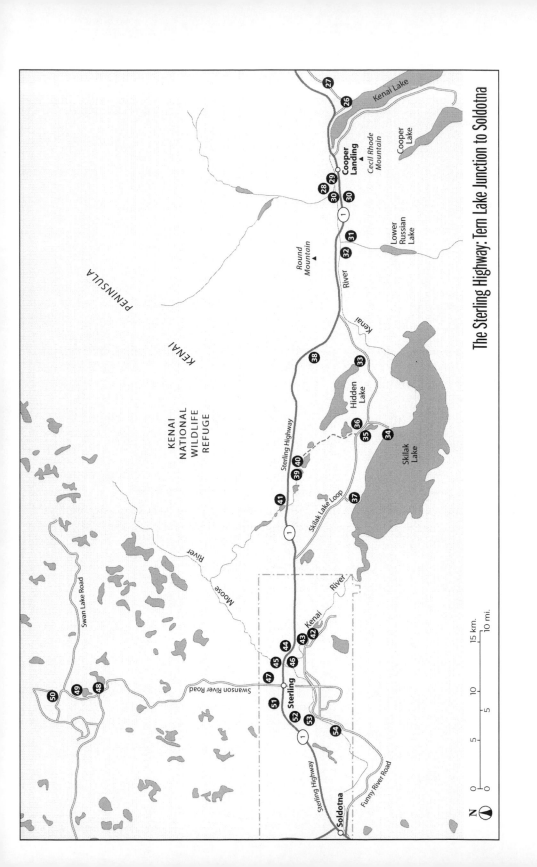

The Sterling Highway: Tern Lake Junction to Soldotna

26 Quartz Creek Campground

Location: Near Cooper Landing
GPS: N 60° 28.744' / W 149° 43.680'
Season: Mid-May through September
Sites: 45 basic sites
Maximum length: 45 feet
Facilities: Tables, fire pits, covered picnic area, potable water, flush and vault toilets, fishing/lake access, boat launch
Fee per night: $-$$
Maximum stay: 14 days
Management: USDA Forest Service, Seward Ranger District, (907) 224-3374, www.fs.fed.us/r10/chugach; reservations at www.recreation.gov, (877) 444-6777
Finding the campground: From mile 44.9 of the Sterling Highway at the Sunrise Inn, turn south onto Quartz Creek Road. Drive 0.3 mile to the campground on your right.
About the campground: This refined campground is the most luxurious public campground of the Kenai. It's located among small spruce with clean-cut landscaped walkways; there are forty-five spacious campsites dispersed along two paved loops. A few pull-thrus will take rigs of any size.

A moose grazes with her young calf near Skilak Lake Loop Road.

The lakefront sites have unsurpassed views of Kenai Lake and brilliant photo and wildlife-viewing opportunities. Equally impressive are the crisp, cool sites located along Quartz Creek. Like all the facilities at this campground, the airy vault toilets seem new, along with the tables and structures of the day-use area. This campground also has some flush toilets and running water in the bathrooms. The campsites that overlook the lake here are hard to walk away from when your time is up. It's no wonder these sites are the first to fill all summer long.

27 Crescent Creek Campground

Location: Near Cooper Landing
GPS: N 60° 29.871' / W 149° 41.074'
Season: Mid-May through October
Sites: 9 basic sites
Maximum length: 25 feet
Facilities: Tables, fire pits, potable water, vault toilets, hiking/creek/fishing access
Fee per night: $- $$
Maximum stay: 14 days
Management: USDA Forest Service, Seward Ranger District, (907) 224-3374, www.fs.fed.us/r10/chugach
Finding the campground: From mile 44.9 of the Sterling Highway at the Sunrise Inn, turn south onto Quartz Creek Road. Drive 3 miles to the campground on your left.
About the campground: With older facilities, this small rustic campground isn't as improved as its Quartz Creek counterpart. In fact, the rugged isolation and wilderness access are what make Crescent Creek popular with its fans. It fills up on the weekends pretty quickly since there are only nine sites. The sites are small and basic, located in a heavily wooded grove, within a few feet of nearby Crescent Creek Trailhead. A 6-mile hike to Crescent Lake links campers with further backcountry adventure.

28 Kenai Princess RV Park

Location: Near Cooper Landing
GPS: N 60° 29.461' / W 149° 51.006'
Season: Mid-May through mid-September
Sites: 40 full-hookup RV sites
Maximum length: 50 feet
Facilities: Tables, potable water, flush toilets, showers, dump station, laundry, WiFi, shuttle, restaurant, spa, hot tubs, gym, gift shop
Fee per night: $$$$–$$$$$
Maximum stay: None
Management: Kenai Princess Wilderness Lodge, (907) 595-1425, (800) 426-0500, www.princesslodges.com

Finding the campground: From mile 47.7 of the Sterling Highway, just east of the Kenai River, turn north onto Bean Creek Road. Drive 1.8 miles to the RV park and lodge.

About the campground: The Kenai Princess Wilderness Lodge is part of the Princess empire of cruises, trains, buses, and everything a luxury tour company could need in Alaska. The RV park is no exception to the high standards of Princess tours. If you're looking for a vacation from a vacation, these fancy grounds allow access to lodge amenities at no extra charge. The RV park is a basic gravel lot located just beneath the lodge. Since the hill is steep, the lodge is not visible from the site. In fact, the views of surrounding mountains and forest are impressive, even though usually it's the amenities, not the vistas, that bring customers here. The open lot consists of forty side-by-side spaces; most sites have tables, but fires are not allowed. Within the RV park there is an office with toilets, laundry, and showers, but you'll have to trek up the hill for most other amenities.

29 Kenai Riverside Campground and RV Park

Location: Near Cooper Landing
GPS: N 60° 29.185' / W 149° 51.708'
Season: Late May through September
Sites: 18 partial-hookup RV sites, 10 basic sites, open tent area
Maximum length: Any
Facilities: Some tables, fire pits, and grills, potable water, flush and portable toilets, showers, dump station, laundry, WiFi, fishing/river access, charters
Fee per night: $$-$$$$
Maximum stay: None
Management: Kenai Riverside Campground and RV Park, (907) 595-1406, (888) 536-2478, www.kenairv.com
Finding the campground: On the banks of the Kenai River at mile 49.7 on the Sterling Highway.
About the campground: This big-rig-friendly campground has eighteen pull-thru sites. As you glance toward the campground from the highway, it doesn't seem like the snugly placed camping area would be so spacious—it appears packed between the river and the road. But once you get in, you'll find plenty of room. Tents are allowed here, a bonus if you're looking to stay close to a shower (at extra cost). The tenting area is a combination of earth and gravel in an open area. You can get your fishing license here, book a charter, or fish the Kenai right from the campground.

30 Cooper Creek Campground

Location: Near Cooper Landing
GPS: N 60° 29.052' / W 149° 53.124'
Season: May through September
Sites: 26 basic sites, 3 tent sites
Maximum length: 45 feet
Facilities: Tables, fire pits, potable water, vault toilets, fishing/river access
Fee per night: $

Maximum stay: 14 days
Management: USDA Forest Service, Seward Ranger District, (907) 224-3374, www.fs.fed.us/r10/chugach; reservations at www.recreation.gov, (877) 444-6777
Finding the campground: This campground is located at mile 50.5 of the Sterling Highway on both sides of the roadway.
About the campground: This small campground rests under the shade of cottonwood and spruce trees. The camping area is divided into two loops, one on the north side of the Sterling Highway and the other on the south. All campsites are rather small and basic with a table and fire pit. The north loop has seven campsites, a few of which are located directly on the rushing Kenai River. Three campsites are tent-only walk-ins. The south loop has thirteen thickly wooded back-in sites. On weekends or when the fish are running, expect the campground to be full. Views are spectacular here, but as with most grounds in the Cooper Landing area, people are likely here to fish for salmon.

31 Russian River Campground

Location: Near Cooper Landing
GPS: N 60° 28.921' / W 149° 56.586'
Season: April through November
Sites: 83 basic sites
Maximum length: 55 feet
Facilities: Tables, fire pits, potable water, flush and vault toilets, dump station, fish-cleaning facilities, hiking/fishing/river access
Fee per night: $$–$$$
Maximum stay: 3 days
Management: USDA Forest Service, Seward Ranger District, (907) 224-3374, www.fs.fed.us/r10/chugach; reservations at www.recreation.gov, (877) 444-6777
Finding the campground: From mile 53 of the Sterling Highway, follow the signs south along the paved road for 1.8 miles to the campground.
About the campground: When the salmon are running, the Russian River Campground is a sight to see. During summer from late June through August, the campground is buzzing with activity. Gorgeous mountain views seem to fade among human action, creating a scenic backdrop for the real show—the anglers. The driveways and walkways are a blur of waders. Makeshift fishing gear camps overtake the area where you expect to find a tent. Rangers and staff seem to be everywhere ensuring people don't overextend their three-day limit during the runs, and the hosts are the busiest in the state. Watching the commotion can be an exciting experience, but if you're not here to fish, you will be a fish out of water.

The camping area is located in a spruce grove on a bluff between the Kenai and Russian rivers. The grounds are divided into three loops, all similar, with small basic back-in sites separated by trees and brush. With talent, a rig of up to 40 feet can fit in some of the sites, but you will have to drive cautiously. The loop roads are extremely narrow and hard to maneuver (notice the rocks painted neon orange on the road's edge). When the fish aren't stealing the show, hiking is a major draw here. Several trails spawn from the grounds, and you'll find these parking areas full on most days as well. The most heavily traveled jaunts include a 2-mile hike to the falls and an easy stroll to a fish-viewing platform. Enthusiastic backpackers set out on the 21-mile Russian Lakes Trail.

32 Russian River Ferry

Location: Near mile 54 of the Sterling Highway
GPS: N 60° 29.209' / W 150° 00.277'
Season: Late May through September
Sites: 60 side-by-side stalls, 10 tent sites
Maximum length: Any
Facilities: Some tables, potable water, vault toilets, fish-cleaning facilities, fishing/river access, boat launch, ferry
Fee per night: $$
Maximum stay: 2 days
Management: US Fish and Wildlife Service, Kenai National Wildlife Refuge, (907) 262-7021, http://kenai.fws.gov

Sportsman's Landing.

Finding the campground: The campground is located on the south side of the Sterling Highway at mile 54.8. From June through August you can't miss the cars lining the road.

About the campground: The confluence of the Kenai and Russian rivers is the hottest spot for summer sportfishing in all of Alaska. For a small fee, a ferry carries anglers across the Kenai River, allowing excellent access to the mouth of the Russian River. The ferry is operated by a private company and shuffles thousands of anglers across the water every season. From there they line shoulder-to-shoulder combat fishing for salmon as far as the eye can see. It is not uncommon to see a fisherman get hooked. Acclimated bears frequent the area and are spotted on an almost daily basis. Even though the gates lock, fishing goes on most hours of the night, a very Alaskan experience. The old lodge was removed to make room for the RV parking area. The campground is simply a gravel parking area that allows an overnight stay of up to two nights to accommodate the fishing madness. The parking spaces are located at the entrance to the ferry.

33 Hidden Lake Campground

Location: Skilak Lake Loop Road
GPS: N 60° 27.884' / W 150° 12.062'
Season: May through September
Sites: 44 basic sites, 10 overflow sites
Maximum length: 40 feet
Facilities: Tables, fire pits, covered picnic area with barbecue, potable water, vault toilets, dump station, fishing/hiking/lake access, boat launch
Fee per night: $
Maximum stay: 14 days
Management: US Fish and Wildlife Service, Kenai National Wildlife Refuge, (907) 262-7021, http://kenai.fws.gov
Finding the campground: From mile 58 of the Sterling Highway, drive south onto Skilak Lake Loop Road. Continue 3.3 miles down the gravel road and turn right at the sign to Hidden Lake. Drive 0.5 mile to the campground.
About the campground: Skilak Lake Loop Road may not be paved, but the roads through Hidden Lake Campground are. This is the largest and nicest of the refuge's campgrounds, with supersize sites and nearly new facilities. The campsites are located off loops with an amphitheater as the center of weekend events. The lower loop has impressive lakefront sites and a picnic area. If you miss out on the lower loop, the upper sites have wonderful mountain views and access to trails. Along with a picturesque backdrop, campers also come to Hidden Lake to fish for trout. The highly developed grounds have a dump station on site.

34 Upper Skilak Lake Campground

Location: Skilak Lake Loop Road
GPS: N 60° 26.400' / W 150° 19.263'
Season: May through September
Sites: 15 basic sites, 10 tent sites
Maximum length: 35 feet
Facilities: Tables, fire pits, covered picnic area, potable water, vault toilets, hiking/fishing/lake access, boat launch
Fee per night: $
Maximum stay: 14 days
Management: US Fish and Wildlife Service, Kenai National Wildlife Refuge, (907) 262-7021, http://kenai.fws.gov
Finding the campground: From mile 58 of the Sterling Highway, turn south at Skilak Lake Loop Road. Drive 8 miles and turn left onto a gravel road; continue 2 miles to the campground.
About the campground: Clean and well kept, Upper Skilak Lake is—along with Hidden Lake—a pleasant upgraded surprise along gravel Skilak Lake Loop Road. Most people are utilizing the boat launch at this popular campground. The campsites are basic, several have lake views, but all sites have great views. There are ten walk-in tent sites.

35 Lower Ohmer Lake Campground

Location: Skilak Lake Loop Road
GPS: N 60° 27.646' / W 150° 19.159'
Season: May through October
Sites: 3 basic sites
Maximum length: 25 feet
Facilities: Tables, fire pits, lake/fishing access; there are toilets at Ohmer Lake, but they don't appear to have been maintained—consider them unusable
Fee per night: Free
Maximum stay: 14 days
Management: US Fish and Wildlife Service, Kenai National Wildlife Refuge, (907) 262-7021, http://kenai.fws.gov
Finding the campground: From mile 58 of the Sterling Highway, turn south onto Skilak Lake Loop Road and drive 8.2 miles to Lower Ohmer Lake Campground.
About the campground: This small area has three sites and remains rather undeveloped. Each site has an older table and fire pit. There is direct access to the lake from the grounds, as well as a popular canoe launch.

36 Engineer Lake Campground

Location: Skilak Lake Loop Road
GPS: N 60° 28.437' / W 150° 19.654'
Season: May through October
Sites: 4 basic sites
Maximum length: 25 feet
Facilities: Tables, fire pits, potable water, vault toilet, fishing/lake access, boat launch
Fee per night: Free
Maximum stay: 14 days
Management: US Fish and Wildlife Service, Kenai National Wildlife Refuge, (907) 262-7021, http://kenai.fws.gov
Finding the campground: This campground is located 9.5 miles from either entrance of Skilak Lake Loop Road. From mile 58 or 75.3 of the Sterling Highway, turn south onto Skilak Lake Loop Road and drive 9.5 miles to the campground.
About the campground: Complete with a boat launch, Engineer Lake is stocked with silver salmon—but it's not as popular as other Skilak counterparts. This campground consists of just a few spots across a gravel lot from the lake. The basic sites have tables and fire pits and are separated by trees and brush. The trailhead for the 4.4-mile trek to Kelly Lake is located on site.

37 Lower Skilak Lake Campground

Location: On Skilak Lake Loop Road
GPS: N 60° 28.275' / W 150° 28.091'
Season: May through September
Sites: 14 basic sites
Maximum length: 25 feet
Facilities: Tables, fire pits, potable water, vault toilets, fishing/lake access, boat launch
Fee per night: Free
Maximum stay: 14 days
Management: US Fish and Wildlife Service, Kenai National Wildlife Refuge, (907) 262-7021, http://kenai.fws.gov
Finding the campground: From mile 75.3 of the Sterling Highway (the western junction of the 19-mile Skilak Lake Loop Road), turn south onto Skilak Lake Loop Road. Drive 5.3 miles, turn right, and continue 1 mile down the gravel road to the campground.
About the campground: An older version of its newer counterpart, this campground has fourteen basic sites. About half are acceptable for rigs up to 25 feet; the rest are tent sites. You'll find these to be smaller but with the same basic amenities. Each site has a table and fire pit. Lower Skilak Lake is popular with boaters.

38 Jean Lake Campground

Location: Near mile 60 of the Sterling Highway
GPS: N 60° 30.081' / W 150° 09.929'
Season: May through October
Sites: 3 basic sites
Maximum length: 20 feet
Facilities: Tables, fire rings, pit toilet, fishing/lake access
Fee per night: Free
Maximum stay: 14 days
Management: US Fish and Wildlife Service, Kenai National Wildlife Refuge, (907) 262-7021, http://kenai.fws.gov
Finding the campground: From mile 60 on the Sterling Highway, turn south onto the unlabeled road at milepost 60; since there isn't a sign and the road is behind thick bushes, watch for the milepost. Exercise extreme caution while turning into and out of this campground. A car is the last thing most drivers expect to see come out of this patch of greenery on the side of the road.
About the campground: There are only two developed campsites at this campground, although there is a clearing for a third. If you're looking for a seemingly private lake to fish or even just relax and enjoy a quiet campfire, this is a great spot. Aside from a few fishermen, people hardly ever wander down here. The sites are earthen back-ins relatively far apart and divided by a small circle driveway. Both are waterfront with spectacular views of Jean Lake, where you can fish for Dolly Varden and rainbow. This is a rustic camping area; while there is an outhouse uphill from the site, it's found through a mesh of overgrown weeds. The facilities are not well maintained.

39 Kelly Lake Campground

Location: Near mile 68 of the Sterling Highway
GPS: N 60° 31.263' / W 150° 23.340'
Season: May through October
Sites: 3 basic sites
Maximum length: Any
Facilities: Tables, fire pits, potable water, vault toilets, hiking/fishing/lake access, boat launch
Fee per night: Free
Maximum stay: 14 days
Management: US Fish and Wildlife Service, Kenai National Wildlife Refuge, (907) 262-7021, http://kenai.fws.gov
Finding the campground: From mile 68.8 of the Sterling Highway, turn south onto the unlabeled road with the signs to Kelly and Peterson lakes. Drive 0.6 mile to Kelly Lake.
About the campground: This campground has three lakefront sites located on a small gravel pad beside Kelly Lake. The large circular gravel lot is suitable for rigs of any size. The campsites are fairly well developed. Kelly Lake is a smaller lake, but people often come here to fish or just to get away from the busy atmosphere of the larger campgrounds. You can't beat the price, especially on the Kenai!

40 Peterson Lake Campground

Location: Near mile 68 of the Sterling Highway
GPS: N 60° 31.493' / W 150° 23.806'
Season: May through October
Sites: 3 basic sites
Maximum length: Any
Facilities: Tables, fire pits, potable water, vault toilets, fishing/lake access, boat launch
Fee per night: Free
Maximum stay: 14 days
Management: US Fish and Wildlife Service, Kenai National Wildlife Refuge, (907) 262-7021, http://kenai.fws.gov
Finding the campground: From mile 68.8 of the Sterling Highway, turn south onto the unlabeled road with the signs to Kelly and Peterson lakes. Stay right and drive 0.4 mile to Peterson Lake.
About the campground: Much like Kelly Lake, Peterson Lake has a large, very basic gravel lot with a few established sites along the lakefront. The area is suitable for any size rig. You can fish for rainbows or just enjoy the isolated charm of this lake.

41 Watson Lake Campground

Location: Near mile 71 of the Sterling Highway
GPS: N 60° 32.167' / W 150° 27.677'
Season: May through October
Sites: 3 basic sites
Maximum length: Any
Facilities: Tables, fire pits, potable water, fishing access, boat launch
Fee per night: Free
Maximum stay: 14 days
Management: US Fish and Wildlife Service, Kenai National Wildlife Refuge, (907) 262-7021, http://kenai.fws.gov
Finding the campground: From mile 71.2 of the Sterling Highway, just east of the East Fork Moose River, turn north onto the unlabeled gravel road at a very small and difficult-to-see sign for Watson Lake. Drive 0.4 mile to the campground at the road's end. Since there aren't signs for the campground, watch your mileage.
About the campground: Small and pleasant Watson Lake is known for good rainbow trout fishing, and the camping area was recently redone. The three campsites are off a large gravel circle amid spruce trees. The campground isn't labeled from the road; it simply says WATSON LAKE, so you'll find mostly locals, and traffic is low-key. This is a remarkably quiet campground for being only 0.4 mile off the Sterling.

42 Bing's Landing Campground

Location: In Sterling
GPS: N 60° 31.244' / W 150° 42.247'
Season: Mid-May through September
Sites: 31 basic sites, 5 tent sites
Maximum length: Any
Facilities: Tables, covered picnic area, fire pits, potable water, vault toilets, fish-cleaning facilities, hiking/fishing/river access, boat launch
Fee per night: $–$$
Maximum stay: 7 days
Management: Alaska State Parks, Kenai Area Office, (907) 262-5581, www.dnr.state.ak.us/parks
Finding the campground: In Sterling, from mile 80.2 of the Sterling Highway, turn south at a sign for Bing's Landing State Recreation Site. Continue 0.5 mile to campground.
About the campground: This campground is made popular by its access to the Kenai River with a busy boat launch. Rafters, kayakers, and anglers often utilize this spot. The campsites are very deep back-ins separated by trees and brush. Five walk-in tent sites are completely wheelchair-accessible.

43 Real Alaskan Cabins and RV Park

Location: In Sterling
GPS: N 60° 31.421' / W 150° 42.558'
Season: Mid-May through mid-September
Sites: 34 full-hookup RV sites
Maximum length: 60 feet
Facilities: Tables, fire pits, communal picnic area, potable water, flush toilets, showers, charters, gift shop
Fee per night: $$$
Maximum stay: None
Management: Real Alaskan Cabins and RV Park, (907) 262-6077, www.realalaskan.com
Finding the campground: In Sterling, from mile 80.3 of the Sterling Highway, turn south at the sign for Bing's Landing State Recreation Site. Drive 0.1 mile to the campground in a thickly wooded area on your immediate right.
About the campground: If you're looking for full hookups next to the recreation opportunities of Bing's Landing, this full-service RV park is for you. Real Alaskan has thirty-four spacious sites on wooded grounds. Less like a RV park, and more of a traditional campground, these sites are separated by towering birch trees, each with a fire pit and table. Reservations are recommended during salmon runs.

44 Bing Brown's RV Park and Motel

Location: In Sterling
GPS: N 60° 31.622' / W 150° 43.581'
Season: Mid-May through late September
Sites: 16 full-hookup RV sites, 10 partial-hookup RV sites, open tent camping
Maximum length: 50 feet
Facilities: Tables, communal fire pit, potable water, flush toilets, dump station, laundry, fish-cleaning facilities, WiFi, small store
Fee per night: $$–$$$
Maximum stay: None
Management: Bing Brown's RV Park and Motel, (907) 262-4780
Finding the campground: Look for this campground on the north side of the Sterling Highway at mile 81.
About the campground: This typical roadhouse-style operation has a gravel area for camping behind a motel/liquor store on the Sterling Highway. Trees outline the property, but the sites are open side-by-sides in gravel. There is a grassy area for tent camping. People who stay here are likely utilizing the day-use facilities of Bing Brown's State Recreation Site and looking for full hookups at night. The lot does fill up, not because the sites are superb, but rather as overflow from the popular fishing area. A small sportsman's store on site serves anglers' needs.

45 Moose River RV Park

Location: In Sterling
GPS: N 60° 32.099' / W 150° 44.553'
Season: May through September
Sites: 2 full-hookup RV sites, 2 partial-hookup RV sites, open tent camping
Maximum length: 45 feet
Facilities: Tables, communal fire pit, potable water, flush toilets, showers, laundry, cafe, small store, WiFi, charters
Fee per night: $$–$$$$$
Maximum stay: None
Management: Moose River RV Park, (907) 260-7829, mooseriverresort.com
Finding the campground: This campground is located on the north side of the Sterling Highway at mile 81.5.
About the campground: This gravel lot is pretty nice for the side of the highway and even has a few trees to break up the open space. The facilities are kept clean and tidy. Within walking distance you can check out the confluence of the Moose and Kenai rivers. The staff can also organize canoe rentals and transport if you'd like to paddle the placid Moose River. On site you can rent fishing and basic camping gear. The sites are available only seasonally or monthly.

46 Izaak Walton Campground

Location: In Sterling
GPS: N 60° 32.157' / W 150° 45.274'
Season: Mid-May through late September
Sites: 31 basic sites
Maximum length: 32 feet
Facilities: Tables, fire pits, potable water, vault toilets, fish-cleaning facilities, fishing/river access, boat launch
Fee per night: $$
Maximum stay: 7 days
Management: Alaska State Parks, Kenai Area Office, (907) 262-5581, www.dnr.state.ak.us/parks
Finding the campground: From mile 81.9 of the Sterling Highway, turn south just east of the bridge and follow the signs
About the campground: Where the brownish mucky water of the calming Moose River mixes with the clear turquoise water of the rushing Kenai, you'll find a major meeting point for fishing charters, rafters, and sightseers alike. Fishing guides often launch their charters from this point, which also meets one terminus of the Swan Lake canoe trail.

The Izaak Walton campground is held between these two rivers, and cornered by the conflux. Suitably, the boat launch and river access are the main attraction here, and the campsites are cramped. They offer some shade but very little privacy, and they will not hold large RVs. Camping remains popular here, mostly with those utilizing the canoe trail or putting in for a Kenai rafting adventure. Gracious hosts can point you in the direction of fishing and rafting opportunities.

47 Jana House Hostel and RV Park

Location: In Sterling
GPS: N 60° 32.484' / W 150° 47.656'
Season: June through October
Sites: 10 full-hookup RV sites, open tent area
Maximum length: Any
Facilities: Tables, communal kitchen, potable water, flush toilets, showers, fish-cleaning facilities, WiFi
Fee per night: $$–$$$
Maximum stay: None
Management: Jana House Hostel and RV Park, (907) 260-4151
Finding the campground: From mile 83.4 of the Sterling Highway, turn north onto Swanson River Road. Drive 0.4 mile to the hostel on your right.
About the campground: Jana House has hostel amenities and camping prices. The simple gravel lot behind the big yellow building has room for ten RVs and an open area for tenters. The camping area is clean and organized, with surrounding forest along the edges. There is plenty of room for big rigs here, and the sixty-amp electric connections are more than inviting. This is a larger-scale hostel with about fifty beds, so activity in the communal areas can be busy. If you like the hostel atmosphere, this is a great place to meet some new people and organize a canoeing trip.

48 Dolly Varden Lake Campground

Location: 14 miles north of Sterling
GPS: N 60° 42.042' / W 150° 47.891'
Season: Mid-May through October
Sites: 12 basic sites
Maximum length: 25 feet
Facilities: Tables, fire pits, water, vault toilets, lake/canoe/fishing access, boat launch
Fee per night: Free
Maximum stay: 14 days
Management: US Fish and Wildlife Service, Kenai National Wildlife Refuge, (907) 262-7021, http://kenai.fws.gov
Finding the campground: From the west end of Sterling at mile 83.4 of the Sterling Highway, drive north on Swanson River Road for 14 miles. The narrow road through the campground is suitable for only the smallest campers and RVs.
About the campground: Swanson River Road allows access to a small portion of the two-million-plus acres of the Kenai National Wildlife Refuge. Here you can find the most popular canoeing sites in the area. From Swanson River Road you can connect to two canoe routes linking more than forty lakes by 80 miles of trails. The channels are noted for spectacular scenery, wildlife viewing, and trout fishing.

Dolly Varden Lake Campground is the first of the three located on Swanson River Road. This sublime lakefront campground takes on the atmosphere of a summer novel. If you manage to camp at one of the waterfront sites, you'll be pleased with beautiful views of the placid lake despite the thickly wooded grounds. The sites have basic amenities with a table and fire pit, while tenters are rewarded with earthen and leaf-covered places to pitch. As with all Swanson River Road campgrounds, this is a popular launch for canoeing and provides productive year-round fishing for arctic char and rainbows. It should be noted that the quality of the water available in this part of the refuge often changes. Be prepared to boil water before it is of drinking quality. Water-quality signs will be posted.

49 Rainbow Lake Campground

Location: 16 miles north of Sterling
GPS: N 60° 43.067' / W 150° 49.107'
Season: May through October
Sites: 3 basic sites
Maximum length: 25 feet
Facilities: Tables, fire pits, water, vault toilets, fishing/lake/canoe access, boat launch
Fee per night: Free
Maximum stay: 14 days
Management: US Fish and Wildlife Service, Kenai National Wildlife Refuge, (907) 262-7021, http://kenai.fws.gov

Finding the campground: From the west end of Sterling at mile 83.4 of the Sterling Highway, drive north on Swanson River Road for 15.4 miles.

About the campground: This small campground is located in a clearing on the edge of Rainbow Lake. The campsites lack the woodsy feel of Dolly Varden but offer a quieter lakeshore setting. The handful of basic sites are less developed than at neighboring Dolly Varden but still adequate and without a fee.

50 Swanson River Campground

Location: 17 miles north of Sterling
GPS: N 60° 44.604' / W 150° 48.067'
Season: May through October
Sites: 4 basic sites
Maximum length: 25 feet
Facilities: Tables, fire pits, vault toilets, fishing/river/canoe access, boat launch
Fee per night: Free
Maximum stay: 14 days
Management: US Fish and Wildlife Service, Kenai National Wildlife Refuge, (907) 262-7021, http://kenai.fws.gov
Finding the campground: From the west end of Sterling at mile 83.5 of the Sterling Highway, drive north on Swanson River Road for 17.5 miles to the campground entrance (2 miles past the entrance to Rainbow Lake Campground).

About the campground: This small campground is similar to Rainbow Lake and has four clean sites located on open grounds near the parking lot. There is direct access to the water. The sites are a little larger and more comfortable for RVs and campers here. This is the terminus of the Swanson River route, so expect a busier scene than at nearby Rainbow Lake.

51 Alaska Canoe & Campground

Location: In Sterling
GPS: N 60° 32.213' / W 150° 48.158'
Season: May through October
Sites: 24 full-hookup RV sites, open area for tents
Maximum length: 35 feet
Facilities: Tables, some fire pits, picnic area, potable water, flush toilets, showers, dump station, laundry, fish-cleaning facilities, WiFi, charters, boat/gear rentals
Fee per night: $$-$$$$
Maximum stay: None
Management: Alaska Canoe and Campground, (907) 262-2331, www.alaskacanoetrips.com
Finding the campground: This campground is located on the north side of the Sterling Highway at mile 84.

About the campground: Located close to paddling access for the Kenai National Wildlife Refuge, Alaska Canoe & Campground is a popular base camp in the summer. The Swanson River and Swan Lake canoe routes offer not only the most accessible, but arguably the most pristine paddling opportunities in the state. Alaska Canoe & Campground rents any and all needed equipment for trips ranging from half a day to two weeks, as well as shuttling customers to access points on Swanson River Road. The staff here have a remarkable reputation and selection of equipment to outfit you, from water vessels to camping and fishing gear, beginners to advanced. The quaint camping area is located behind the office. There are twenty-five RV sites separated by trees. The lot is a combination of gravel and grass. Tents are allowed. Spaces are often booked July through August, so make reservations.

52 Morgan's Landing Campground

Location: In Sterling
GPS: N 60° 30.051' / W 150° 51.882'
Season: Mid-May through September
Sites: 41 basic sites
Maximum length: Any
Facilities: Tables, fire pits, potable water, vault toilets, fish-cleaning facilities, fishing/river access
Fee per night: $
Maximum stay: 7 days
Management: Alaska State Parks, Kenai Area Office, (907) 262-5581, www.dnr.state.ak.us/parks
Finding the campground: From mile 84.9 of the Sterling Highway, drive south on Scout Lake Loop Road for 1.5 miles. Turn right onto Lou Morgan Road and drive 2.4 miles to the campground.
About the campground: There are two main draws at Morgan's Landing: the Alaska State Parks Management Area Headquarters, and direct access to fish from the banks of the Kenai. From mid- to late summer, the salmon runs honor Morgan's Landing's place on the map, and the day-use parking area is likely packed. Unlike the grounds at the Russian River Ferry, the campground here has traditional wooded sites separated from the neighbors by grass and trees, offering shade and fire pits. Ten pull-thrus and several supersize sites can accommodate those who camp in luxury, but big-rig captains should note that Lou Morgan Road is a narrow, winding road. Sites are likely to fill on busy weekends throughout the summer and often in July. An "overflow" parking area offers a place to shack up for one day in the attempt to fit in the grounds the following day.

53 Cast Away Riverside RV Park

Location: In Sterling
GPS: N 60° 30.492' / W 150° 51.318'
Season: May through September
Sites: 10 partial-hookup RV sites, 3 tent sites
Maximum length: Any

Facilities: Tables, some fire pits, potable water, flush toilets, showers, dump station, laundry, fish-cleaning facilities, espresso bar
Fee per night: $$$
Maximum stay: None
Management: Cast Away Riverside RV Park, (907) 262-7219, (800) 478-6446, castawayak.com, www.goingnorth.com
Finding the campground: From mile 84.9 of the Sterling Highway, drive south on Scout Lake Loop Road for 1.5 miles and turn right onto Lou Morgan Road. Drive 0.7 mile and turn left onto Martins Road. Continue 0.5 mile to the T and turn left.
About the campground: A small 140-foot dock allows campers to fish directly from the grounds here, and guests seem to appreciate the exclusive offer. This rather quiet riverfront park is located well off the road in a settled residential neighborhood, literally casting you away from the often busy environment of the Kenai. Even with the small lodge on site, things are rather low-key, and the fishing is serene. Each large campsite here has plenty of room for pop-outs and awnings, and also its own personal lawn area. Some sites have fire pits; a few along the river are suitable for tents. Ten sites have electric hookups. There is a dump and water-fill station on the grounds. The desirable sites are often booked, and there seems to be a transition to long-term rentals with a minimum of 7 day stay and tendency to rent RV sites for the season.

54 Funny River Campground

Location: Near Soldotna
GPS: N 60° 29.547' / W 150° 51.807'
Season: May through September
Sites: 10 basic sites
Maximum length: 40 feet
Facilities: Tables, fire pits, vault toilets, fishing/river access
Fee per night: $
Maximum stay: 7 days
Management: Alaska State Parks, Kenai Area Office, (907) 262-5581, www.dnr.state.ak.us/parks
Finding the campground: From mile 96.1 of the Sterling Highway, turn east onto Funny River Road (just opposite Kalifornsky Beach Road). Drive 11.2 miles to the campground on your left just over the Funny River Bridge.
About the campground: Before the mid-July salmon run, this area is closed to fishing and practically abandoned, which might be hard to believe if you arrive later in summer. Not far from the campground, a Kenai River fish walk offers fishing access that draws the crowds. Fishing from the platform not only creates less erosion on the banks but also allows access to the steep or inaccessible banks of the river. The camping area consists of just a few rustic camping spots that are close together and shaded by trees and shrubs. Hosts sometimes appear here, though the grounds are rather undeveloped and most of the time you will have to pack out your own trash.

55 Diamond M Ranch

See map on page 44

Location: Near mile 96 of the Sterling Highway
GPS: N 60° 31.045' / W 151° 11.403'
Season: Year-round
Sites: 40 full-hookup RV sites, open dry camping
Maximum length: Any
Facilities: Communal picnic area and fire pit, potable water, flush toilets, showers, dump station, laundry, fish-cleaning facilities, playground, WiFi
Fee per night: $$–$$$$$
Maximum stay: None
Management: Diamond M Ranch, (907) 283-9424, www.diamondmranch.com
Finding the campground: From mile 96.1 of the Sterling Highway in Soldotna, turn west onto Kalifornsky Beach Road. Drive 5.5 miles to the campground on your right.
About the campground: Located on eighty acres, this unique farm-style RV park stays true to its ranching roots and has been run by the same family for several generations. Along with cabins and a bed-and-breakfast, the park can host up to 120 RVs. Forty of the sites are equipped with full hookups; twelve oversize pull-through spaces can accommodate any size of rig. Most sites are located in a dry gravel lot, although there are a few established sites with trees, and tent camping is in an open field. The facilities are very cozy and personal and the restrooms are clean. This is a popular campground for families in summer and can fill up quickly. The owners and staff entertain and organize groups and social events daily, creating a kid-friendly family-style community.

Kenai Highway and Soldotna

Kenai Highway and Soldotna	Hookup Sites	Total Sites	Max. RV Length	Hookups	Toilets	Showers	Drinking Water	Fires	Dump Station	Recreation	Fee	Reservations
56 Kenai RV Park	12	22	35	WES	F	Y	Y	Y	N	N	$$-$$$$$	Y
57 Discovery Campground	0	52	40	N	NF	N	Y	Y	N	H	$$	Y

56 Kenai RV Park

Location: In Kenai
GPS: N 60° 33.195' / W 151° 15.759'
Season: May through September
Sites: 22 full-hookup RV sites, 10 tent sites
Maximum length: 50 feet
Facilities: Tables, grills, potable water, flush toilets, showers, laundry, fish-cleaning station, WiFi
Fee per night: $$-$$$$$
Maximum stay: None
Management: Kenai RV Park, (541) 281-1609, www.kenairv.net
Finding the campground: The Kenai RV Park is located on Migrate Road about three miles south of Kenai near the intersection of Bridge Access Road and Kalifornsky Beach Road.
About the campground: This campground is essentially a gravel parking lot with full-hookup RV spaces and a few electric-only spaces. There is an open area for tent camping with minimal ambience. Still, if you're looking for a clean in-town location with hot showers, this site is conveniently situated just a few blocks from town and the Kenai River.

57 Discovery Campground

Location: About 25 miles north of Kenai
GPS: N 60° 48.198' / W 151° 00.520'
Season: May through mid-September
Sites: 52 basic sites
Maximum length: 40 feet
Facilities: Tables, fire pits, picnic area, potable water, vault toilets, beach access
Fee per night: $$
Maximum stay: 15 days
Management: Alaska State Parks, Kenai Area Office, (907) 262-5581, www.dnr.state.ak.us/parks

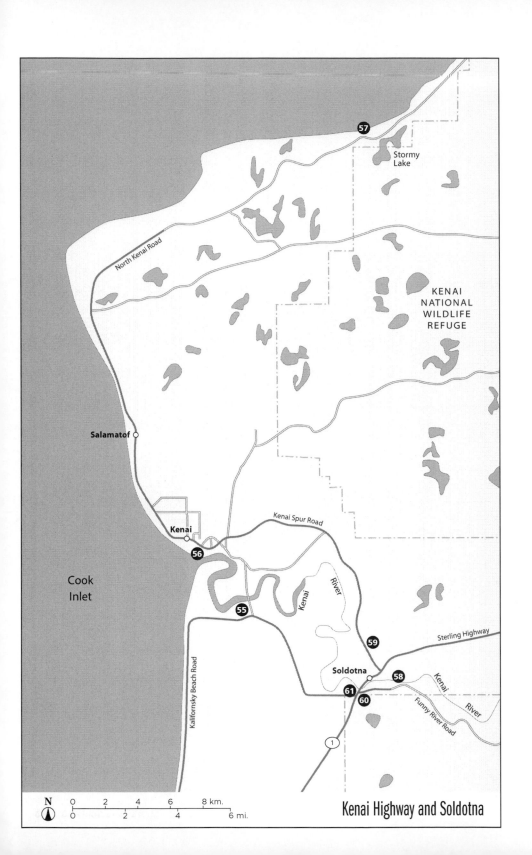

Stormy
Lake

KENAI
NATIONAL
WILDLIFE
REFUGE

North Kenai Road

Salamatof

Cook
Inlet

Kenai

Kenai Spur Road

Kenai River

Soldotna

Sterling Highway

Kenai River

Funny River Road

Kalifornsky Beach Road

N

0   2   4   6   8 km.
0   2   4   6 mi.

Kenai Highway and Soldotna

Finding the campground: From Kenai drive 25 miles north on North Kenai Road. Turn right near milepost 36 at the sign for Discovery Campground in the Captain Cook State Recreation Area. Follow the signs into the campground.

About the campground: The Captain Cook State Recreation Area covers about 3,500 acres tucked far off the beaten path 25 miles north of Kenai. The Discovery Campground is located on a high coastal bluff overlooking the Cook Inlet with beautiful views of the snowcapped Alaska-Aleutian Range. This is a quiet campground, even in summer, away from the highway and the fishing scene. The main attractions in this area are wildlife, peacefulness, beachcombing for agates, and canoeing and boating Stormy Lake.

Unless you visit on a holiday or special-event weekend, this campground is likely to be only half full. The camping area hosts spectacular coastal views from many campsites, and all are located in a lush setting of cottonwoods, spruce, and birch trees. The nicely spaced back-in sites are rather private. Watch out for heaps of the thorny devil's club that have overtaken the grounds, a painful prickly shrub to disturb.

The Sterling Highway: Soldotna to Anchor Point

The Sterling Highway: Soldotna to Anchor Point

	Hookup Sites	Total Sites	Max. RV Length	Hookups	Toilets	Showers	Drinking Water	Fires	Dump Station	Recreation	Fee	Reservations
58 Swiftwater Park	0	40	40	N	NF	N	Y	Y	Y	FBL	$$	N
59 King Salmon RV Park	39	39	Any	WES	F	Y	Y	N	N	N	$$$$	N
60 Klondike RV Park and Cabins	27	27	60	WESC	F	Y	Y	Y	N	N	$$$$$	Y
61 Centennial Park Campground	0	176	Any	N	NF	N	Y	y	Y	FBL	$$	N
62 Decanter Inn	55	55	50	E	F	Y	Y	Y	Y	F	$$$	Y
63 Crooked Creek State Recreation Site	0	80	50	N	NF	N	Y	Y	N	HF	$	N
64 Crooked Creek Guides RV Park	45	55	Any	WES	F	Y	Y	Y	Y	F	$$$$$	Y
65 Cohoe Cabins and RV Park	0	26	Any	N	F	N	Y	Y	Y	FBL	$$	Y
66 Johnson Lake State Recreation Area	0	48	30	N	NF	N	Y	Y	N	FBL	$	N
67 Kasilof RV Park	34	34	40	WESC	F	Y	Y	Y	Y	F	$$$$	Y
68 Clam Gulch State Recreation Area	0	136	30	N	NF	N	Y	Y	Y	F	$$	N
69 Scenic View RV Park	19	19	30	WES	F	Y	Y	Y	Y	N	$$$-$$$$	Y
70 Ninilchik River Campground	0	45	40	N	NF	N	Y	Y	N	HF	$$	N
71 Ninilchik Scenic Overlook Campground	0	25	Any	N	NF	N	Y	Y	N	N	$$	N
72 Alaskan Angler RV Resort	65	72	Any	WESC	F	Y	Y	Y	Y	N	$$-$$$$$	Y
73 Ninilchik View Campground	0	15	40	N	NF	N	Y	Y	Y	N	$$	N
74 All Seasons Campground	52	52	60	WESC	F	Y	Y	Y	N	N	$$$	Y
75 Deep Creek View Campground	15	30+	40	E	F	Y	Y	Y	Y	N	$$$	Y
76 Deep Creek Beach Campground	0	189	Any	N	NF	N	Y	Y	N	FBL	$$	N
77 Deep Creek North Campground	0	25	35	N	NF	N	Y	Y	N	F	$$	N
78 Deep Creek South Campground	0	18	35	N	NF	N	N	Y	N	F	$$	N
79 Ninilchik Volcano View RV Park	24	38	40	WE	F	Y	Y	Y	Y	N	$$-$$$$$	Y
80 Stariski Creek Campground	0	13	30	N	NF	N	Y	Y	N	N	$$	N
81 Whiskey Point Cabins and RV Park	25	26	Any	WES	F	Y	Y	Y	Y	N	$$-$$$$$	Y
82 Anchor River State Recreation Area	138	Any	N	NF	N	Y	Y	N	N	F	$$	N
83 Kyllonen RV Park	25	25	40	WES	Y	Y	Y	Y	N	N	$$$-$$$$	Y

58 Swiftwater Park

See map on page 44

Location: In Soldotna
GPS: N 60° 28.986' / W 151° 02.509'
Season: May through September
Sites: 40 basic sites
Maximum length: 40 feet
Facilities: Tables, fire pits, covered picnic area, potable water, vault toilets, dump station, river/fishing access, boat launch
Fee per night: $$
Maximum stay: 14 days
Management: City of Soldotna Parks and Recreation, (907) 262-3151, www.ci.soldotna.ak.us/parks_rec.html
Finding the campground: From mile 94.1 of the Sterling Highway, head east on East Redoubt Avenue for 0.4 mile. Turn right onto Swiftwater Park Road and drive another 0.4 mile to the campground.
About the campground: Even though this campground is smaller than nearby Centennial Campground, you will find it to be just as busy with the endless buzz of fishing traffic. The back-in campsites are in a wooded grove; some smaller sites more suited for tents are located along the river. There is a covered picnic area with a grill, and a boat launch. Most campers will be headed toward the boat launch or the 800-foot fish walk in search of salmon.

59 King Salmon RV Park

See map on page 44

Location: In Soldotna
GPS: N 60° 29.763' / W 151° 04.179'
Season: Mid-May through late September
Sites: 39 full-hookup RV sites
Maximum length: Any
Facilities: Tables, potable water, flush toilets, showers, laundry, WiFi
Fee per night: $$$$
Maximum stay: None
Management: King Salmon RV Park , (907) 262-5857, kingsalmonrvpark.com
Finding the campground: This campground is actually on the Kenai Spur Road, but it was one of the first in Soldotna. From mile 94 of the Sterling Highway, turn north onto Kenai Spur Road and drive 0.6 mile to the motel on your right.
About the campground: They don't take reservations, which can be nice if you decided to stay in Soldotna on a whim. Camping is limited to RVs and consists of a gravel parking area with thirty-nine full-hookup RV sites. There is a laundry facility and a restaurant nearby.

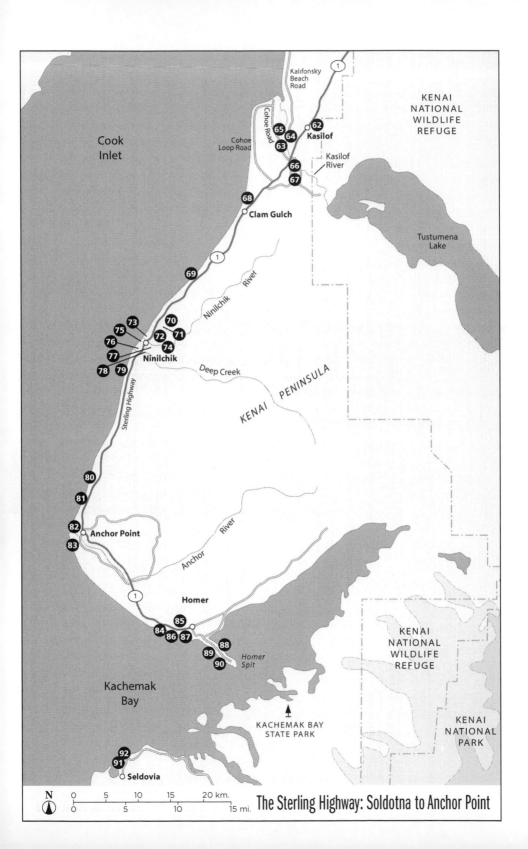

KENAI
NATIONAL
WILDLIFE
REFUGE

Cook
Inlet

Kalifonsky
Beach
Road

Cohoe Road

Cohoe
Loop Road

65
64
63
62 **Kasilof**

66
67

Kasilof
River

Tustumena
Lake

68 ○ **Clam Gulch**

1

69

Ninilchik River

73
75 **70**
76 **72** **71**
77 **74**
78 **79** **Ninilchik**

Deep Creek

KENAI PENINSULA

Sterling Highway

Anchor River

80

81

82 ○ **Anchor Point**

83

1

Homer

85
84 **87**
86

88

89
90

Homer
Spit

KENAI
NATIONAL
WILDLIFE
REFUGE

Kachemak
Bay

KACHEMAK BAY
STATE PARK

KENAI
NATIONAL
PARK

92
91
○ **Seldovia**

N
0   5   10   15   20 km.
0   5   10   15 mi.

The Sterling Highway: Soldotna to Anchor Point

60 Klondike RV Park and Cabins

See map on page 60

Location: In Soldotna
GPS: N 60° 28.452' / W 151° 04.612'
Season: Mid-May through September
Sites: 27 full-hookup RV sites
Maximum length: 60 feet
Facilities: Some tables and fire pits, potable water, showers, laundry, WiFi
Fee per night: $$$$$
Maximum stay: None
Management: Klondike RV Park and Cabins, (907) 262-6035, (800) 980-6035, www.klondikervpark.com
Finding the campground: From mile 96.1 of the Sterling Highway, turn east onto Funny River Road and drive 0.1 mile to the campground on the right side of the road.
About the campground: Just one block from the Kenai River, this newer RV park and campground will likely gain popularity given its location and squeaky-clean facilities. The RV sites are spacious and can accommodate large rigs. Each has a small lawn; some have trees. These grounds do not have restrooms since all sites are full hookups, so you want to be in a self-contained rig. The grounds do have clean showers and a laundry, along with free WiFi.

A bald eagle takes off from the Clam Gulch State Recreation Area.

61 Centennial Park Campground

See map on page 44

Location: In Soldotna
GPS: N 60° 28.798' / W 151° 05.536'
Season: Mid-May through mid-September
Sites: 176 basic sites
Maximum length: Any
Facilities: Tables, some fire pits, some grills, covered picnic area, potable water, vault toilets, dump station, river/fishing access, boat launch
Fee per night: $$
Maximum stay: 14 days
Management: City of Soldotna Parks and Recreation, (907) 262-3151, www.ci.soldotna.ak.us/parks_rec.html
Finding the campground: From mile 96.1 of the Sterling Highway in Soldotna, turn west onto Kalifornsky Beach Road and make an immediate right at the sign for the campground.
About the campground: With a 96-foot fish walk and 650 feet of elevated river access, more than a dozen sets of river-access stairs, and a popular boat launch, you'll find a lot of people on a quest for fish here. Centennial is home to over 150 wooded campsites, about half of which are quite large. Smaller sites near the boat launch are just a step away from the river action. If you're pulling a large RV, you'll be happy to find nine new oversize pull-thrus in an open lot near the entrance.

62 Decanter Inn

Location: Near Kasilof
GPS: N 60° 20.442' / W 151° 13.667'
Season: May through September
Sites: 55 partial-hookup RV sites
Maximum length: 50 feet
Facilities: Some tables, some fire pits, potable water, flush toilets, showers, dump station, fishing access, fish-cleaning station, restaurant, bar
Fee per night: $$$
Maximum stay: None
Management: The Decanter Inn, (907) 262-5933, (907) 262-5917, www.decanterinn.com
Finding the campground: The inn is located on the east side of the Sterling Highway at mile 107.
About the campground: Run in conjunction with the Decanter Inn, this small, mostly gravel lot is located on sixty wooded acres. Camping is in an open area with combination of small back-ins, a couple of pull-thrus, and basic parking-lot-style sites that are snug. Many campers who choose to stay here appreciate warm meals at the restaurant and a nightcap at the bar. There are also two small lakes on the premises; Rogue is stocked with salmon by Fish and Game. Given the close proximity to Kasilof fishing holes, reservations are recommended.

63 Crooked Creek State Recreation Site

Location: Near Kasilof
GPS: N 60° 19.300' / W 151° 17.233'
Season: May through November
Sites: 80 parking-lot-style sites
Maximum length: 35 feet
Facilities: Some tables and fire pits, potable water, vault toilets, hiking/fishing/river access
Fee per night: $
Maximum stay: 7 days
Management: Alaska State Parks, Kenai Area Office, (907) 262-5581, www.dnr.state.ak.us/parks
Finding the campground: At milepost 111 of the Sterling Highway, turn northwest onto North Cohoe Loop Road. The campground is 1.6 miles down this loop road.
About the campground: Located at the confluence of the Kasilof River and Crooked Creek, the popularity of this state recreation site in May and June can be attributed to the king salmon fishing. The campsites are all parking-lot-style side-by-side stalls that lack aesthetics. The main reason to stay here is for the fish. In fact, the site is run as a sportfishing access location in a cooperative effort between Alaska State Parks and Alaska Fish and Game. The area continues to stay moderately busy (with fishing) as the season endures. Although the camping atmosphere is nil, the fish run through here all season long.

64 Crooked Creek Guides RV Park

Location: Near Kasilof
GPS: N 60° 19.263' / W 151° 17.053'
Season: May through October
Sites: 37 full-hookup RV sites, 8 partial-hookup RV sites, 10 tent sites
Maximum length: Any
Facilities: Tables, grills, fire pits, potable water, flush toilets, showers, dump station, fish-cleaning facilities, fishing/river access, WiFi, charters, snack bar
Fee per night: $$$$$
Maximum stay: None
Management: Crooked Creek Guides RV Park, (907) 262-1299, www.crookedcreekguides.com
Finding the campground: At milepost 111 of the Sterling Highway, turn northwest onto North Cohoe Loop Road. The campground is 1.8 miles down this loop road, just past the state park campground at 23434 Trespass Street.
About the campground: This is a very nice campground for both RVs and tents, well off the main road with earthen side-by-side spaces and shady surroundings. The park is located next to a parking-lot-style state campground, the Crooked Creek State Recreation Site. In a rare change, the RV park has the natural camping atmosphere and the government campground has the bleak parking lot. Fringe benefits of staying at the private park include flush toilets, hot showers, and wireless internet. As with its neighbor, the main attraction here is fishing. These grounds are the closest to the Kasilof River and have access to a private bank on Crooked Creek. You can still access the

state fishing area. The standard established sites can take rigs up to 45 feet, and the overflow can accommodate any size.

65 Cohoe Cabins and RV Park

Location: Near Kasilof
GPS: N 60° 19.797' / W 151° 18.521'
Season: May through September
Sites: 26 basic sites
Maximum length: Any
Facilities: Tables, fire pits, potable water, flush toilets, dump station, fish-cleaning facilities, fishing/river access, boat launch, small store
Fee per night: $$
Maximum stay: None
Management: Cohoe Cabins and RV Park, (907) 953-5949
Finding the campground: At milepost 111 of the Sterling Highway, turn west onto North Cohoe Loop Road. Drive 2.5 to the campground on the right.
About the campground: This campground is just down the road from the Crooked Creek campgrounds and hosts twenty-six basic sites, thirteen of which are located along the Kasilof River with 900 feet of fishing access.

66 Johnson Lake State Recreation Area

Location: In Kasilof
GPS: N 60° 17.803' / W 151° 15.958'
Season: May through October
Sites: 48 basic sites
Maximum length: 30 feet
Facilities: Tables, fire pits, covered picnic area, potable water, vault toilets, fishing/lake access, boat launch
Fee per night: $
Maximum stay: 15 days
Management: Alaska State Parks, Kenai Area Office, (907) 262-5581, www.dnr.state.ak.us/parks
Finding the campground: From mile 110.3 of the Sterling Highway, turn east onto Ptarmigan Road. Drive 0.1 mile and turn left onto Johnson Lake Road. Continue for 0.3 mile and turn left at the sign for Tustumena Lake Area. Drive 0.1 mile and turn right at the sign into Johnson Lake Campground.
About the campground: This peaceful 332-acre wooded campground edges picturesque Johnson Lake and is a popular summer destination for local families. The lake is stocked with rainbows. Many come to fish directly from the waterfront sites, resting along the calm shores and quietly watching the lines. Brave kids swim in the cold, calm waters, and canoeing is always popular.

There are forty-eight basic sites, most surrounded by trees, though a few lack shade. Smaller RVs can nestle up to the shore in the desirable lakefront sites along with tenters who will find the spaces roomy. Reservations aren't accepted, so a lake spot can be hard to get; the campsites fill up during the weekends all summer. The grounds are open until they freeze up, then are maintained again in May when the host arrives.

67 Kasilof RV Park

Location: In Kasilof
GPS: N 60° 17.398' / W 151° 16.255'
Season: Late May through September
Sites: 9 full-hookup RV sites, 25 partial-hookup RV sites
Maximum length: 40 feet
Facilities: Tables, fire pits, potable water, flush toilets, showers, dump station, laundry, lake/fishing access, WiFi, charters, gift shop
Fee per night: $$$$
Maximum stay: None
Management: Kasilof RV Park, (907) 262-3704, www.kasilofrvpark.com
Finding the campground: From mile 110.3 of the Sterling Highway, turn east onto Ptarmigan Road. Drive 0.1 mile and turn right onto Johnson Lake Road. Drive 0.4 mile and turn left onto Crooked Creek Road. The campground is 0.5 mile down Crooked Creek Road on your right.
About the campground: This cute RV park is located down a gravel road away from the highway. Kasilof RV is situated directly across from calm Johnson Lake and is an excellent alternative to the parking-lot-style facilities along the Sterling Highway. Most of the sites are shaded and well spaced for an RV park. Plenty of landscaping keeps things fresh and organized. The full-service facilities are very clean, and the owners are on site and helpful. Reservations are recommended and there is a minimum 7-night stay.

68 Clam Gulch State Recreation Area

Location: Near mile 117 of the Sterling Highway
GPS: N 60° 14.324' / W 151° 23.741'
Season: Mid-May through mid-September
Sites: 116 parking-lot-style spaces, 20 basic sites
Maximum length: 30 feet
Facilities: Some tables and fire pits, covered picnic area, potable water, vault toilets, fishing/beach access
Fee per night: $$
Maximum stay: 15 days
Management: Alaska State Parks, Kenai Area Office, (907) 262-5581, www.dnr.state.ak.us/parks
Finding the campground: At milepost 117.4 of the Sterling Highway, turn west at the sign to Clam Gulch State Recreation Area, then drive 0.2 mile to the campground.

About the campground: Hundreds of thousands of clams are harvested from the beaches on the west coast of the Kenai. Clam Gulch State Recreation Area—originally intended as a day-use area to accommodate clammers—has been transformed into a campground. At the entrance to the 500-acre grounds, there are 116 unimpressive gravel parking-lot-style spaces that you can over-night in. Farther down the grounds, closer to the beach on a coastal bluff, there are about twenty basic sites with some greenery. Suitable to its name, the main attraction at this campground is the direct access to one of the better beaches for razor clamming in Alaska.

69 Scenic View RV Park

Location: Near mile 127 of the Sterling Highway
GPS: N 60° 07.871' / W 151° 32.131'
Season: Year-round
Sites: 10 full-hookup RV sites, 9 partial-hookup RV sites
Maximum length: 30 feet
Facilities: Picnic area with fire pit, potable water, flush toilets, showers, dump station, laundry, fish-cleaning facilities, charters, WiFi
Fee per night: $$$-$$$$
Maximum stay: None
Management: Scenic View RV Park, (907) 567-390
Finding the campground: The campground is on the west side of the Sterling Highway near mile-post 127.
About the campground: This aptly named campground has spectacular views of the Aleutians. Scenic View RV Park is home to a few gravel sites on a high bluff overlooking the Aleutian Range. The owners are friendly and provide nightly campfires and conversations to complement the backdrop. With clean yet basic facilities and an excellent location, this park can fill up quickly with clammers during time of a minus tide or anytime the fish are running.

70 Ninilchik River Campground

Location: In Ninilchik
GPS: N 60° 03.134' / W 151° 39.023'
Season: Mid-May through mid-September
Sites: 45 parking-lot-style spaces
Maximum length: 40 feet
Facilities: Some tables and fire pits, covered picnic area, potable water, vault toilets, hiking/fishing/river access
Fee per night: $$
Maximum stay: 15 days
Management: Alaska State Parks, Kenai Area Office, (907) 262-5581, www.dnr.state.ak.us/parks

Finding the campground: This is the northernmost of the Ninilchik State Recreation Area quad of campgrounds. From the east side of the Sterling Highway at mile 134.5, turn at the sign for the SRA and drive 0.2 mile to the campground.

About the campground: The Ninilchik State Recreation Area hosts popular salmon runs. Along with offering spectacular inlet and Aleutian views, this is a staging area for salmon and halibut fishing. It is no surprise, then, that the facility is more a parking lot allotted for multiday anglers than a campground in the traditional sense. That said, Ninilchik River has the most organic environment of the Ninilchik quad. The campsites back up to the woods, and an access trail leads to the river. There are still quite a few sites that are a tight squeeze. There is a lot of traffic here, and spaces fill quickly when the fish run.

71 Ninilchik Scenic Overlook Campground

Location: In Ninilchik
GPS: N 60° 02.917' / W 151 39.227'
Season: May through mid-September
Sites: 25 parking-lot-style spaces
Maximum length: Any
Facilities: Some tables and fire pits, potable water, vault toilets
Fee per night: $$
Maximum stay: 15 days
Management: Alaska State Parks, Kenai Area Office, (907) 262-5581, www.dnr.state.ak.us/parks
Finding the campground: This campground is located a tad south of Ninilchik River Campground and just north of the Ninilchik River, at mile 134.6 of the Sterling Highway.

About the campground: Functioning mostly as an overflow lot for Ninilchik River Campground, this campground has twenty-five extra sites that also fill up quickly during the fishing season. Since the camping area consists of an open lot with parking-lot-style spaces, you can fit rigs of any size here, but tenters won't have much luck when looking for a cozy place to pitch.

72 Alaskan Angler RV Resort

Location: In Ninilchik
GPS: N 60° 02.712' / W 151° 40.028'
Season: Year-round
Sites: 55 full hook-up RV sites, 10 partial hook-up RV sites, 7 tent sites
Maximum length: Any
Facilities: Tables, covered picnic area, communal fire pit, potable water, flush toilets, showers, dump station, laundry, fish-cleaning facilities, WiFi, charters, small store
Fee per night: $$–$$$$$
Maximum stay: None
Management: Alaskan Angler RV Resort, (907) 567-3393, www.alaskabestrvpark.com

Finding the campground: From mile 135.3 of the Sterling Highway, turn east onto Kingsley Road; the park is on your immediate left.

About the campground: True to its name, this full-service RV park was designed with the angler in mind. The campground is on the east side of the highway, about a 0.25-mile walk from the beach, and therefore away from the view. The on-site fishing charters cater to any local fresh- or saltwater fishing desire. The campground is complete with fish-cleaning facilities, a fish smoker, and a walk-in fish freezer. The owners can even assist with overnight shipping of your catch. The hookup sites are in a well-groomed gravel lot, with several supersize spaces suitable for any size of rig. A separate wooded area has dry RV sites and tent space.

73 Ninilchik View Campground

Location: In Ninilchik
GPS: N 60° 02.811' / W 151° 40.226'
Season: Mid-May through mid-September
Sites: 15 basic sites
Maximum length: 40 feet
Facilities: Tables, fire pits, potable water, vault toilets, dump station
Fee per night: $$
Maximum stay: 8 days
Management: Alaska State Parks, Kenai Area Office, (907) 262-5581, www.dnr.state.ak.us/parks
Finding the campground: From mile 135.7 of the Sterling Highway, turn west at the sign for Ninilchik State Recreation Area.

About the campground: As the name states, this campground is located above Ninilchik Beach on a high bluff with excellent views of the ocean and the village. There are fifteen basic back-in sites separated by stout spruce. A brief wooded trail connects this campground with the Ninilchik Beach Campground and water access below. These grounds are located beyond the water/dump station.

74 All Seasons Campground

Location: Near mile 136 of the Sterling Highway
GPS: N 60° 01.419' / W 151° 35.617'
Season: May through late September
Sites: 52 full-hookup RV sites
Maximum length: 60 feet
Facilities: Tables, communal fire pit, picnic area, potable water, flush toilets, showers, laundry, fish-cleaning facilities, WiFi, restaurant, gift shop
Fee per night: $$$
Maximum stay: None
Management: All Seasons Campground, (907) 567-3396, www.allseasonsalaska.com

Finding the campground: From mile 135.9 of the Sterling Highway, drive east on Oil Well Road for 3.1 miles to the All Seasons Campground on your left.

About the campground: This Wild West–themed campground is located about 3 miles from the Sterling Highway. Despite being a few miles from the popular fishing areas, there are still fish-cleaning facilities, and charters can be arranged through the park. All Seasons has fifty-two full-hookup parking-lot-style RV sites. About a quarter are pull-thrus that can accommodate rigs of any size. The country-style grounds are complete with a restaurant called the "Up-chuck Saloon"; although alcohol is not served, the theme is engaging.

75 Deep Creek View Campground

Location: Near mile 136 of the Sterling Highway
GPS: N 60° 02.192' / W 151° 41.329'
Season: May through mid-September
Sites: 15 RV partial-hookup RV sites, 15 dry RV sites, open overflow area
Maximum length: 40 feet
Facilities: Tables, fire pits, potable water, flush toilets, showers, dump station, fish-cleaning facilities, WiFi, charters
Fee per night: $$$
Maximum stay: None
Management: J & J Smart Charters, (888) HALIBUT, May through September (907) 567-3320, www.smartcharters.com
Finding the campground: From mile 136.2 of the Sterling Highway, at the sign for J & J Smart Charters, drive west on Julia Steik Avenue for 0.3 mile to a T. Turn right onto Erikson Avenue. The campground is on your left at 0.1 mile.

About the campground: This family-run campground and charter operation is a refreshing change from the standard gravel RV parks in the area. Located on the classic high bluff along the Cook Inlet, J & J offers a feeling of coastal isolation even though you're not far from the highway. There are about thirty cozy back-in sites; most have tables and fire pits, and half have electrical hookups. An open grassy pad is available for tenters. Some sites overlook Deep Creek River and the inlet, an excellent chance to watch serene sunsets and sunrises over Mounts Redoubt and Iliamna. There is no direct beach access from this campground, but the elevation provides a lofty view of the water below. Not surprisingly, most guests here book fishing charters through the owners, J & J Smart Charters. Reservations are available for the sites with hookups, which often fill.

76 Deep Creek Beach Campground

Location: Near mile 137 of the Sterling Highway
GPS: N 60° 01.878' / W 151° 42.147'
Season: May through September
Sites: 189 basic sites
Maximum length: Any

Facilities: Some tables and fire pits, communal picnic area and fire pits, potable water, vault toilets, fishing/beach/creek access, boat launch
Fee per night: $$
Maximum stay: 15 days
Management: Alaska State Parks, Kenai Area Office, (907) 262-5581, www.dnr.state.ak.us/parks
Finding the campground: At mile 137.2 of the Sterling Highway, turn west at the sign for Deep Creek State Recreation Area and drive 0.3 mile to the campground.
About the campground: This 172-acre beachfront campground has brilliant coastal views. With the mouth of Deep Creek draining into the sea, fishing is productive. In late spring the marshy areas are inhabited by sandhill cranes. The campsites are impersonal open side-by-side spaces suitable for any size of RV or camper; some have tables and fire pits. Many commercial charters launch from this campground, so there is a very busy and well-developed boat launch.

77 Deep Creek North Campground

Location: Mile 137 of the Sterling Highway
GPS: N 60° 01.827' / W 151° 40.865'
Season: Year-round
Sites: 25 parking-lot style spaces
Maximum length: 35 feet
Facilities: Some tables and fire pits, communal picnic area, potable water, vault toilets, fishing/creek access
Fee per night: $$
Maximum stay: 15 days
Management: Alaska State Parks, Kenai Area Office, (907) 262-5581, www.dnr.state.ak.us/parks
Finding the campground: This site is located on the north shore of Deep Creek at mile 137.
About the campground: This campground was originally designed as day-use area and lacks any camping ambience. Still, it's a clean, reasonably inexpensive place to stay if you're looking to camp close to fishing access. All sites are back-in parking-lot-style stalls. A dull open area behind the lot is suitable for pitching a tent. The services for this campground close down in September but the gates remain unlocked for campers.

78 Deep Creek South Campground

Location: Mile 137 of the Sterling Highway
GPS: N 60° 01.732' / W 151° 41.057'
Season: Mid-May through September
Sites: 18 basic sites
Maximum length: 35 feet
Facilities: Some tables and fire pits, picnic area, vault toilets, fishing/creek access
Fee per night: $$
Maximum stay: 15 days

Management: Alaska State Parks, Kenai Area Office, (907) 262-5581, www.dnr.state.ak.us/parks

Finding the campground: This campground is located just across the water from Deep Creek North, on the south shore of Deep Creek at mile 137.

About the campground: A smaller version of its northern counterpart, this site was also originally designed as a day-use area. It similarly lacks camping ambience. Still, it's a clean, inexpensive place to park if you're looking to stay close to fishing access, and the grounds do fill. All sites are back-in parking-lot-style stalls, with an unremarkable open area behind the lot suitable for pitching a tent.

79 Ninilchik Volcano View RV Park

Location: Near mile 137 of the Sterling Highway

GPS: N 60° 01.606' / W 151° 41.981'

Season: May through September

Sites: 24 partial-hookup RV sites, 14 basic sites

Maximum length: 40 feet

Facilities: Some tables and fire pits, picnic area with grills, potable water, flush toilets, showers, dump station, laundry, fish cleaning facilities, beach access, WiFi, charters

Fee per night: $$-$$$$$

Maximum stay: None

Management: Ninilchik Volcano View RV Park, (907) 567-3220, www.discoverakadv.com

Finding the campground: From mile 137.2 of the Sterling Highway, drive west onto the Deep Creek Beach access road. Follow the signs for 0.2 mile to the campground.

About the campground: This large gravel lot with basic parking-lot-style sites is located on a high bluff with a good view of the Aleutian Range and has direct access to the beach. Guests are also within walking distance of the Deep Creek State Recreation Area facilities. The full-service RV park is run in conjunction with the full-service fishing charters, and the area is also popular with clammers.

80 Stariski Creek Campground

Location: Near mile 151 of the Sterling Highway

GPS: N 59° 50.503' / W 151° 48.734'

Season: May through October

Sites: 13 basic sites

Maximum length: 30 feet

Facilities: Tables, fire pits, covered picnic area, potable water, vault toilets

Fee per night: $$

Maximum stay: 15 days

Management: Alaska State Parks, Kenai Area Office, (907) 262-5581, www.dnr.state.ak.us/parks

Finding the campground: This campground is located at the west side of the Sterling Highway at mile 151.9.

About the campground: Stariski is a smaller, quieter campground on a wooded hilltop with views of Mounts Augustine, Iliamna, and Redoubt. This campground is also a mile from beach access, so it's not as popular as other campgrounds in the area that have direct water and fishing access. Still, if you're looking for a less busy alternative to the Anchor River campgrounds, yet want to be close to the good fishing spots, Stariski is a fine choice. The only trade-off is the highway noise, which is inescapable in many Sterling Highway campgrounds. The campsites here are practical and best suited for RVs 30 feet and under.

81 Whiskey Point Cabins and RV Park

Location: Mile 152 of the Sterling Highway
GPS: N 59° 49.854' / W 151° 48.949'
Season: Late May through September
Sites: 25 full hookups sites, tent site
Maximum length: Any
Facilities: Some tables, communal fire pit, potable water, flush toilets, showers, dump station, laundry, WiFi
Fee per night: $$$–$$$$$
Maximum stay: None
Management: Whiskey Point Cabins and RV Park, (907) 235-1961, www.whiskeypointalaska.com
Finding the campground: This campground is on the west side of mile 152.5 of the Sterling Highway.
About the campground: On a clear day you can have sweeping views of the three volcanoes from the bluff at this ocean side campground. The sites are in a gravel lot with tent space available.

82 Anchor River State Recreation Area

Location: Near mile 157 of the Sterling Highway
GPS: N 59° 46.264' / W 151° 50.270'
Season: May through late September
Sites: 138 basic sites
Maximum length: Any
Facilities: Some tables and fire pits, vault toilets, potable water, fishing/river access.
Fee per night: $$
Maximum stay: 15 days
Management: Alaska State Parks, Kenai Area Office, (907) 262-5581, www.dnr.state.ak.us/parks
Finding the campground: From mile 156.9 of the Sterling Highway in Anchor Point, turn west onto the Old Sterling Highway and drive 0.3 mile. Take the first right after you cross the bridge at the sign for the Anchor River State Recreation Area. The Silverking Campground is on your immediate right; Coho is 0.2 mile farther down the road, followed by Steelhead at 0.4 mile, Slidehole at 0.7, and Halibut at 1.2 miles. If you were to drive to the dead end of Anchor River Road, you'd be at the westernmost point of the westernmost road in North America accessible by the continuous road system.

About the campground: The Anchor River State Recreation Area encompasses five camping sections—and since the Anchor River is one of Alaska's premier fishing locales, expect the area to be busy all summer. You'll find an exceptionally crowded river during the king salmon run in late May and early June. The fishing holes stretch for a couple of miles, and the line of anglers seems never-ending. Anchor Point is an interesting historical area (legend has it that Captain Cook lost his anchor on this point—hence the name) and the area is a wonderful spot for viewing all kinds of Alaskan wildlife. At the lookout, spectacular views of the Aleutian Chain's photogenic Mounts Augustine, Iliamna, and Redoubt are available. The campsites, however, are for the most part tucked behind brush without quality scenery.

Camping is divided into five sections, the first four of which are respectively similar. Silverking, Coho, Steelhead, and Slidehole Campgrounds contain parking-lot-style side-by-side stalls. Some have tables and fire pits and a few are located directly on the river. Halibut is the last campground on the park road and is closest to the beach at Anchor Point. It is far removed from the fishing but by far the best locale in the Anchor Point series if you're looking for atmosphere. Several beachfront sites have magnificent Aleutian views. Most of the sites are spaciously placed and include the basic government amenities of a place to park, a place to pitch a tent, a table, and a fire pit. The first three campgrounds are big-rig friendly, the latter two are best for RVs 35 feet and under.

83 Kyllonen RV Park

Location: Near mile 157 of the Sterling Highway
GPS: N 59° 46.249' / W 151° 51.603'
Season: Mid-May through September
Sites: 25 full-hookup RV sites
Maximum length: 40 feet
Facilities: Tables, fire pits, potable water, flush toilets, showers, laundry, fish-cleaning facilities, WiFi, gift shop
Fee per night: $$$–$$$$
Maximum stay: None
Management: Kyllonen RV Park, (907) 235-7762, (888) 848-2589, www.kyllonenrvpark.com
Finding the campground: From mile 156.9 of the Sterling Highway, go right onto the Old Sterling Highway at the Y in the road between the two highways, drive west on the Old Sterling Highway for 0.3 mile. Turn right onto the road that takes you to the Anchor River State Recreation Area. Drive 1.2 miles down the beach access road to the Kyllonen RV Park on your right.
About the campground: This small private RV park is located in the middle of the Anchor River State Recreation quad of public campgrounds. The forested park has lovely views of the Cook Inlet across the marshes at the mouth of the Anchor River. Wildlife-viewing opportunities, especially for birders, are greatly enhanced by sites overlooking the marsh. Camping is divided into two sections joined by a short footpath. Most sites are fairly close together, but the owners invested a lot of time and talent into creating a cozy and charming environment. It may be a snug fit here for many RVs, so call ahead and make a reservation! Each site has a fire pit, and free firewood is available. The park—proudly proclaimed "North America's Most Westerly RV Park"—is located near the end of the westernmost road in the continuous road system of North America.

Homer

Homer and Seldovia

	Hookup Sites	Total Sites	Max. RV Length	Hookups	Toilets	Showers	Drinking Water	Fires	Dump Station	Recreation	Fee	Reservations
84 Homer/Baycrest KOA Holiday	66	75	45	WES	F	Y	Y	Y	Y	N	$$$$-$$$$$	Y
85 Karen A. Hornaday Hillside Park	0	33	30	N	NF	N	Y	Y	N	N	$-$$	N
86 Ocean Shores RV Park	83	92+	45	WESC	F	Y	Y	N	N	N	$$-$$$$	Y
87 Driftwood Inn and RV Park	22	22	40	WESC	F	Y	Y	N	N	HF	$$$$$	Y
88 Heritage RV Park	107	107	Any	WESC	F	Y	Y	Y	Y	HF	$$$$$	Y
89 Homer Spit City Campground	30	80	Any	E	F & NF	N	Y	Y	Y	HF	$-$$	N
90 Homer Spit Campground	99	123	50	EC	F	Y	Y	Y	Y	HF	$$$-$$$$$	Y
91 Outside Beach	0	20	Any	N	NF	N	N	Y	N	HF	$	N
92 Seldovia RV Park	0	19	35	N	NF	N	Y	Y	N	HF	$	N

84 Homer/Baycrest KOA Holiday

Location: In Homer
GPS: N 59° 39.472' / W 151° 38.3922'
Season: Early May to mid-September
Sites: 66 full hookup RV sites, 6 partial hookups, 3 tent sites
Maximum length: 45 feet
Facilities: Tables, some fire pits, potable water, flush toilets, showers, laundry, WiFi, gift shop
Fee per night: $$$$-$$$$$
Maximum stay: None
Management: Homer/Baycrest KOA Holiday, (907) 435-7995, www.koa.com/campgrounds/homer
Finding the campground: This campground is located on the west side of the Sterling Highway at mile 169 next to the gas station.
About the campground: This newer high bluff campground has sweeping ocean views clear to the volcanoes across the inlet. Most of the sites are well kept gravel RV pads, and there are a handful of partial hookups and tent sites.

85 Karen A. Hornaday Hillside Park

See map on page 48

Location: In Homer
GPS: N 59° 39.090' / W 151° 33.307'
Season: April through October
Sites: 33 basic sites
Maximum length: 30 feet
Facilities: Tables, fire pits, potable water, vault toilets
Fee per night: $-$$
Maximum stay: 14 days
Management: City of Homer Department of Parks and Recreation, Public Works Department, (907) 235-3170, www.ci.homer.ak.us
Finding the campground: This site can be difficult to find, but the city has posted signs. From the Sterling Highway at the west end of Homer, drive north on Bartlett Street for 0.1 mile; turn left at the second street onto West Fairview. Take the first right onto Campground Road. The campground is at the end of the road.
About the campground: This campground is located above the Karen A. Hornaday city park on a steep hillside overlooking the city of Homer. Some of the sites have views of the bay, but most are secluded in willow brush. The steep, narrow roads throughout the grounds are extremely hard to maneuver; only the first couple sites are recommended for RVs or campers of any length. Scout out any farther on foot. Tenters will find soft grass and earthen grounds to pitch a tent. As one of Homer's two public campgrounds, this is an appealing spot to escape the roaring wind of the spit, enjoy the quiet hills, and see the twinkle of the city lights or the spectacular sunset from high above the city. As with most city-operated campgrounds, the facilities are not as clean or open as those in state or federal counterparts, and not as well maintained. The public park beneath the site has a playground, baseball field, and large covered picnic area.

86 Ocean Shores RV Park

See map on page 48

Location: In Homer
GPS: N 59° 38.365' / W 151° 32.717'
Season: May through October
Sites: 68 full-hookup RV sites, 15 partial-hookup RV sites, 9 tent sites, open overflow
Maximum length: 45 feet
Facilities: Communal picnic area with grills, potable water, flush toilets, showers, laundry, WiFi, beach access, gift shop, hiking/fishing access
Fee per night: $$-$$$$
Maximum stay: None
Management: Ocean Shores RV Park, (907) 435-0800, www.homeralaskarvpark.com

Finding the campground: This park is located at mile 172.7 on the Sterling Highway in old town Homer. It's the first campground you'll see on your right as you approach Homer from the north.

About the campground: Ocean Shores is a large-scale RV park and probably the nicest beach location for RVs to set up outside the Homer Spit. The scenic beachfront sites have mountain views and direct access down to Bishop Beach. The gravel sites are terraced. Level sites are set above one another on a gentle slope, so most campers have stunning Kachemak Bay views. The campground is complete with a landscaped grassy lawn and clean restrooms. About half of the sites can accommodate rigs up to 45 feet; the rest are smaller back-ins. All are rather narrow. There is a separate open area for tent camping and an area for beach viewing.

87 Driftwood Inn and RV Park

See map on page 48

Location: In Homer
GPS: N 59° 38.365' / W 151° 32.717'
Season: Year-round
Sites: 22 full-hookup RV sites
Maximum length: 40 feet
Facilities: Tables, picnic area with grill, potable water, flush toilets, showers, laundry, fish-cleaning facilities, hiking/fishing/beach access, charters
Fee per night: $$$$$
Maximum stay: None
Management: Driftwood Inn, (907) 235-8019, (800) 478-8019, www.thedriftwoodinn.com
Finding the campground: From Homer, drive south on Main Street from its intersection with the Sterling Highway. Drive 0.1 mile and turn left onto Ohlsen Lane. The back of the Driftwood Inn RV park is on your immediate right.
About the campground: Wedged between the beach and the inn, this small, open campground has snug side-by-side sites. The grounds are cramped and neighbors are very close together, so maneuvering room is limited. Those parking fifth wheels will be in for a challenge. Several of the back-in sites face the bay. Location wins over many campers here: The park is just a few feet from beach access and within walking distance of downtown. The grounds are also across the street from a bar, so some nights can get noisy.

88 Heritage RV Park

See map on page 48

Location: In Homer
GPS: N 59° 36.630' / W 151° 26.515'
Season: May through early September
Sites: 107 full-hookup RV sites

Maximum length: Any
Facilities: Tables, communal fireplace, picnic area, potable water, flush toilets, showers, laundry, beach access, WiFi, restaurant, gift shop, putting green, clubhouse
Fee per night: $$$$$
Maximum stay: None
Management: Heritage RV Park, (907) 226-4500, (800) 380-7787, www.alaskaheritagervpark.com
Finding the campground: From downtown Homer, follow the Sterling Highway through town (now labeled the Homer-Bypass Road) to its end as it turns into Lake Street. Drive 0.4 mile down Lake Street and follow the road left as it becomes Ocean Drive. After 0.5 mile, Ocean Drive turns into Homer Spit Road. Drive 3.3 miles down Homer Spit Road to the campground on your left.
About the campground: This is by far the plushest RV park in the Homer area; it's also the most expensive, with the beachfront sites running $75 a day. The high price accompanies the newest and most luxurious facilities in the area, complete with a small putting green. Camping is in a large open gravel lot. The sites are spacious parking-lot-style stalls, many of which are oversize and can accommodate any size of rig. All have full hookups. The pricey beachfront sites have direct beach access and amazing views of Upper Kachemak Bay. The most popular fishing hole of the spit is just a few feet away.

89 Homer Spit City Campground

See map on page 48

Location: In Homer
GPS: N 59° 36.477' / W 151° 26.200'
Season: April through October
Sites: 30 partial-hookup RV sites, 50 basic sites
Maximum length: Any
Facilities: Some tables, open fires, potable water, vault and flush toilets, dump station, hiking/fishing access
Fee per night: $-$$
Maximum stay: 14 days
Management: City of Homer Department of Parks and Recreation, (907) 235-3170, www.ci.homer.ak.us
Finding the campground: From downtown Homer, follow the Sterling Highway through town (now labeled the Homer-Bypass Road) to its end as it turns into Lake Street. Drive 0.4 mile down Lake Street and follow the road left as it becomes Ocean Drive. After 0.5 mile, Ocean Drive turns into Homer Spit Road. Mariner Park is on your right 0.4 mile down Homer Spit Road. Three miles down the road, the Camp Fee Collections Cabin is in the center of the tent (on your right) and RV sections (left) of the spit camping.
About the campground: Many say that in order to become "sourdough" (a seasoned Alaskan), you must spend some time camped out on the Homer Spit. The public beach camping here is legendary. Located across the road from the boat harbor, deep-water docks, and Alaska Marine Highway ferry terminal, fishermen used to camp out on the spit waiting for the next boat to go out. In the last few years, however, the city has made a successful effort to regulate beach camping. Fees

are not only imposed but also enforced, discouraging long stays for campers. The grounds are now highly regulated, so be sure to post your receipts after you pay the fee at one of the drop boxes.

The city-operated campground on Homer Spit is divided into three sections. Mariner Park is located at the base of the spit about 0.4 mile down the Spit Road as you begin your drive down the narrow strip of land. Camping in Mariner Park is in open unassigned parking-lot-style spaces in an open gravel lot. Tenters have the option of camping along the beachfront, in front of the RVs, where there are some fire rings and tables. Many traveling in campers and RVs will also be able to enjoy the spectacular panorama of the waterfront, peering over the tents from the open lot.

As you reach the 3-mile mark heading down the spit, you'll find yourself at the wooden Camp Fee Collection Cabin on the west side of the spit; if it's open, you can pay your fees here and talk to staff. Next to the collection cabin, along the beach on the west side, you will notice small wooden signs with numbers marking the city camping areas. This is the small RV and tent camping area. The spit can get windy, and tent stakes aren't often sufficient; think about bringing sand stake bags and possibly a tarp for added protection. Wind-whipping nights aren't guaranteed; sometimes the beach is serene. Several fire pits have been built along this stretch of the beach.

Across the road from the cabin lie the paved and gravel lots of the city-run RV section. Some brave souls will pull an RV into the sinking sand of the western side of the spit, but if you are unsure of your rig's sand-immersed driving capabilities, stick to the east. Park in the boundaries of the designated signs and avoid camping in any other area—charters and such strictly enforce their parking regulations. There is also a city-operated dump and water-fill station by the fishing lagoon restrooms if you're camping in an RV.

Campers on the Homer Spit City Campground.

90 Homer Spit Campground

See map on page 48

Location: In Homer
GPS: N 59° 36.047' / W 151° 25.003'
Season: Mid-May through mid-September
Sites: 99 partial-hookup RV sites, 24 basic sites
Maximum length: 50 feet
Facilities: Tables, some fire rings, potable water, flush toilets, showers, dump station, laundry, hiking/fishing/beach access, WiFi, charters, gift shop
Fee per night: $$$-$$$$$
Maximum stay: None
Management: Homer Spit Campground, (907) 235-8206, www.homerspitcampground.com
Finding the campground: From downtown Homer, follow the Sterling Highway through town (now labeled the Homer-Bypass Road) to its end as it turns into Lake Street. Drive 0.4 mile down Lake Street and follow the road left as it becomes Ocean Drive. After 0.5 mile, Ocean Drive turns into Homer Spit Road. Drive 4 miles down Homer Spit Road to the campground.
About the campground: This attractive campground is located at the end of the Homer Spit, where the road literally ends and the water spans for miles. There are ninety-nine electric-only sites in an open area and twenty-four dry sites directly on the beach, offering dramatic views away from the crowds of the city-run campground. Thirteen pull-thrus are suitable for rigs up to 50 feet. Reservations are recommended.

91 Outside Beach

See map on page 48

Location: In Seldovia
GPS: N 59° 27.326' / W 151° 42.586'
Season: Year-round
Sites: 20 primitive campsites
Maximum length: Any
Facilities: Some tables and fire rings, covered picnic area, vault toilet, hiking/fishing/beach access
Fee per night: $
Maximum stay: 14 days
Management: City of Seldovia, (907) 234-7643, www.cityofseldovia.com
Finding the campground: To reach Outside Beach from downtown Seldovia, take Jakolof Bay Road north and turn left onto the unlabeled road just before milepost 1. Drive 0.3 mile to the vault toilets and covered picnic area. Camping begins here and stretches along the road for about another mile. Those traveling in RVs or pulling trailers will want to be very cautious—the road can get muddy, and many parking areas are in thick sand. To pay the camp fees, visit the city offices at 245 Dock Street, immediately next to the ferry dock.

About the campground: Rumor is that the road ends in Homer, but in fact the Alaska Marine Highway just begins here. Seldovia, the closest hop along the Marine Highway from Homer, is a popular local getaway. Water taxis, as well as the state ferry system, sail this way nearly daily. You have two choices in campgrounds—Outside Beach and Wilderness RV Park. You can't get closer to the action than Outside Beach, and it can get rowdy here on weekends and summer holidays. The beach is popular with locals and covered with anglers during the salmon runs. The camping area stretches along the gravel shores of the sea to one side of the road and tucks into the adjoining woods on the other. The sites are primitive, although there are a few tables; most camp spots are identifiable by a lone makeshift fire ring. Tables or not, the beach is a bargain at a low cost. This campground doesn't have self-registration boxes; you must pay your fee and register at the city or harbormaster's offices.

92 Seldovia RV Park

See map on page 48

Location: In Seldovia
GPS: N 59° 27.674' / W 151° 42.275'
Season: Year-round
Sites: 16 basic sites, 3 walk-in tent sites
Maximum length: 35 feet
Facilities: Tables, fire pits, potable water, vault toilets, hiking/fishing/beach access
Fee per night: $
Maximum stay: 14 days
Management: City of Seldovia, (907) 234-7643, www.cityofseldovia.com
Finding the campground: To reach the campground from Seldovia, take Jakolof Bay Road north for 1.5 miles and turn left at the sign for the RV park. Drive 0.1 mile to the campsites. To pay the camp fees, visit the city offices at 245 Dock Street, just next to the ferry dock.
About the campground: These wooded sites are not directly on the water, but they feature enjoyable bay views and trail access to Outside Beach. The Seldovia RV Park is a city-operated campground more resembling a traditional government campground than an RV park. The campsites are basic back-ins with tables and fire pits. All of the facilities are well kept. Most of the sites are located under the thick branches of old spruce; some have more open views of the sea. Like its counterpart, this campground is a bargain for campers. Don't forget to register and pay your camp fee at the city or harbormaster's office. Seldovia RV Park does not have self-registration boxes, but there is often a caretaker around to ensure that fees are paid. This campground stays open until the snow pushes visitors out.

Anchorage and Chugach State Park

Located at the edge of south-central Alaska, nestled between the roily shores of the Cook Inlet and the towering peaks of the Chugach Range, the gulf-coast city of Anchorage is the taming ground of the Alaskan wilderness and the gateway to some of the most enthralling outdoor opportunities the state has to offer.

Topographically known as the Anchorage Bowl, the city and vicinity are nearly at sea level but are surrounded by towering mountains on three sides, including the Chugach Range, one of the highest coastal mountain ranges in the world. More impressive are the peaks that lie beyond. In fact, on a clear day it's possible to view six mountain ranges from the city, and often the tallest peak in North America, Denali.

With mountains a short drive from their doorsteps, locals will commonly joke that Anchorage is only "twenty minutes from Alaska." From the classics to the unconventional—hiking to dogsledding, flight-seeing across glaciers to gold panning at midnight—calling Anchorage the home base of Alaskan adventure is appropriate, with the city just minutes from some of the state's premier sites. Whether you're fishing for salmon in the lucid waters of the Kenai Peninsula, viewing a dramatic bore tide, or catching a short flight to an area glacier, a plethora of activities await you not far from the city lines.

But you don't have to leave Anchorage to access a lifetime of adventures. Landscapes within the city include thick spruce forests and light deciduous groves, saltwater marshes and alpine tundra. Activities from bird-watching to mountaineering are all accessible from the city stretch. The surplus of opportunities is partially due to the geographic size of Anchorage. In a state known for vastness, the largest city is no exception. The municipality of Anchorage encompasses almost 2,000 square miles, stretching far past the city proper, covering a sprawl about the size of the state of Delaware. Public-access wilderness lands within Anchorage abound, including the half-million-acre Chugach State Park.

Anchorage is also Alaska's most populated city. Roughly half the state's population lives here, with about 280,000 residents calling it home. For many the Anchorage area seasonally hosts the perfect hiking and camping weather with short and deceitfully idyllic summers. In a pocket between the moderating ocean breezes and protective mountains, the city is gifted with a nearly mild maritime climate. Summer highs range from fifty to seventy degrees Fahrenheit, and combined with the late-night sun, this camper's playground seems to be full of endless choices.

The Anchorage trail system is impressive evidence that when it comes to aesthetics, locals would rather spend their time looking at nature than architecture. In summer months more than 200 miles of trails are available for exploration within the city. You'll find these trails well groomed and well traveled. The 11-mile Tony Knowles Coastal Trail follows the coastline in downtown with spectacular views of the inlet and panoramic mountains. Located at the eastern edge of Anchorage is Alaska's most climbed peak, Flattop Mountain. During the summer solstice Flattop is a mecca

Nestled between the Chugach Range and Cook Inlet, Anchorage has a mild, nearly maritime climate.

where residents can soak in the everlasting sun on the horizon. Of course, no discussion of the Anchorage outdoors would be complete without mentioning the magnet of Alaskan travel—fishing. Within the city four species of salmon can be found. During salmon runs, anglers line shoulder-to-shoulder along downtown's Ship Creek, a stark contradiction to the skyscrapers that frame this image.

Anchorage began as a railroad construction camp, and it remains true to its working-class roots. In a successful attempt to join the urban ranks and express a unique cultural heritage, the downtown has made great strides in museums and art. The Alaska Center for the Performing Arts hosts many events. The twenty-five-acre Alaska Native Heritage Center offers an inside view of the people who thrived in this area for thousands of years. The Alaska Museum of Natural History is also a must; don't miss the ice age mammal displays and volcano simulator.

Anchorage may be most famous as the center of Alaskan shopping. Most campers begin their travels here, given that the city hosts a major airport, and both the Glenn and Seward highways pass through town. Before they leave, campers may take advantage of Alaska's most economical choices for stocking the ice chest or pack. Anchorage is home to many discount stores and outdoor retailers. In a land where things are often shipped thousands of miles before they hit the shelf, pricing your necessities in the city is a wise move.

Camping in the Anchorage vicinity, particularly for RVs, has become a challenge. For the past few years it has not been uncommon to find RV campgrounds booked solid. With the largest private campground closing in the city (to make room for more discount stores!), campers are now faced with hundreds fewer sites. Do your research ahead of time to ensure that your trip will end with a cozy night of camping instead of a frantic search for a berth. Reservations are almost always necessary from May through September. Pricing has changed dramatically in Anchorage and continues to rise rapidly. It's not unusual to find RVs parking in the Wal-Mart and Fred Meyer's parking lot or at the Alaska Parking Authority downtown. Another reasonable option is to stay forty-five minutes north of the city in the agricultural spread of the Matanuska Valley. Both Palmer and Wasilla are home to many government campgrounds and full-service RV parks.

In short, Anchorage may not be the glittery urban metropolis that so many other cities are, but the area thrives as a cultural hot spot with all the big-city amenities—in the company of urban moose, salmon runs, and wilderness trails. You find both rush-hour traffic and elegant restaurants, but of the Alaskan variety—wear your nicest fleece! Anchorage is the perfect spot for the camper to visit museums, sample an Alaskan original restaurant, and stock up for the journey to Alaska, likely only a short twenty minutes away!

Anchorage

Anchorage

	Hookup Sites	Total Sites	Max. RV Length	Hookups	Toilets	Showers	Drinking Water	Fires	Dump Station	Recreation	Fee	Reservations
93 Creekwood Inn	68	68	45	WESC	F	Y	Y	N	N	H	$$$–$$$$$	Y
94 Golden Nugget Camper Park	215	215	45	WESC	F	Y	Y	N	N	N	$$$$–$$$$$	Y
95 Centennial Camper Park	0	100	60	N	F	Y	Y	Y	Y	H	$$–$$$	N
96 Ship Creek Landings Downtown RV Park	157	177	40	WES	F	Y	Y	N	N	N	$$–$$$$	Y

93 Creekwood Inn

Location: In Anchorage
GPS: N 61° 12.054' / W 149° 52.144'
Season: Year-round
Sites: 58 full-hookup RV sites, 10 partial-hookup RV sites
Maximum length: 45 feet
Facilities: Picnic area, some grills, potable water, flush toilets, showers, laundry, WiFi, hiking access
Fee per night: $$$–$$$$$
Maximum stay: None
Management: Creekwood Inn, (907) 258-6006, www.creekwoodinn-alaska.com
Finding the campground: From mile 126 of the Seward Highway, just south of East 20th Avenue in midtown Anchorage, turn west into the Creekwood Inn parking lot. The several-lane highway is separated by dividers and creates one-way traffic in both directions. At this point the highway is Gambell Street heading south, and Ingra Street heading north. If you approach from Ingra Street, you will have to pass the inn on your left and turn around in the city. If you head south on Gambell Street, the park is on your right just after the Sullivan Arena.
About the campground: This midtown RV park is located on the side of the Seward Highway within a short walk of many stores. The camping area is behind the motel, but the roar of the booming highway is inescapable. Campsites are simple gravel back-in parking-lot-style stalls. They may be close together, but if you're looking for miles of open space, the grounds are situated next to the impressive Chester Creek Trail. A short, pleasant walk along the creek infuses you with a feeling of nature, and if you're enthusiastic, Chester Creek adjoins the coastal trail just a few miles west, so you'll likely spend little time in the cramped park.

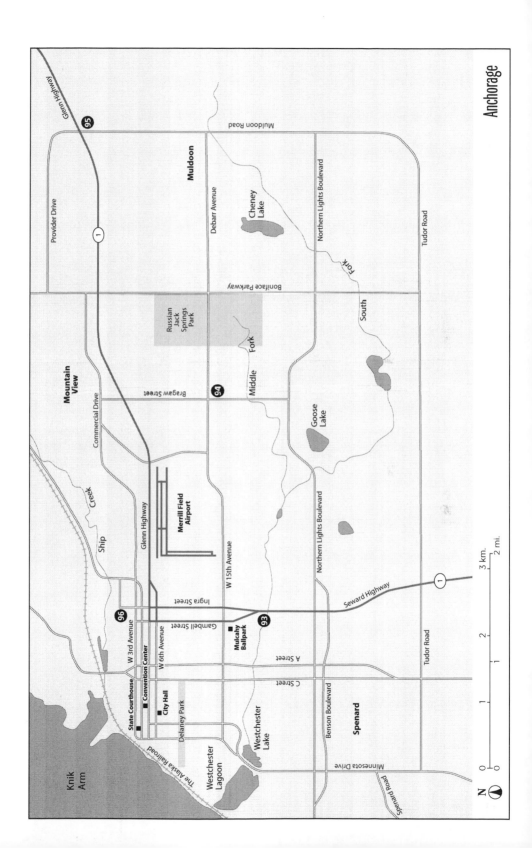

Anchorage

94 Golden Nugget Camper Park

Location: In Anchorage
GPS: N 61° 12.524' / W 149° 48.045'
Season: Year-round
Sites: 190 full-hookup RV sites, 25 partial-hookup RV sites
Maximum length: 45 feet
Facilities: Tables, picnic area with fire pit, potable water, flush toilets, showers, laundry, WiFi, gift shop, playground, volleyball, horseshoes
Fee per night: $$$$–$$$$$
Maximum stay: None
Management: Golden Nugget Camper Park, (907) 333-2012, (800) 449-2012, www.goldennuggetcamperpark.com
Finding the campground: From mile 3 of the Glenn Highway in Anchorage, take the Boniface Parkway/Mountain View exit and head south on North Boniface Parkway. Drive 1.1 miles and turn right onto Debarr Road. Drive 0.8 mile to the campground on your left.
About the campground: This well-kept RV park has landscaped grounds lined with mature trees. There are more than 200 campsites, a combination of back-ins and pull-thrus, each with its own table and sufficient room for pop-outs. The facilities get a lot of traffic but are kept clean. Campers are also located within decent proximity of Anchorage amenities—not to mention next door to Russian Jack Springs Park. To entertain the masses, this campground offers live music and other social events most nights of the week.

95 Centennial Camper Park

Location: In Anchorage
GPS: N 61° 13.711' / W 149° 43.353'
Season: Late May through September
Sites: 100 basic sites
Maximum length: 60 feet
Facilities: Tables, fire pits, flush toilets, dump station, showers, hiking access, potable water
Fee per night: $$–$$$
Maximum stay: 14 nights
Management: Municipality of Anchorage, Department of Parks and Recreation, May through October (907) 343-6986, winter (907) 343-6992, www.muni.org/parks/camping.cfm
Finding the campground: From mile 4.4 of the Glenn Highway, take the Muldoon exit south and turn left onto Boundary Avenue. Then make an immediate left onto the frontage road. Drive 0.5 mile to campground on your right.
About the campground: This city-operated park is set far enough off the freeway and in a natural enough setting that you can feel miles from an urban area. It's run in conjunction with a day-use park, so there's a nearby playground and acres of open space for kids to explore. The forested grounds provide a nice amount of shade. The well-spaced, earthen sites are dispersed along the comfort of a paved road. Seventeen units are set aside for RVs only, and not many sites can

accommodate large rigs, so if you're arriving in style it's best to call ahead and make reservations. Although there aren't hookups at this campground, you will find a dump station, flush toilets, and showers; every site has a table and fire pit. As with many city-run operations, the bathroom facilities are basic and a bit gloomy.

96 Ship Creek Landings Downtown RV Park

Location: In Anchorage
GPS: N 61° 13.320' / W 149° 52.254'
Season: May through late September
Sites: 157 full-hookup RV sites, 20 tent sites
Maximum length: 40 feet
Facilities: Some tables, potable water, flush toilets, showers, laundry
Fee per night: $$–$$$$
Maximum stay: None
Management: Ship Creek Landings Downtown RV Park, (907) 277-0877, (888) 778-7700, www.alaskatraveladventures.com
Finding the campground: From the Glenn Highway in downtown Anchorage (East 5th Avenue), turn north onto Ingra Street. Drive 0.2 mile and turn right onto East 1st Avenue. Make a quick sharp left onto North Ingra Street; the campground is on your left.
About the campground: For those backpacking or wishing to park their RV and enjoy the amazing downtown area, Ship Creek Landings is a great option. Located in downtown, just a hop away from the coast and a few blocks from touristy 4th Street, this clean campground is also a short walk from the famous Ship Creek salmon-viewing area, a must-see during the season. Most of the campsites are gravel back-ins with small grassy areas; there are four pull-thrus for larger RVs. Despite the urban atmosphere, you'll find trees and a decent amount of open space for a downtown RV park. Unfortunately, it's next to the railyards, so when a train is running the noise is intense.

Chugach State Park

97 Bird Creek

Location: 20 miles southeast of Anchorage
GPS: N 60° 58.316' / W 149° 27.617'
Season: Mid-May through mid-September
Sites: 23 basic sites, 12 tent sites, 15 overflow sites
Maximum length: 30 feet
Facilities: Tables, fire pits, potable water, vault toilets, hiking/cycling/fishing/creek access, bike rentals
Fee per night: $$
Maximum stay: 7 nights
Management: Alaska State Parks, Potter Section House, (907) 345-5014, www.dnr.state.ak .us/parks
Finding the campground: On the west side of the Seward Highway at mile 101.2, just east of the Bird Creek Bridge.
About the campground: The Bird Creek area is a never-ending center of summer activity surrounded with excellent fishing and hiking. The newly blasted mountainside parking areas are an impressive display of the area's popularity. Along with fishing and hiking, Bird Creek is a great location for viewing the Turnagain Arm bore tide, one of the largest tidal fluxes in the world. A bore tide is a large wave or series of waves that rush in after an extreme minus low tide. Since the waves stretch 50 miles across Turnagain Arm, many people climb the Bird Ridge Trail to absorb the big picture. During the summer migration, watching for whales after the tide rushes in is also a popular activity.

The Bird Creek campground fills up quickly, but there is an overflow area. The main campground sits on the west side of the highway under a towering birch and spruce forest, visually masking the road with thick woods and foliage. However, the sound of traffic is apparent. Most of the sites are located off the bumpy, narrow road that loops the grounds. The sites are large, lush, and well spaced; a few are suitable for RVs up to 30 feet. There are 12 walk-in tent sites for backpackers and cyclists. The overflow parking up the hill costs less and is not nearly as nice, consisting of 15 basic sites and a day-use area with fire pits and tables.

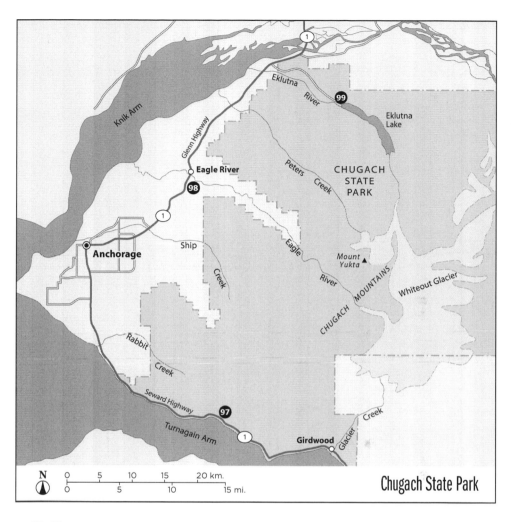

Chugach State Park

98 Eagle River Campground

Location: 12 miles north of Anchorage
GPS: N 61° 18.375' / W 149° 34.261'
Season: May through mid-September
Sites: 49 basic sites, 8 tent sites, 10 overflow sites
Maximum length: Any
Facilities: Tables, fire pits, covered picnic area with grills, potable water, flush and vault toilets, dump station, hiking/fishing/river access
Fee per night: $$
Maximum stay: 4 nights

Management: Alaska State Parks, Potter Section House, (907) 345-5014, www.dnr.state.ak.us/parks; campground management privately contracted through Lifetime Adventures (907) 746-4644, (800) 952-8624, www.lifetimeadventures.net

Finding the campground: From mile 11.6 of the Glenn Highway, take the Hiland Road exit northeast. Follow the signs on the frontage road north for 1.3 miles to the campground.

About the campground: This popular campground in Eagle River is also the only campground within Chugach State Park that takes reservations. It's a great opportunity to snag a campsite during the high season. Activities are centered on the rushing river; the campground's management is privately contracted to a charter company that offers a variety of float trips from the grounds. When campers aren't gearing up in the river staging area, they are likely indulging in fishing or a short hike from the site.

Camping is located off paved loops. The Rapid Loop has the only riverfront sites. The eight walk-in tent sites allow you to hear the roar of the rapids and feel the cool moist air in your tent. The rest of the sites are basic deep back-ins, a few forested; some have good mountain views. There is also an overflow lot up the hill near the dump station that holds about ten large RVs or campers. Here you'll find a block of flush toilets and only a few fire pits and tables in the trees at the edge of the lot. All of the facilities at Eagle River are impressively clean given the amount of

Just south of Anchorage along Turnagain Arm, a family stops along the Seward Highway to view the wild mountain goats.

traffic that passes through. Hosts are on site. The Chugach State Park Nature Center is nearby—a highly recommended stop for information on the park and the ecology of the area.

99 Eklutna Lake

Location: 26 miles northeast of Anchorage
GPS: N 61° 24.641' / W 149° 08.785'
Season: Mid-May through mid-September
Sites: 42 basic sites, 8 tent sites, 15 overflow sites
Maximum length: 45 feet
Facilities: Tables, fire pits, covered picnic area, potable water, vault toilets, hiking/cycling/lake/fishing access
Fee per night: $$
Maximum stay: 15 nights

A hiker surveys Eklutna Lake.

Management: Alaska State Parks, Potter Section House, (907) 345-5014, www.dnr.state.ak
.us/parks

Finding the campground: From mile 25.6 of the Glenn Highway, take the Eklutna Lake Road exit east. Follow park signs for 9 miles east on the gravel Eklutna Lake Road to Eklutna Lake and the campground.

About the campground: Eklutna Lake is possibly the most popular lake in the state—and with one look around, it's no wonder. The bright blue lake is surrounded by cascading peaks, home to Eklutna Glacier and steep canyon walls. The level 12.7-mile one-way Eklutna Lakeside Trail leads to the glacier, waterfalls, gravel bars, and beyond. The stroll along this old roadbed is one of the most popular campsite hikes in the state. Whether you're looking to hike, backpack, camp, kayak, canoe, fish, mountain bike, windsurf, sail, boat (nonmotorized or electric only), horseback ride, berry pick, or bustle around on an ATV, there is a trail for you at Eklutna Lake. Parts of the trail system shift between motorized and nonmotorized days during the week; if you're planning a journey, call ahead and check the status of the trail. In summer months the on-site charter company offers tours as well as equipment rentals. They rent everything from sleeping bags to camp stoves and kayaks. An eighty-car parking lot and day-use picnic area with more than twenty tables attests to the popularity of the lake.

The camping area is divided into three sections—main, overflow, and group. The main campground has completely paved roads with deep back-in basic sites and one pull-thru. A thick forest of spruce and birch lends shade and privacy to the well-developed sites. An impressive amount of wildlife and forest ambience makes this popular site still a pleasure for the nature enthusiast to visit. Telescopes and interpretive displays are available at the trailhead to watch life on the lake; binoculars could add to the opportunity. If you're traveling in a large RV or the main grounds are full, the overflow lot has room for about fifteen large RVs or campers in an open gravel area with tables, fire pits, and portable toilets. Still, if the bustle is too much, there are two free backpack-in campgrounds along Lakeside Trail at 8 miles and 11 miles. Each pack-in site features a pit toilet, fire pit, and picnic table.

The George Parks Highway and Denali National Park

Often referred to as the road through the heart of Alaska, stretching from Anchorage to Fairbanks, the 362-mile George Parks Highway etches across some of the state's most dramatic mountain panoramas. The highway was completed in 1971. Until that time the state's two biggest cities were a long detour apart. The new connecting road was originally called the Anchorage–Fairbanks Highway and later renamed the George Parks Highway to commemorate George A. Parks, an early Alaskan governor.

Still, when most campers hear parks, they think Denali National Park, the six-million-acre camper's dreamland located roughly midpoint down the highway. If you travel the Parks Highway from south to north, you'll pass up through the Susitna River Valley. The scenery transitions quickly from the thick forests of the south into dwarfed trees, rolling tundra, and expansive vistas. This is the Alaskan interior. You may drive across miles without human residents. Instead you find wild views in every direction, from fields of low-lying tundra to the highest peak in North America.

The glorious peaks of the Alaska Range tower to the west. This range is home to the tallest base-to-top mountain in the world. Climbing out of the ground at a mere 2,000 feet, Alaska's Denali tops off at 20,320 feet, showcasing more than 18,000 feet of solid rock and ice for the spectator. (Everest stands the tallest in the world at over 29,000 feet, but because its base is at an elevation of 17,000 feet, the total rise is only

12,000 feet.) The name "Denali" means "the Great One." Although the mountain is located deep within the national park, on clear days it is possible to view snow blanketed Denali directly as far south as Anchorage. Several wayside viewpoints have been set aside along the Parks Highway, offering the perfect glimpse of the valiant giant if it isn't tucked away behind the clouds.

Mountaineers travel to Alaska from all over the world to take a shot at summiting the mammoth beauty. They begin their journey in Talkeetna, an authentic interior town turned intellectual colony. Talkeetna is located off mile 98.7 of the Parks Highway down a paved 15-mile spur road. The city caters to tourists and climbers alike with festivals, art galleries, unique restaurants, and the aviation base for expeditions up the High One. During peak climbing months, Talkeetna transforms into the mountaineering mode. Climbers sit in anticipation over pizza and live music or discuss the triumph or tribulations of their daring journeys at local bars.

The lesser-traveled Denali Highway connects the Richardson to the Parks Highway at mile 210 and was once the link to Denali National Park. Today this gravel road is a scenic side trip for many travelers. Still reminiscent of the unpaved days of Alaska, the 134-mile road is a chance to sample the flavor of frontier times. Wild and breathtaking, the drive passes through brilliant scenery just south of the Alaska Range.

Spanning over the Alaska Range, the interior's subarctic prize, Denali National Park and Preserve, is accessed by the entrance at mile 237 of the Parks Highway. Once threatened by a gold rush in the Kantishna hills, this park and preserve was established in 1917. This unique park is open to private vehicles for only a few miles; beyond that you'll have to board a bus to explore the 90-mile road. The sealed-road system controls the environmental pressure that nearly half a million annual visitors have on the park's delicate ecosystem. This stewardship has allowed wildlife to flourish within the gates, and even along the quiet roadside. From the bus it is often possible to view Dall sheep, caribou, grizzly bears, wolves, moose, and many other mammals, or some of the more than 150 different species of birds within the park. At Denali National Park there are six campgrounds and six million acres of backcountry just waiting to be explored.

North of Denali the Parks Highway follows the Nenana Valley toward Fairbanks. Campgrounds and services become few and far between. The highway eventually climbs a ridge just before the city and showcases sweeping views of the valley below. Then the road finally returns to an urban empire—well, at least by Alaskan standards. Through mountains and valleys and back again, city to city, the Parks Highway connects the people of Alaska.

The Parks Highway: Wasilla to Denali

The Parks Highway: Wasilla to Denali

	Hookup Sites	Total Sites	Max. RV Length	Hookups	Toilets	Showers	Drinking Water	Fires	Dump Station	Recreation	Fee	Reservations
100 Big Bear RV Park	42	42+	Any	WESC	F	Y	Y	Y	Y	N	$$-$$$$$	Y
101 Lake Lucille Park	0	59	45	N	NF	N	Y	Y	N	HF	$$	N
102 Finger Lake State Recreation Site	0	36	Any	N	NF	N	Y	Y	N	HFBL	$$	N
103 Government Peak Campground	0	8	30	N	NF	N	Y	Y	N	H	$$	N
104 Alaska Forget Me Not Campground	0	30	30	N	NF	N	N	Y	N	N	$$	N
105 Big Lake South	0	20	45	N	NF	N	Y	Y	N	FBL	$$	N
106 Big Lake North	0	40	35	N	NF	N	Y	Y	N	FBL	$$	N
107 Rocky Lake	0	10	35	N	NF	N	Y	Y	N	FBL	$$	N
108 Little Susitna River Campground	0	86	45	N	NF	N	Y	Y	Y	F	$	N
109 Riverside Camper Park	56	58	Any	WESC	F	Y	Y	Y	Y	FBL	$$-$$$$$	Y
110 Nancy Lake State Recreation Site	0	30	Any	N	NF	N	Y	Y	N	FBL	$$	N
111 South Rolly Campground	0	98	35	N	NF	N	Y	Y	N	FBL	$$	N
112 Willow Creek State Recreation Area	0	120	Any	N	NF	N	Y	Y	N	FBL	$$	N
113 Hatcher Pass RV and Cabins	48	48	Any	E	N	N	Y	Y	Y	N	$$	N
114 Pioneer Lodge	25	37	Any	WES	F	Y	Y	Y	Y	F	$$-$$$	Y
115 Willow Creek Resort	39	50	Any	WES	F	Y*	Y	Y	Y	F	$$-$$$	Y
116 Susitna Landing	5	35	45	E	NF	N	Y	Y	N	FBL	$-$$	N
117 Sheep Creek Lodge	55	75	Any	WESC	F	Y	Y	Y	Y	N	$	Y
118 Montana Creek Campground	18	102	Any	E	NF	N	Y	Y	Y	F	$-$$$$	Y
119 Talkeetna Camper Park	34	34	40	WESC	F	Y	Y	Y	Y	N	$$$-$$$$$	Y
120 Talkeetna Alaska RV and Boat Launch	0	60	45	N	NF	Y	Y	Y	N	FBL	$$	N
121 Talkeetna Hostel International	0	10	T	N	F	Y	Y	Y	N	N	$$	Y
122 Talkeetna Riverfront Park	0	10	T	N	F	N	Y	Y	N	N	$	N
123 H&H	10	10+	Any	E	F	Y	Y	Y	Y	F	$$-$$$$	Y
124 Trapper Creek Inn and RV Park	18	37	60	WESC	F	Y	Y	Y	Y	N	$$-$$$	Y
125 K'esugi Ken Campground	0	30	Any	N	NF	N	Y	Y	N	HF	$	N
126 Lower Troublesome Creek Campground	32	42	Any	E	F	N	Y	Y	Y	H	$$-$$$	Y
127 Byers Lake Campground	0	74	35	N	N	Y	Y	Y	Y	HFBL	$$	N
128 East Fork Chulitna Wayside	0	11	Any	N	NF	N	Y	Y	N	N	$	N
131 Cantwell RV Park	76	79	55	WE	F	Y	Y	Y	Y	N	$$$-$$$$	Y
132 Denali Grizzly Bear Cabins and Campground	56	86	Any	WE	F	Y	Y	Y	Y	N	$$$-$$$$$	Y

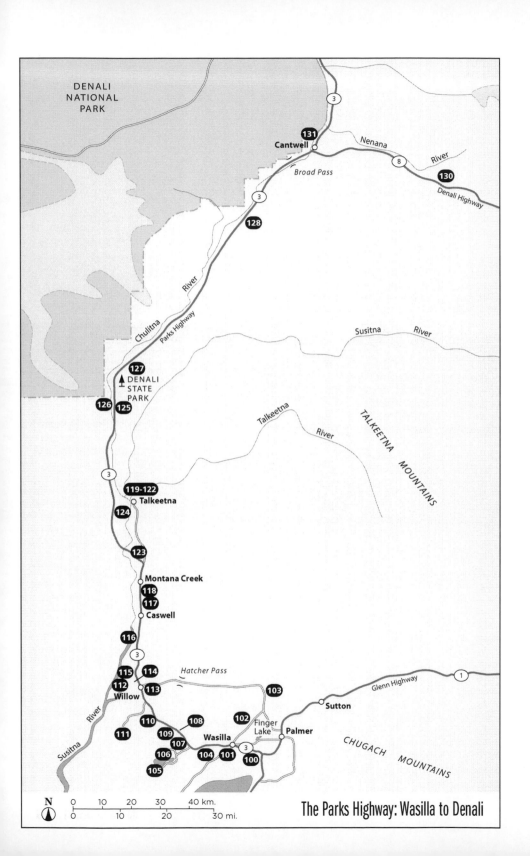

DENALI
NATIONAL
PARK

131 Cantwell

Nenana

3

Broad Pass

River

8

130
Denali Highway

3

128

Chulitna

River

Susitna River

Parks Highway

127
▲ DENALI
STATE
PARK

126 **125**

Talkeetna River

TALKEETNA MOUNTAINS

3

119-122 Talkeetna

124

123

Montana Creek

118
117
Caswell

116

3

Hatcher Pass

115 **114**

112 **113**

Willow

103

Glenn Highway

1

Sutton

102

Finger
Lake

100

Palmer

110

108

111

109

107

Wasilla

CHUGACH MOUNTAINS

106

104 **101**

Susitna River

105

3

N

0   10   20   30   40 km.

0   10   20   30 mi.

The Parks Highway: Wasilla to Denali

100 Big Bear RV Park

Location: In Wasilla
GPS: N 61° 33.669' / W 149° 17.524'
Season: Year-round
Sites: 16 full-hookup RV sites, 26 partial-hookup RV sites, open tent camping
Maximum length: Any
Facilities: Tables, fire pits, potable water, flush toilets, showers, dump station, laundry, WiFi
Fee per night: $$$-$$$$$
Maximum stay: None
Management: Big Bear Campground & RV Park, (907) 745-7445, www.alaskarvpark.net
Finding the campground: From mile 36.1 of the Parks Highway, take the Trunk Road exit south and make the first right onto East Fireweed Road. Drive 0.7 mile and turn left onto Church Street; the campground is on your immediate right. Look for the giant big bear sign with a cutout of two dancing bears as you drive by.
About the campground: This clean, open lot is located along the Parks Highway, a couple of miles from Wasilla's shopping centers. The campground has plenty of grassy areas and nicely kept facilities. Camping is located in an open gravel lot with twenty oversize pull-thrus suitable for large RVs. The large sites include tables and plenty of room for pop-outs. The park is open year-round.

101 Lake Lucille Park

Location: In Wasilla
GPS: N 61° 34.041' / W 149° 28.854'
Season: Late May through November
Sites: 59 basic sites
Maximum length: 45 feet
Facilities: Tables, fire pits, covered picnic area, potable water, vault toilets, soccer field, playground, volleyball, hiking/fishing/river access
Fee per night: $$
Maximum stay: 10 days
Management: Matanuska-Susitna Borough, Parks and Outdoor Recreation, (907) 745-4801
Finding the campground: From mile 42.2 of the Parks Highway, drive south on Knik Goose Bay Road for 2.2 miles and turn right onto Endeavor Street. Continue 0.6 mile to campground.
About the campground: With a couple of soccer fields, sand volleyball court, horseshoe pit, and picnic pavilion, this eighty-acre park is popular for day use among local families. Camping is also available at this large city park. Campsites are divided between two loops, the first of which is a bit older and open to tents and small RVs. Here there are seventeen basic sites among a few sparse trees without a lot of privacy. These sites are also older and overgrown with foliage compared with the newer RV loop just below them. The RV section has larger campsites in an enchanting grove of birch and cottonwood trees. There are only a couple of pull-thrus that could accommodate large RVs. Tents are allowed on the RV loop for a maximum stay of three days, after which they have to

Visitors to Denali National Park board a bus to travel the sealed road.

go back to the degraded tent loop, or seek permission for a longer stay. Lake Lucille Park opens for camping by Memorial Day and doesn't close until the snow pushes everyone out in fall.

102 Finger Lake State Recreation Site

Location: In Wasilla
GPS: N 61° 36.627' / W 149° 15.905'
Season: May through mid-September
Sites: 36 basic sites
Maximum length: Any
Facilities: Tables, fire pits, picnic area, potable water, vault toilets, hiking/lake/fishing access, boat launch
Fee per night: $$
Maximum stay: 7 days
Management: Alaska State Parks, Mat-Su/CB Area Office (907) 745-3975, www.dnr.state.ak.us/parks
Finding the campground: From mile 36.1 of the Parks Highway, turn north onto Trunk Road. Drive 4 miles (1 mile past the Palmer–Wasilla Highway) and turn left onto Bogard Road. Drive 0.9 mile to the campground entrance.

About the campground: Finger Lake is the largest stocked lake in the Matanuska-Susitna Valley and is known for excellent rainbow fishing. The boat launch has recently been upgraded and the addition of a wheelchair-accessible fishing dock has increased access to the water. Paddlers also enjoy Finger Lake, which is located on the 7-mile canoe route connecting Wasilla and Cottonwood lakes. Camping is divided into two small loops of back-in sites under cottonwoods. A few lucky tenters might be able to squeeze into a small string of the sites along the lakefront. If you're traveling in a large RV, you will have to sacrifice the wooded basic sites for a parking-lot-style gravel lot away from the water.

103 Government Peak Campground

Location: Near Wasilla
GPS: N 61° 44.566' / W 149° 13.868'
Season: Late May through September
Sites: 8 basic sites
Maximum length: 30 feet
Facilities: Tables, fire pits, vault toilets
Fee per night: $$
Maximum stay: 7 days
Management: Alaska State Parks, Mat-Su/CB Area Office (907) 745-3975, www.dnr.state.ak
.us/parks
Finding the campground: This campground is located at mile 11 of Hatcher Pass Road.
About the campground: Depending on the year, Hatcher Pass may still be snowy in mid-summer, so be sure to check in with state parks before you drive up. This small campground has 8 basic sites, three of which are tent only. If the sites are full, RVs can park at the Gold Mint Trailhead at mile 13.7 of Hatcher Pass Road.

104 Alaska Forget Me Not Campground

Location: Mile 51 of the Parks Highway
GPS: N 61° 34.208' / W 149° 43.037'
Season: Late May through September
Sites: 30 basic sites
Maximum length: 30 feet
Facilities: Some tables, some fire pits, vault toilets.
Fee per night: $$
Maximum stay: None
Management: Alaska Forget Me Not Campground, (907) 892-3733, www.forgetmenotrvpark.com
Finding the campground: This campground is located on the south side of the Parks Highway at mile 51.8.
About the campground: The Alaska Forget Me Not is a no-frills place to camp near Wasilla and Big Lake. The basic sites have some trees around them, and some back up to Johnson Pond.

105 Big Lake South

Location: In Big Lake
GPS: N 61° 31.964' / W 149° 50.015'
Season: Mid-May through mid-September
Sites: 20 parking-lot-style spaces
Maximum length: 45 feet
Facilities: Some tables, fire pits, picnic area, potable water, vault toilets, boat launch, fishing/lake access
Fee per night: $$
Maximum stay: 7 days
Management: Alaska State Parks, Mat-Su/CB Area Office, (907) 745-3975, www.dnr.state.ak.us/parks
Finding the campground: From mile 52.3 of the Parks Highway, turn west onto Big Lake Road and drive 3.6 miles to a Y in the road. Stay left on South Big Lake Road and drive 1.5 miles to the campground.
About the campground: Big Lake is a magnet for locals on the weekend, popular for just about every summer water-related activity. The lake is buzzing with the sounds of motors all summer long. Boating, jet skiing, and fishing top the list of activities. Camping on the lake is not in traditional government-campground-style sites; instead both Big Lake campgrounds resemble parking lots. At Big Lake South, camping is in a day-use area turned campground with even less character than its northern partner. The campsites are basic stalls in an open gravel lot next to the boat launch. Most of the campers who stay here do so to be close to lake access and their boats. A nearby sandy beach draws swimmers.

106 Big Lake North

Location: In Big Lake
GPS: N 61° 32.752' / W 149° 51.262'
Season: Mid-May through mid-September
Sites: 30 RV sites, 10 tent sites
Maximum length: 35 feet
Facilities: Some tables and fire pits, covered picnic area, potable water, vault toilets, fishing/lake access, boat launch
Fee per night: $$
Maximum stay: 7 days
Management: Alaska State Parks, Mat-Su/CB Area Office, (907) 745-3975, www.dnr.state.ak.us/parks
Finding the campground: From mile 52.3 of the Parks Highway, turn southwest onto Big Lake Road and drive 3.6 miles to a Y. Stay right, following the signs to Big Lake North SRS, on North Shore Road. Drive 1.4 miles to the campground.
About the campground: You can tell that Big Lake North was originally intended to be a parking area and has been recently modified into a campground. In fact, little attempt has been made

to clarify the new rules. Old signs reading NO CAMPING are still posted next to new signs that simply state the price of overnight parking. The area in which camping is now allowed is also unclear. It would be best to find the host to clarify the campsite locations. The sites are basically parking spaces in a large asphalt lot; a few are congregated in a wooded area with tables and fire pits.

107 Rocky Lake

Location: In Big Lake
GPS: N 61° 33.400' / W 149° 43.037'
Season: Mid-May through mid-September
Sites: 10 basic sites
Maximum length: 35 feet
Facilities: Some tables and fire pits, potable water, vault toilets, fishing/lake access, boat launch
Fee per night: $$
Maximum stay: 7 days
Management: Alaska State Parks, Mat-Su/CB Area Office, (907) 745-3975, www.dnr.state.ak .us/parks
Finding the campground: From mile 52.3 of the Parks Highway, turn west onto Big Lake Road, drive 3.3 miles, and turn right onto Beaver Lake Road. Drive 0.5 mile and turn left onto Rocky Road. The campground is on your immediate left down a gravel road.
About the campground: This campground has more of an organic feeling than the pavement of the Big Lake duo. It's suitable for those looking for a good campground as opposed to the closest link to the launches of Big Lake. The camping area is in a natural wooded setting with basic sites next to small Rocky Lake. The lake is stocked with petite salmon and can be popular on weekends, but still shadows the crowds of Big Lake. Here ten wooded campsites are well dispersed in light woods, with fire pits and tables, and some are located on the shore of the lake.

108 Little Susitna River Campground

Location: In Houston
GPS: N 61° 37.816' / W 149° 47.941'
Season: Late May through October
Sites: 86 basic sites
Maximum length: 45 feet
Facilities: Tables, fire pits, potable water, vault toilets, dump station, playground, fishing/river access
Fee per night: $
Maximum stay: 10 days
Management: Matanuska-Susitna Borough, Parks and Outdoor Recreation, (907) 745-4801
Finding the campground: From mile 57.3 of the Parks Highway, turn north onto Armstrong Road and make an immediate right at the sign for the campground. Follow the gravel road 0.2 mile to the campground.

About the campground: When the salmon are running on the Little Susitna, people don't seem to mind shacking up at this worn-down campground. At other times, the grounds appear abandoned and are not well kept, with unruly grasses taking over most sites. Camping is located off a confusing mangle of loops labeled A through G. Large spruce and birch trees lend some shade to the earthen sites. Most have aging tables and fire pits fashioned out of barrels cut in half. There are a couple of pull-thrus for larger RVs. The toilets are extremely dingy. The center of the grounds features a large children's playground. The campground opens for Memorial Day and closes at freeze-up in fall.

109 Riverside Camper Park

Location: In Houston
GPS: N 61° 37.775' / W 149° 48.804'
Season: April through October
Sites: 56 full-hookup RV sites, 2 tent sites
Maximum length: Any
Facilities: Tables, some fire pits, covered picnic area with grill, potable water, flush toilets, showers, dump station, laundry, fish-cleaning facilities, WiFi, fishing/river access, boat launch, charters, small store
Fee per night: $$$–$$$$$
Maximum stay: None
Management: Riverside Camper Park, (907) 892-9020, www.riversiderak.com
Finding the campground: This campground is located on the west side of the Parks Highway at mile 57.7.
About the campground: Not surprisingly, this campground is on the Little Susitna River, a fishing hot spot where five species of salmon can be caught throughout the season. Expect Riverside Camper Park to be full of campers and activity during the runs. Camping is in an open area along grass with back-in sites and a few pull-thrus. There is a large covered picnic pavilion. The groomed grounds include well-maintained outbuildings with showers, laundry, and a small store.

110 Nancy Lake State Recreation Site

Location: Near mile 66 of the Parks Highway
GPS: N 61° 42.130' / W 150° 00.335'
Season: Late May through October
Sites: 30 basic sites
Maximum length: Any
Facilities: Tables, fire pits, covered picnic area, potable water, vault toilets, fishing/lake access, boat launch
Fee per night: $$
Maximum stay: 14 days

Management: Alaska State Parks, Mat-Su/CB Area Office, (907) 745-3975, www.dnr.state.ak
.us/parks

Finding the campground: From mile 66.5 of the Parks Highway, turn south onto Buckingham Palace and follow the road as it heads east for 0.2 mile to the campground on your right.

About the campground: Located within the 22,000-acre Nancy Lake State Recreation Site, this favorable lakefront campground sits in a spruce, birch, and aspen forest. The basic earthen sites are located off a small gravel loop road. There is also a covered picnic area. Camping here most often serves those looking to explore the Nancy Lake area's boating, fishing, and hiking opportunities. The 8-mile Lynx Lake Loop canoe route can be accessed from Nancy Lake and inspires canoeing as the most popular summer activity.

111 South Rolly Campground

Location: Near mile 67 of the Parks Highway
GPS: N 61° 40.021' / W 150° 08.449'
Season: Late May through October
Sites: 98 basic sites
Maximum length: 35 feet
Facilities: Tables, fire pits, picnic area, potable water, vault toilets, boat launch, fishing/lake access, canoe rentals
Fee per night: $$
Maximum stay: 14 days
Management: Alaska State Parks, Mat-Su/CB Area Office, (907) 745-3975, www.dnr.state.ak
.us/parks

Finding the campground: From mile 67.3 of the Parks Highway, turn west onto Nancy Lake Road and drive 6.5 miles to the campground on your left.

About the campground: The Red Shirt trailhead is located at the South Rolly Campground, and this lake also links with the Lynx Lake Canoe Route, so you'll often find paddlers camped along these shores. On site, a private company offers watercraft rentals if you decide to venture out on the water. The earthy campground has large and well-spaced campsites divided by lush greenery and wild shrubs. There are some stunning views from the lakeside sites as well as those elevated along a hill. Much of the camping area is crawling in devil's club, a pesky thorny plant known to prick a camper or two, so be cautious. If you're looking for more of a backcountry adventure but want to stay within an established camping area, the 3-mile Red Shirt Trail leads to the SRS's largest lake and several secluded lakefront campsites. Don't forget your water purifier—these primitive campsites are not developed like those at the main campground!

112 Willow Creek State Recreation Area

Location: In Willow
GPS: N 61° 46.463' / W 150° 09.671'
Season: Late May through October

Sites: 120 parking-lot-style spaces
Maximum length: Any
Facilities: Tables, fire pits, potable water, vault toilets, fishing access, boat launch
Fee per night: $$
Maximum stay: 7 days
Management: Alaska State Parks, Mat-Su/CB Area Office, (907) 745-3975, www.dnr.state.ak
.us/parks
Finding the campground: From mile 70.8 of the Parks Highway, turn west onto the paved Willow
Creek Parkway and drive 3.7 miles to the dead end into the campground.
About the campground: This campground is located where the south channel and the main
channel of Willow Creek meet with the Susitna River, a busy salmon-fishing area and popular raft
take-out. The camping area has parking-lot-style side-by-side spaces that back up to tables and
fire pits among trees. These sites may be a tight squeeze, but you don't see many people in the
camping area—everyone's out on the river throwing a line. If this campground fills up, there are a
few RV sites at the Willow Trading Post.

113   Hatcher Pass RV and Cabins

Location: In Willow
GPS: N 61° 45.685' / W 150° 02.894'
Season: Mid-May through mid-September
Sites: 48 partial-hookup RV sites
Maximum length: Any
Facilities: Tables, fire rings, potable water, portable toilets, dump station
Fee per night: $$
Maximum stay: None
Management: Hatcher Pass RV and Cabins, (907) 495-4955, www.hatcherpassrv.com
Finding the campground: From mile 71.2 of the Parks Highway, turn east onto Fishhook Willow
Road and drive 0.6 mile, just over the railroad tracks. Turn right onto a gravel road; the camp-
ground is on your left.
About the campground: This campground is only 0.5 mile off the highway but it feels much more
remote. Lightly forested by tall birch trees, the sites are very large pull-thrus in a clean gravel lot.
There are no outbuildings on site and no showers, but there is a water-fill and dump station as
well as a portable toilet.

114   Pioneer Lodge

Location: In Willow
GPS: N 61° 45.990' / W 150° 04.041'
Season: April through October
Sites: 7 full-hookup RV sites, 18 partial-hookup RV sites, 12 tent sites
Maximum length: Any

Facilities: Tables, fire pits, potable water, flush and portable toilets, dump station, laundry, fish-cleaning facilities, fishing/river access, restaurant, bar, charters
Fee per night: $$–$$$
Maximum stay: None
Management: Pioneer Lodge, (907) 495-6884
Finding the campground: On the west side of the Parks Highway at mile 71.4, just south of Willow Creek.
About the campground: Willow Creek is known for blue-ribbon king salmon as well as good silver and rainbow catches. At the Pioneer Lodge there are eighteen campsites that back up directly to the water, a real treat for guests. There are also a few pull-thru sites for larger RVs farther back from the action. These grounds resemble a roadhouse-style operation, with a restaurant, bar, small liquor store, and charter services.

115 Willow Creek Resort

Location: In Willow
GPS: N 61° 46.087' / W 150° 04.124'
Season: Year-round
Sites: 27 full-hookup RV sites, 12 partial-hookup RV sites, 11 basic sites
Maximum length: Any
Facilities: Tables, fire pits, flush and portable toilets, showers, dump station, laundry, WiFi, fishing/river access, small store, charters
Fee per night: $$–$$$
Maximum stay: None
Management: Willow Creek Resort, (907) 495-6343, www.willowcreekresortalaska.com
Finding the campground: On the west side of the Parks Highway at mile 71.4, just north of Willow Creek.
About the campground: Located across the water from the Pioneer Lodge, this aesthetically pleasing riverside resort has access to the same first-class fishing opportunities. With direct fishing access from the campground, these prime sites also fill throughout the season. A combination of partial hookups and dry sites line the river, and there is also an open area with full hookups that can accommodate large rigs. This campground has a parklike setting with plenty of grass and some large mature trees, as well as an interesting infestation of domestic rabbits roaming the grounds.

116 Susitna Landing

Location: Near mile 82 of the Parks Highway.
GPS: N 61° 54.786' / W 150° 05.909'
Season: Year-round
Sites: 5 partial-hookup RV sites, 30 basic sites
Maximum length: 45 feet

Facilities: Some tables, fire pits, covered picnic area, potable water, vault toilets, fishing/river access, boat launch, small store, espresso bar, charters
Fee per night: $$
Maximum stay: None
Management: Alaska Department of Fish and Game, (907) 495-7700
Finding the campground: From mile 82.5 of the Parks Highway, turn west onto Susitna Landing Road. Drive 1 mile until the road dead-ends at the campground.
About the campground: The camping mariner themed camping area is run in conjunction with the charter services, offering fishing charters, float trips, and boat tours. The landscaped waterfront sites are side-by-side, and many suitable for large rigs, in an open area near a clipped lawn. The facilities are basic and clean. Only a few of these sites have hookups, and the campground is run on a first-come, first-served basis.

117 Sheep Creek Lodge

Location: Mile 88 of the Parks Highway
GPS: N 61° 59.504' / W 150° 03.0444'
Season: May through September
Sites: 35 basic sites
Maximum length: 25 feet
Facilities: Some tables, some firepits, potable water, WiFi
Fee per night: $
Maximum stay: None
Management: Sheep Creek Lodge, (907) 495-6227, www.sheepcreeklodgeak.com
Finding the campground: This campground is located on the east side of the Parks Highway at Mile 88.
About the campground: The Sheep Creek Lodge has a restaurant, bar, lodge with cabins, and campground. The basic sites are surrounded by woods and were only $15 in 2021.

118 Montana Creek Campground

Location: Near mile 96 of the Parks Highway
GPS: N 62° 06.200' / W 150° 03.581'
Season: Mid-May through late September
Sites: 18 partial-hookup RV sites, 84 basic sites
Maximum length: Any
Facilities: Tables, some fire pits and grills, outhouses, river/fishing access, small store
Fee per night: $$–$$$$
Maximum stay: None
Management: Montana Creek Campground, (907) 566-2267, (877) 475-CAMP; Alaska State Parks, Mat-Su/CB Area Office, (907) 745-3975, www.dnr.state.ak.us/parks

Finding the campground: These campgrounds are on both sides of the Parks Highway at mile 96.5 just south of Montana Creek.

About the campground: If you follow the trail of anglers streaming out of this RV park, it will lead you to the mouth of Montana Creek and the Susitna River. This area is known for prime salmon and trout fishing, and the campground caters to this draw. On site there is a small store for tackle and licenses, so your basic needs are set.

Camping is divided into two creekside sections across the highway from each other, although one is Alaska State Parks land; both are privately managed. On the eastern side, the Montana Creek campground has rustic wooded sites on gravel and earthen pads, with plenty of grass for tenters and large spaces for RVs. The sites are a combination of back-ins and pull-thrus suitable for RVs of any size. Labeled RECREATION PARK, the Alaska State Parks camping area on the west side of the highway is in more of an open lot, with parking-lot-style spaces also suitable for large RVs. Sites here also have tables, fire pits, and outhouses. Sixteen of these sites have tent pads; the rest are standard parking stalls. This section is not as forested as its eastern counterpart, but campers are rarely here for shade. As with most area campgrounds, they're here to fish.

119 Talkeetna Camper Park

Location: In Talkeetna
GPS: N 62° 19.036' / W 150° 06.251'
Season: Mid-April through October
Sites: 5 full-hookup RV sites, 29 partial-hookup RV sites
Maximum length: 40 feet
Facilities: Communal fire pit, potable water, flush toilets, showers, dump station, laundry, WiFi, gift shop
Fee per night: $$$–$$$$
Maximum stay: None
Management: Talkeetna Camper Park, (907) 733-2693, www.talkeetnacamper.com
Finding the campground: From mile 98.7 of the Parks Highway, drive east on Talkeetna Road for 13.9 miles to the campground on your right just before you pull into town.
About the campground: Talkeetna's only full-service RV park is also within walking distance of town. The camping area offers side-by-side stalls in a gravel lot with some trees, about half in pull-thrus and half, back-ins. There are five full hookups; the remainders are water/electric with a dump station on site. The park is directly beside the train station, which means that there's a lot of foot traffic as people board and exit the popular rail excursion to Talkeetna. Trains blow by quite often.

120 Talkeetna Alaska RV and Boat Launch

Location: In Talkeetna
GPS: N 62° 19.551' / W 150° 06.406'
Season: Late May through September
Sites: 60 basic sites

Maximum length: 45 feet
Facilities: Tables, fire rings, covered picnic area, potable water, vault toilets, showers, dump station, boat launch, fishing/river access, small store
Fee per night: $$
Maximum stay: None
Management: Alaska Department of Fish and Game concessionaire Talkeetna River Adventures RV Park and Campground, (907) 733-2604, www.talkeetna-rv.com
Finding the campground: From mile 98.7 of the Parks Highway, drive east on Talkeetna Road for 14.1 miles. As you enter town, follow the signs toward the airport by turning east onto 2nd Street; then make an immediate left onto South F Street and drive 0.3 mile to the campground on your left.
About the campground: This rustic campground and boat launch is privately operated for Fish and Game. The boat launch is more popular than the campground and is the base for many scenic floats along the river. The campground is wooded and rustic, located off a bumpy earthen road. Lush brush separates some of the scattered campsites, but overall boundaries are not well defined. You'll find a combination of pull-thrus and back-ins, but those with larger RVs and campers will want to stick to the sites near the entrance. These sites are the most accessible, and the road has some tight turns for larger rigs. Tenters will find some cool camp pads near the river. There is also an office with showers if you'd like to spruce up for a night in town. A trail across from the campground leads the trek into downtown.

121 Talkeetna Hostel International

Location: In Talkeetna
GPS: N 62° 19.409' / W 150° 05.850'
Season: May through September
Sites: 10 tent sites
Maximum length: N/A
Facilities: Picnic area with fire pit and barbecue, kitchen, potable water, flush toilets, showers, laundry, Internet, bike rentals
Fee per night: $$
Maximum stay: None
Management: Talkeetna Hostel International, (907) 733-4678, www.talkeetnahostel.com
Finding the campground: From mile 98.7 of the Parks Highway, drive east on Talkeetna Road for 14.1 miles. As you enter town, follow the signs toward the airport by turning east onto 2nd Street. Drive 0.2 mile and turn left onto I Street. The hostel is the third house on your right. Plenty of signs guide your way.
About the campground: Camping is limited to about ten tents at the Talkeetna Hostel International. The camping area is just behind the hostel on a large grassy lawn with picnic tables and a communal fire pit. Showers and toilets are also located near the tenting area, along with lazy hammocks and a permanently parked Volkswagen bus turned hostel bed. The cost of camping includes access to all hostel facilities, free ultraclean showers, and Internet access. A communal room with couches and a kitchen often hosts an international group of climbers and interesting conversation. Helpful and accommodating staff ensure a comfortable and welcoming stay for campers.

122 Talkeetna Riverfront Park

Location: In Talkeetna
GPS: N 62° 19.404' / W 150° 07.122'
Season: May through late September
Sites: 10 tent sites
Maximum length: N/A
Facilities: Tables, grills, communal fire pit, potable water, flush toilets, river access
Fee per night: $
Maximum stay: 14 days
Management: Talkeetna Chamber of Commerce, (907) 733-2330, www.talkeetnachamber.org
Finding the campground: From mile 98.7 of the Parks Highway, drive east on Talkeetna Road for 14.5 miles to the dead end of Main Street.
About the campground: This campground isn't much for atmosphere, but it's right in the center of all the action. If location and proximity to the shops and pub life are on your mind, River Park is only a stumble from both. The campground has ten very tightly spaced campsites that each have a table and grill. There is also a block of restrooms with flush toilets and running water. The sites do not have a view of the river, but access is just 100 feet away. Lounging on the large softly sanded beach and watching the rafts and jet boats float by is a pleasing venture on a sunny day. Hiking along the gravel bars and possibly catching a glimpse of Denali is a photographic opportunity not to be missed.

123 H&H

Location: Near mile 99 of the Parks Highway
GPS: N 62° 08.397' / W 150° 03.364'
Season: Year-round
Sites: 10 partial-hookup RV sites, open RV/tent camping
Maximum length: Any
Facilities: Tables, fire pits, potable water, flush toilets and portable toilets, showers, dump station, laundry, restaurant, gift shop
Fee per night: $$–$$$$
Maximum stay: None
Management: His and Hers Lakeview Lounge and Restaurant, (907) 733-2415
Finding the campground: This campground is located at mile 99.5 of the Parks Highway on the east side of the road.
About the campground: This roadhouse operation has a few pull-thru sites behind the restaurant along a small lake. The highway is elevated above the camping area, so traffic is not overwhelming. The campground is very basic and the facilities are older, but camping here is at a slower pace than at the more packed campgrounds, and some sites have a wooded and lake view. Laundry and showers are available as well as a dump and water-fill station. The nearby Tesoro gas station also has a few hookups in the back parking lot.

124 Trapper Creek Inn and RV Park

Location: Near mile 114 of the Parks Highway
GPS: N 62° 18.865' / W 150° 13.932'
Season: Year-round
Sites: 18 full-hookup RV sites, 19 basic sites
Maximum length: 60 feet
Facilities: Covered picnic area with grill, potable water, flush and portable toilets, showers, dump station, laundry, WiFi, gas station, deli
Fee per night: $$–$$$
Maximum stay: None
Management: Trapper Creek Inn, (907) 733-1444, www.trappercreek.biz
Finding the campground: The campground is located behind the Trapper Creek Inn/Tesoro gas station on the east side of the Parks Highway at mile 114.8. The park is masked by the ground's lovely trees, so look for the blue Tesoro station as you near milepost 115.
About the campground: Attached to a gas station, these campsites are a bargain along the Parks Highway. The camping area is a combination of pull-thrus and back-ins throughout trees. There are full-hookup RV sites as well as basic dry sites for tents or RVs. An attractive wooden covered picnic area has a couple of picnic tables and a large grill for campers' enjoyment. The sites are not spacious, but they're separated by thick woods and well maintained. Recently remodeled facilities include four full private bathrooms and an industrial-style laundry, both available for use by non-guests.

125 K'esugi Ken Campground

Location: Near mile 135 of the Parks Highway
GPS: N 62° 37.522' / W 150° 13.670'
Season: Mid-May through late September
Sites: 32 partial hookup RV sites, 10 walk-in tent sites, open overflow parking
Maximum length: Any
Facilities: Tables, fire pits, covered picnic area with fire pit, potable water, vault toilets, interpretive center, river/fishing/hiking access
Fee per night: $$–$$$
Maximum stay: 7 days
Management: Alaska State Parks, Mat-Su/CB Area Office, (907) 745-3975, www.dnr.state.ak.us/parks
Finding the campground: On the east side of the Parks Highway at mile 135.4.
About the campground: Alaska's newest state park campground is beautifully designed with several sites overlooking sweeping views of the Alaska Range. Most sites are electric-only RV sites with varying amps and lengths. There are also ten easy walk-in tent sites. Around the campground numerous trails connect to a well-developed trail system including graded gravel loops with interpretive signs. According to Alaska State Parks "Kesugi" is a Tanaina Indian dialect word meaning "The Ancient One" and is a fitting complement of the Tanana Indian word "Denali" which means

"The High One." If this posh and popular campground is full they offer overflow parking on site or at the Denali Viewpoint South just across the street or at Denali Viewpoint North at mile 162.

126 Lower Troublesome Creek Campground

Location: Near mile 137 of the Parks Highway
GPS: N 62° 37.522' / W 150° 13.670'
Season: Mid-May through late September
Sites: 20 parking-lot-style spaces, 10 tent sites
Maximum length: Any
Facilities: Some tables and fire pits, covered picnic area with fire pit, potable water, vault toilets, river/fishing/hiking access
Fee per night: $$
Maximum stay: 15 days
Management: Alaska State Parks, Mat-Su/CB Area Office, (907) 745-3975, www.dnr.state.ak.us/parks
Finding the campground: On the west side of the Parks Highway at mile 137.3.
About the campground: In typical wayside fashion, most of the "camping" spots at Lower Troublesome Creek are parking-lot-style spaces suitable for any size vehicle. Also located on the grounds are ten forested walk-in tent sites with tables, benches, and fire pits. Some are located in clusters of three, creating a less impersonal environment, but refreshingly out of the paved lot. Watch out for the painful devil's club shrub; as signs in the area aptly state, the thorns from this shrub can be the source of "festering splinters" and a painful experience. Yet the real drawback here for tenters is the seemingly loudest section of the Parks Highway. When large vehicles cross the bridge, a particularly unpleasant screeching noise screams from the overpass. With big rigs roaring by all night, tenters might want to gauge their tolerance to the noise before they hit the sack. From the campground a small 0.6-mile trail leads to the Chulitna River.

127 Byers Lake Campground

Location: Mile 147 of the Parks Highway
GPS: N 62° 44.631' / W 150° 07.704'
Season: Late May through late September
Sites: 74 basic sites
Maximum length: 35 feet
Facilities: Tables, fire pits, picnic area, potable water, vault toilets, dump station, hiking/lake access, boat launch, rentals, charters
Fee per night: $$
Maximum stay: 15 days
Management: Alaska State Parks, Mat-Su/CB Area Office, (907) 745-3975, www.dnr.state.ak.us/parks
Finding the campground: On the east side of the Parks Highway at mile 147.

A backpacker at Wonder Lake in Denali National Park.

About the campground: One of Alaska's model campgrounds, Byers Lake offers picturesque forested campsites beside a peaceful large lake, home to trumpeter swans, excellent fishing, and a chance to view Denali. The main campground is not located directly on the lake. There are seventy-four large sites located on four sections of a large loop. Several sites are pull-thrus; thick brush, mainly high-bush cranberries and the thorny devil's club—Alaska's most famous pesky plant—separate the sites. Along with the main campground, there is a lakeshore campground accessible by either a 0.7-mile paddle across the lake or a 1.8-mile hike. If you get a chance to stay at one of these six lakeshore spots, you will be rewarded with panoramic beauty, especially when wildflowers take over the campground and "the Great One" is out for a show. At times the weather is warm enough to draw a swimmer or two into the clear cool water.

From the campground, hikes connect to more than five different trails, ranging from the 1-mile stroll to Byer's Creek Bridge to a 27.5-mile trek to the Little Coal Trailhead.

128 East Fork Chulitna Wayside

Location: Near mile 185 of the Parks Highway
GPS: N 63° 09.028' / W 149° 24.590'
Season: Mid-May through mid-September
Sites: 7 basic sites, 4 tent sites
Maximum length: Any
Facilities: Tables, some fire pits and grills, vault toilets
Fee per night: $
Maximum stay: 7 days
Management: Alaska State Parks, Mat-Su/CB Area Office, (907) 745-3975, www.dnr.state.ak
.us/parks
Finding the campground: This wayside is located on the east side of the Parks Highway at
mile 185.6.
About the campground: This is a good example of a wayside camping area if you've never seen
one. The campground resembles a large rest area with picnic tables, fire pits, and grills. There are
eleven established camping spots, but it is easy to tell this was not originally intended to be an
overnight area. Many sites are completely paved, without any earth or gravel to pitch a tent. RVs of
any length, however, will be able to fit on the large paved shoulder of the loop road. There are also
four walk-in tent sites near large trees. One looks to have been designed as a group picnic area,
and indeed it would make a nice site for a group as it includes a large covered picnic shelter with
two large picnic tables. With sparkling-clean vault toilets, this is a rather popular quick stop for
Parks Highway travelers.

Denali Highway

	Hookup Sites	Total Sites	Max. RV Length	Hookups	Toilets	Showers	Drinking Water	Fires	Dump Station	Recreation	Fee	Reservations
129 Tangle Lakes Campground	0	23	Any	N	NF	N	Y	Y	N	FBL	Free	N
130 Brushkana Campground	0	22	Any	N	NF	N	Y	Y	N	HF	$	N

129 Tangle Lakes Campground

See map on page 179

Location: 21 miles west of Paxson
GPS: N 63° 02.982' / W 146° 00.452'
Season: Mid-May through October
Sites: 23 basic sites
Maximum length: Any
Facilities: Tables, fire pits, potable water, vault toilets, lake/fishing access, boat launch
Fee per night: $
Maximum stay: 14 days
Management: Bureau of Land Management, Glennallen Field Office, (907) 822-3217, www.blm.gov/ak
Finding the campground: This campground is located just west of the Tangle River on the Denali Highway, 21.3 miles west of Paxson. The Denali Highway is paved up to this campground entrance!
About the campground: This campground is located within the Tangle Lakes Archaeological District, one of the most significant anthropological finds in North America's subarctic region, home to a record number of indigenous artifacts stretching back over 10,000 years. The Tangle Lakes Campground is popular with locals accessing the waters, fishing for arctic grayling and trout, along with float trips. The on-site boat launch is the designated put-in launch for float trips of the Delta River Canoe Trail. You can tell that this campground serves more as a meeting point and less as an aesthetically pleasing place to stay. On the plus side, the sparsely treed grounds lend spectacular views of the surrounding range. Campsites are sporadically scattered, with some low brush around the grounds. Firewood may be available from the on-site hosts, but judging by the vast open land it is not a bad idea to bring your own just in case.

130 Brushkana Campground

See map on page 84

Location: 31 miles east of Cantwell
GPS: N 63° 17.426' / W 148° 03.081'
Season: Mid-May through October
Sites: 22 basic sites
Maximum length: Any
Facilities: Tables, covered picnic area, fire pits, potable water, vault toilets, hiking/fishing access
Fee per night: $
Maximum stay: 14 days
Management: Bureau of Land Management, Glennallen Field Office, (907) 822-3217, www.blm.gov/ak
Finding the campground: This campground is located on the Denali Highway 31 miles east of Cantwell. To reach it, head east from milepost 209.9 of the Parks Highway onto the Denali Highway. Drive 31 miles to the campground on the north side of the road. The highway is paved for only the first 3 miles.
About the campground: You might be surprised to find hosts here, and even more surprised to find they're volunteers excited about your trip down the Denali Highway. Odds are you're dropping by just to take in the spectacular scenery away from road stops or roadhouses, traffic lights, or even pavement. This campground allows you to experience the feel of the Alaskan bush yet still arrive by road. Trees shield the camping area from the road. The gravel sites feel more remote than they are. There are well-dispersed basic sites, a couple of pull-thrus, and a large gravel lot with a few sites for any size of RV or camper. The gravel lot backs up to picnic tables and fire pits for the corresponding site numbers. A covered picnic area directly on the Brushkana River makes for a scenic lunch spot. If you're in the mood for hiking, a small trail leads for a couple of miles to an expanse of views and the Brushkana River.

131 Cantwell RV Park

Location: Near mile 210 of the Parks Highway
GPS: N 63° 23.567' / W 148° 54.837'
Season: Mid-May through mid-September
Sites: 76 partial-hookup RV sites, 3 tent sites
Maximum length: 55 feet
Facilities: Picnic area, communal fire pit, some tables, potable water, flush toilets, dump station, laundry, WiFi, small store, gift shop
Fee per night: $$$–$$$$
Maximum stay: None
Management: Cantwell RV Park, (907) 888-6850, www.cantwellrvpark.wordpress.com
Finding the campground: From mile 210 of the Parks Highway, turn west onto the unlabeled road to Cantwell. Drive 0.3 mile to the campground on your right.

About the campground: The owners at Cantwell RV Park pride themselves on their well-kept grounds, advertising "the cleanest facilities you've seen since you were home." They live up to their reputation with some of the tidiest restrooms and showers around. Campsites are in good shape as well. They are located in a large open gravel lot. Most sites are side-by-side pull-thrus with mountain views. Some extra-long pull-thrus can hold RVs of up to 55 feet. Each site has a table or spool, and there is a communal fire pit. Sites are water and electric only, with a dump station on site. A small section is set aside for a couple of tents.

132 Denali Grizzly Bear Cabins and Campground

See map on page 112
Location: Near mile 231 of the Parks Highway
GPS: N 63° 39.252' / W 148° 50.080'
Season: Mid-May through mid-September
Sites: 56 partial-hookup RV sites, 30 tent sites
Maximum length: Any
Facilities: Tables, picnic areas with fire pit, potable water, flush toilets, showers, dump station, laundry, WiFi, small store
Fee per night: $$$–$$$$$
Maximum stay: None
Management: Denali Grizzly Bear Resort, (866) 583-2696, October through May (907) 683-2696, www.denaligrizzlybear.com
Finding the campground: On the west side of the Parks Highway at mile 231.1.
About the campground: Next to the Nenana River and close to Denali National Park, this family-operated campground is a good base for tents or RVs. The small earthen and gravel sites are spread among trees; a large gravel lot has back-ins with electric and water hookups. Several walk-in tent sites are located along the river. In conjunction with the campground, rent-a-tents and cabins are available as well as plush rooms at the large lodge. Two well-maintained restroom buildings have flush toilets, and showers are coin operated. The small store on site has groceries and can organize area charters and transportation.

Denali National Park

Denali National Park	Hookup Sites	Total Sites	Max. RV Length	Hookups	Toilets	Showers	Drinking Water	Fires	Dump Station	Recreation	Fee	Reservations
133 Riley Creek Campground	0	150	40	N	F	Y	Y	Y	Y	H	$$$	Y
134 Savage River Campground	0	34	25	N	F	N	Y	Y	N	H	$$$	Y
135 Sanctuary River Campground	0	7	T	N	NF	N	N	N	N	H	$$	N
136 Teklanika River Campground	0	53	Any	N	F	N	Y	Y	N	H	$$	Y
137 Igloo Creek Campground	0	7	T	N	NF	N	N	N	N	H	$	Y
138 Wonder Lake Campground	0	28	T	N	F	N	Y	N	N	H	$	Y

133 Riley Creek Campground

Location: In Denali National Park
GPS: N 63° 43.921' / W 148° 53.645'
Season: Year-round
Sites: 123 basic sites, 27 tent sites
Maximum length: 40 feet
Facilities: Tables, fire pits, food lockers, flush toilets, showers, dump station, laundry, phone, hiking/bus access, post office, groceries, gift shop
Fee per night: $$$
Maximum stay: 14 days
Management: Denali National Park Information, (907) 683-2294, www.nps.gov/dena; Denali National Park Reservations, (800) 622-7275, international (800) 272-7275, fax (907) 264-4684, www.reservedenali.com
Finding the campground: This campground is located on the paved public-access portion of the Park Road fairly close to the Parks Highway. To reach the campground, turn west onto the Park Road from mile 237.5 of the Parks Highway and drive 0.2 mile to the campground on your left.
About the campground: Riley Creek is one of the two Denali National Park campgrounds accessible by personal vehicle on the paved, unsealed portion of the road. It is the first campground as you enter Denali National Park, the largest, and has the most services. Riley Creek caters to crowds, being both the preferred grounds of RVers and home to more than two dozen walk-in tent sites. You may expect sardine-style organization to pack in all the visitors, but the strategically designed sites are impressively spacious, private, and forested. The massive grounds are divided

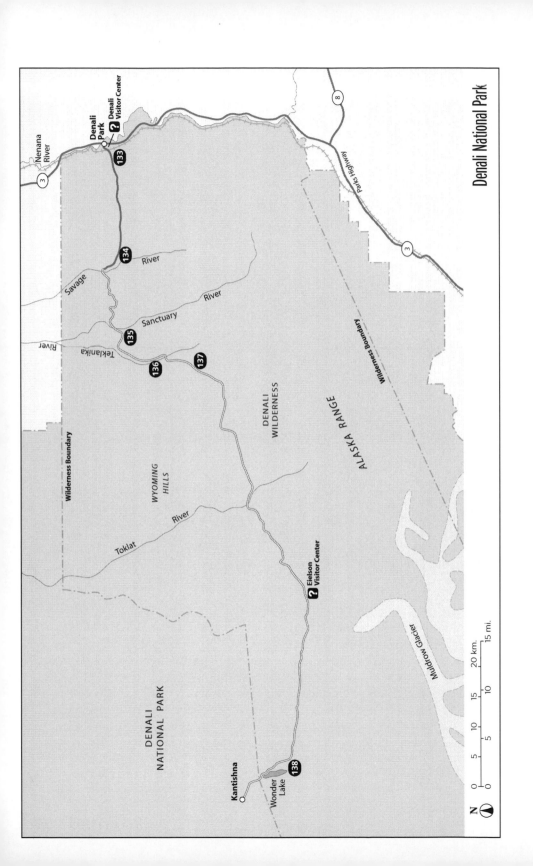

Denali National Park

into three simple loops, two of which are paved. Each site is specifically designated for tents or RVs and wheelchair accessibility. Each has a fire pit and table. Several blocks of flush toilets with cold running water are located throughout the grounds, including the walk-in section.

Despite their location at the bustling epicenter of Denali camping, these sites retain their natural and earthy atmosphere, sited in thick groves of shady spruce. Unfortunately, only a couple of them can accommodate an RV larger than 35 feet, so contact the park well in advance if you will be arriving in a larger rig. The twenty-four walk-in tent sites are pleasantly the same size as their motor-loving neighbors and come complete with food lockers. The nearby Riley Creek Mercantile has a small store with some groceries and firewood, Internet access, laundry, and showers. This campground is open all year with limited facilities from September through May. Winter camping is free.

134 Savage River Campground

Location: In Denali National Park
GPS: N 63° 43.001' / W 149° 15.546'
Season: Mid-May through mid-September
Sites: 34 basic sites
Maximum length: 25 feet
Facilities: Tables, fire pits, potable water, flush toilets, hiking/bus access
Fee per night: $$$
Maximum stay: 14 days
Management: Denali National Park Information, (907) 683-2294, www.nps.gov/dena; Denali National Park Reservations, (800) 622-7275, international (800) 272-7275, fax (907) 264-4684, www.reservedenali.com
Finding the campground: This campground is located on the paved public-access portion of the Park Road at mile 13. To reach the campground, turn west onto the Park Road from mile 237.5 of the Parks Highway and drive 13 miles to the campground on your left.
About the campground: Savage River is the second of the two campgrounds located on the paved, openly accessible portion of the road. The small sites are located off a meandering gravel loop. They are less spacious than Riley Creek but host quintessential park scenery. Many have mountain views along with scattered trees. These grounds are a tight squeeze for even small RVs, so check with the park to make sure a space is available. Many campers are surprised to find that this campground is not actually on the river but about a ten-minute walk away.

135 Sanctuary River Campground

Location: In Denali National Park
GPS: N 63° 43.357' / W 149° 28.420'
Season: Mid-May through mid-September
Sites: 7 tent sites
Maximum length: N/A
Facilities: Tables, chemical toilets, food lockers, hiking/bus access

Fee per night: $$

Maximum stay: 14 days

Management: Denali National Park Information, (907) 683-2294, www.nps.gov/dena

Finding the campground: This campground is located within Denali National Park at mile 23 of the Park Road. The road is sealed to private vehicles after mile 15; to reach it you must ride in on the park's shuttle bus system. Tickets can be purchased at the Wilderness Access Center (WAC). To reach the center, turn west onto the Park Road at mile 237.5 of the Parks Highway and continue 0.5 mile to the WAC on your left.

About the campground: Sanctuary River is the only Denali campground that does not take reservations. Located next to Sanctuary's braided glacial melt waterway, the campground has seven relatively private tent spots in an area popular with hikers and the resident snowshoe hares looking to get away from the crowds. There is also a group site at Savage available for a fee. Contact the park for more information. Staying at this campground is a lot like staying in the backcountry. Campfires are not allowed, and potable water is not available. Many people enjoy the private and quiet atmosphere at this more rustic campground.

136 Teklanika River Campground

Location: In Denali National Park

GPS: N 63° 40.183' / W 149° 34.624'

Season: Mid-May through mid-September

Sites: 53 RV sites

Maximum length: Any

Facilities: Tables, fire pits, flush toilets, hiking/bus access

Fee per night: $$

Maximum stay: 14 days

Management: Denali National Park Information, (907) 683-2294, www.nps.gov/dena; Denali National Park Reservations, (800) 622-7275, international (800) 272-7275, fax (907) 264-4684, www.reservedenali.com

Finding the campground: This campground is located within Denali National Park at mile 29 of the Park Road. The road is sealed to private vehicles after mile 15; to reach this campground you must obtain a special permit. Reservations can be made in advance, or tickets can be purchased at the Wilderness Access Center (WAC). To reach the center, turn west onto the Park Road at mile 237.5 of the Parks Highway and continue 0.5 mile to the WAC on your right.

About the campground: Tucked away almost 30 miles into the park, this campground offers those traveling in a RV or pulling campers a unique opportunity to drive in and camp along the sealed road. With a minimum three-night stay, those camping in hard-shelled vehicles can obtain permission and a special permit to drive their vehicle to and from this campground with no further excursions. Once you're there, the vehicle can't move, but special bus passes allow access through the park via shuttles. Wildlife-viewing opportunities increase as you get farther down the road into Denali's heart, and many take advantage of this chance to take their RV to the backcountry. The basic open campground is in a gravel lot next to the river. Each site has a table and fire pit.

137 Igloo Creek Campground

Location: In Denali National Park
GPS: N 63° 36.526' / W 149° 35.106'
Season: Mid-May through mid-September
Sites: 7 tent sites
Maximum length: N/A
Facilities: Tables, vault toilets, hiking/bus access
Fee per night: $
Maximum stay: 14 days
Management: Denali National Park Information, (907) 683-2294, www.nps.gov/dena; Denali National Park Reservations, (800) 622-7275, international (800) 272-7275, fax (907) 264-4684, www.reservedenali.com
Finding the campground: This campground is located within Denali National Park at mile 34 of the Park Road. The road is sealed to private vehicles after mile 15; to reach it you must ride in on the park's shuttle bus system. Tickets can be purchased at the Wilderness Access Center (WAC). To reach the center, turn west onto the Park Road at mile 237.5 of the Parks Highway and continue 0.5 mile to the WAC on your right.
About the campground: A popular campground and access point for hikers, Igloo Creek includes vault toilets, flooring mountain views, and excellent proximity to popular day-hiking romps.

138 Wonder Lake Campground

Location: In Denali National Park
GPS: N 63° 27.166' / W 150° 51.741'
Season: June through mid-September
Sites: 28 walk-in tent sites
Maximum length: N/A
Facilities: Tables, picnic area, food lockers, potable water, flush toilets, hiking/lake/bus access
Fee per night: $
Maximum stay: 14 days
Management: Denali National Park Information, (907) 683-2294, www.nps.gov/dena; Denali National Park Reservations, (800) 622-7275, international (800) 272-7275, fax (907) 264-4684, www.reservedenali.com
Finding the campground: This campground is located within Denali National Park at mile 85 of the Park Road. The road is sealed to private vehicles after mile 15; to reach it you must ride in on the park's shuttle bus system. Tickets can be purchased at the Wilderness Access Center (WAC). To reach the center, turn west onto the Park Road at mile 237.5 of the Parks Highway and continue 0.5 mile to the WAC on your right.
About the campground: Wonder Lake is the last established campground on Park Road and the indisputable pinup of Denali camping. The odds are you've seen a photograph of Denali taken from the Wonder Lake area at some point in your travels. On a clear day the views of the

The Wonder Lake Campground at Denali National Park.

continent's tallest peak can be spectacular from this campground: Behind the lake the all-white mountain reflects against blue skies and rolling tundra.

But the awe-inspiring scenery doesn't dampen the backpacking atmosphere of this campground. Not only is this area a photographer's and naturalist's haven, but it's also the end of the road and the gateway to the wilderness beyond. Many backcountry adventurers pass through here. The lack of fire rings at this campground inspires communal gathering points at the picnic area and food lockers. Hikers sit around maps discussing expeditions and routes. It is an authentic Denali experience. The campsites are not located on the lake, but on an opposing open hillside with mountain (namely Denali) and valley views. The sites are small walk-ins fairly close together, and each has a table. The well-kept new facilities have clean flush toilets and cold running water, a real treat at this remote campground. Wonder Lake's clear cool waters can come at a cost, especially in July, when horrendous mosquitoes also make camp here. Don't forget your mosquito net!

The Parks Highway: Denali to Fairbanks

The Parks Highway: Denali to Fairbanks

	Hookup Sites	Total Sites	Max. RV Length	Hookups	Toilets	Showers	Drinking Water	Fires	Dump Station	Recreation	Fee	Reservations
139 Denali Rainbow Village RV Park	80	80	Any	WESC	F	Y	Y	Y	Y	N	$$$$$	Y
140 Denali RV Park	89	89	45	WESC	F	Y	Y	N	Y	N	$$$$$	Y
141 Waugaman RV Village	18	18	35	WE	F	Y	Y	N	Y	N	$$	N
142 Tatlanika Trading Company	20	20	Any	WE	F	Y	Y	Y	Y	N	$$$	Y
143 Anderson Riverside Park	20	35+	Any		F	F & NF	Y	Y	Y	Y	N	$$	N

139 Denali Rainbow Village RV Park

Location: Near mile 238 of the Parks Highway
GPS: N 63° 44.828' / W 148° 53.886'
Season: Mid-May through mid-September
Sites: 17 full-hookup RV sites, 63 partial-hookup RV sites
Maximum length: Any
Facilities: Tables, fire pits, potable water, flush toilets, showers, dump station, laundry, WiFi
Fee per night: $$$$$
Maximum stay: None
Management: Denali Rainbow Village, (907) 683-7777, www.denalirv.com
Finding the campground: The campground is located on the east side of the Parks Highway at mile 238.6, within the Denali Park shopping and resort area.
About the campground: Located a short mile north of the entrance, Rainbow Village is the closest private campground to Denali National Park. The campground is located in the dead center of the area's shopping district alongside busy gas stations and gift shop row. With the dozen or so shops in front of the camping area and the very popular Denali Salmon Bake restaurant and bar to the side, foot traffic is consistent at most hours of the day and night. To the area's benefit, restaurants, souvenir shops, and lodges are all within walking distance. The campsites are snugly packed parking-lot-style spaces; most tables and fire rings are shared with neighbors. Only the string of businesses (some are open twenty-four hours) separates the campsites from the highway, so this is a high-traffic, high-noise parking area, but almost always packed due to appealing proximity. Also crammed on site are flush toilets, showers, and laundry.

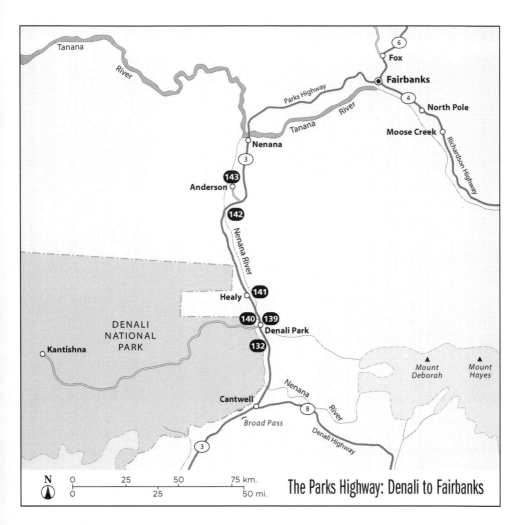

The Parks Highway: Denali to Fairbanks

140 Denali RV Park

Location: Near mile 245 of the Parks Highway
GPS: N 63° 49.266' / W 148° 59.200'
Season: June through September
Sites: 25 full-hookup RV sites, 64 partial-hookup RV sites
Maximum length: 45 feet
Facilities: Tables, picnic area, potable water, flush toilets, dump station, showers, laundry, WiFi, gift shop
Fee per night: $$$$$
Maximum stay: None
Management: Denali RV Park and Motel (907) 683-1500, www.denalirvpark.com

Finding the campground: The Denali RV Park is located on the west side of the Parks Highway at mile 245.1.

About the campground: Run in conjunction with a small motel, this RV park is located in an open gravel lot between the motel and the mountains about 8 miles north of Denali National Park. Sites are basic and close together, with some pull-thrus for RVs of up to 45 feet. Dividing brush offers some privacy. Most sites are electric-only; there are twenty-five full hookups. Several clean, private shower-restroom combinations are available for an extra fee.

141 Waugaman RV Village

Location: In Healy
GPS: N 63° 51.194' / W 148° 56.415'
Season: Late May through September
Sites: 18 partial-hookup RV sites
Maximum length: 35 feet
Facilities: Tables, flush toilets, showers, dump station, laundry
Fee per night: $$
Maximum stay: None
Management: Waugaman Village Motel and RV Park, (907) 683-2737
Finding the campground: From mile 248.7 of the Parks Highway, head east on Healy Road for 3.6 miles to the campground on your left.
About the campground: This lesser-known campground is a great option when all the campgrounds in the Denali area fill. Run in conjunction with a small motel, the Waugaman RV Village rarely packs to the brim—so it's no surprise that the park is simple. At around 4 miles away, the park is a change of pace from most open lots along the highway. There are eighteen gravel back-in sites, along with basic showers and small laundry facilities.

142 Tatlanika Trading Company

Location: Mile 276 of the Parks Highway
GPS: N 64° 13.071' / W 149° 16.449'
Season: June through early September
Sites: 20 partial-hookup RV sites
Maximum length: Any
Facilities: Tables, potable water, flush toilets, showers, dump station,
Fee per night: $$$
Maximum stay: None
Management: Tatlanika Trading Company, (907) 582-2341, www.tatlanika.com
Finding the campground: On the south side of the Parks Highway at mile 276.
About the campground: The Tatlanika Trading Post is a fairly popular restroom and gift shop stop for Parks Highway travelers. You can buy just about any mainstream Alaskan gift here as well as indulge in ice cream and the public picnic area. They offer basic camping in twenty RV sites with

water and electric hookups in a fairly open lot near the Nenana River. There are a few scattered trees and grassy pads, but things are kept very simple here.

143 Anderson Riverside Park

Location: Near mile 283 of the Parks Highway
GPS: N 64° 20.609' / W 149° 12.183'
Season: Mid-May through late September
Sites: 20 partial-hookup RV sites, 15 basic sites, open overflow camping
Maximum length: Any
Facilities: Tables, fire pits, potable water, portable and flush toilets, showers, dump station
Fee per night: $$
Maximum stay: None
Management: City of Anderson, (907) 582-2500
Finding the campground: From mile 283.5 of Parks Highway, drive west on Anderson Road for 6 miles, through the town of Anderson, to the dead end in Riverside Park.
About the campground: If you visit anytime other than July, you might be surprised to find the permanent stage, flush toilets, and showers at Anderson's Riverside Park. Home to the Anderson Bluegrass Festival, this campground hosts a summer meltdown of down-home Alaskan tunes. That's the only time this park will be bustling.

The large camping area is divided into two sections, with a gravel lot near the stage and more secluded sites in the woods. In the huge open area by the stage, you can fit RVs of any size and take advantage of the electrical hookups and nearby restroom facilities. Farther toward the creek are basic campsites tucked in the trees. These slightly more informal sites are located in clearings with fire pits and tables, and nearby portable toilets.

Fairbanks and the Far North

If interior Alaska is the heart of Alaska, it is suitable that Fairbanks is known as the Golden Heart City. In the center of the state, this classic Alaskan metropolis was birthed from the gold rush, and stays true to its pioneer roots. The city was built as a trading post in the early 1900s and has since endured ups and downs as the supply post of the interior, serving the needs of the various projects and the people of the north. Today the city still caters to a modern gold rush, with new caches continuing to be discovered around Fairbanks and deeper in the interior.

Fairbanks is Alaska's second largest city. It is a small city by most standards, with roughly 30,000 people in the city proper and 80,000 in the borough. It feels much larger, sprawled out along a tangle of freeways lacking practical urban planning, tight blocks, or districts. Buy a good map before you roll into this tricky town and try to navigate from one hopscotch neighborhood to another. Fairbanks is wide and flat, spread along the Tanana River Valley and surrounded by foothills. The Chena River snakes through town and provides excellent waterfront camping in this warm summer lowland.

Despite the growing industry, Fairbanks is not dressed up for tourists. Most people will find the city to be far more "Alaskan" than Anchorage. A drive around takes you through some quintessential Alaskan-style living built for practicality. Even the city's promotional Golden Heart Plaza is a small park with only a couple of tables for visitors. If you're looking to tour the city, you might take a different approach than you would in most urban spheres. Tour the University of Fairbanks and stop by the Georgeson Botanical Garden on campus to view a giant cabbage (no, really!). The college also operates the Large Animal Research Station, where you can get up close to a musk ox and ask all the questions you ever had about life in the Arctic. Pioneer Park, a theme park celebrating Alaska through rides and antiques, is free. If you want to really be historic, stop by one of the prospecting shops in town and pick up a gold pan. Staff can send you in the direction of a productive creek, or you can prospect at the original Gold Dredge No. 8 for a small fee.

Most campers will be pleased with their stay in Fairbanks despite the rough edges. The various campgrounds within the city offer excellent locations. There are plenty of campgrounds to choose from, in a variety of styles: from a riverside resort RV park with fine dining to a woodsy tent site at a hostel or just the basic state recreation area. You'll find that the people of Fairbanks don't put on a show; they're down-to-earth and genuine. These campgrounds have some of the most helpful hosts around.

Many campers will continue their journey up the far northern roads of Alaska. In a land without many roads, it is surprising how much roadway there is above Fairbanks. The Steese Highway leads to camping in the White Mountains and the village of Circle on the mighty Yukon River. Forking off the Steese just above Fairbanks, Chena Hot Springs Road takes you to the ecofriendly Chena Hot Springs Resort, a must-see if you're in Fairbanks. Tourists and locals alike flock here year-round to soak their limbs in the hot mineral pools. If you're visiting in spring or fall, book it up to Chena and spend a night aurora-borealis-watching from the hot springs pool in the middle of the night. Fantastic!

If you'd rather get off the beaten path, a long but low-key drive west leads down the Elliott Highway to undeveloped Manley Hot Springs. You can pay a local farmer a few dollars and soak in the cement tubs or visit the Manley Roadhouse, claimed to host Alaska's largest selection of liquor. If Manley's not remote enough, there is always the daring journey that the rental car companies tell you not to take. The Dalton Highway stretches nearly 500 gravel miles up to the Arctic Ocean following the trans-Alaska pipeline to its source. This wild ride has very few services; in fact, there are 244 solid miles without any at all (don't forget your gas can). The Bureau of Land Management's brochure guide to visiting the Dalton Highway reads like a waiver for skydiving, warning of all the risks and dangers on this road where call boxes are nonexistent and big rigs flail by at obscene speeds. You may appreciate the vastness, absorb the rugged environment of the primitive camps, and learn to accept the mosquitoes—either that or you'll loathe it all. This highway ends in Deadhorse, the industrial camp of the oilfields. This area does not cater to tourists, and the last few miles to the Arctic Ocean are on private oilfield land. If you made it this far, you can book a tour up the sealed road to Prudhoe Bay.

The far north and even Fairbanks are not for the weakhearted, which is probably why folks up here are so unique. It is a different journey than the camper takes down south. The summer weather is warmer and the days are basked in light. You might find yourself strangely watching the campfire embers barely flicker under dinnertime sun or forget what time it is in general. There are a lot of unique experiences to be had in the far north. Bring an adventuresome spirit (it deters mosquitoes).

Fairbanks

Fairbanks	Hookup Sites	Total Sites	Max. RV Length	Hookups	Toilets	Showers	Drinking Water	Fires	Dump Station	Recreation	Fee	Reservations
144 Chena River State Recreation Site	11	72	40	E	F	N	Y	Y	Y	HFBL	$$-$$$	N
145 River's Edge RV Park and Campground	190	202	50	WESC	F	Y	Y	N	Y	F	$$$-$$$$	Y
146 Sven's Basecamp Hostel	0	10	T	N	F	Y	Y	Y	N	N	$$	Y
147 Tanana Valley Campground	30	50	40	E	F	Y	Y	Y	Y	N	$$	Y
148 Riverview RV Park	160	166	Any	WESC	F	Y	Y	N	Y	F	$$$-$$$$$	Y
149 Chena Lake Recreation Area	0	85	Any	N	F & NF	N	Y	Y	Y	HFCSBL	$$	N

144 Chena River State Recreation Site

Location: In Fairbanks
GPS: N 64° 50.384' / W 147° 48.554'
Season: Mid-May through mid-September
Sites: 11 partial-hookup RV sites, 56 basic sites, 5 walk-in tent sites
Maximum length: 40 feet
Facilities: Tables, fire pits, covered picnic area, vault and flush toilets, potable water, fish-cleaning facilities, hiking/fishing/river access, boat launch, playground, volleyball, WiFi
Fee per night: $$-$$$
Maximum stay: 15 days; 5 days mid-June through mid-August
Management: Alaska State Parks, Northern Area Office, (907) 451-2695, www.dnr.state.ak.us/parks, www.chenawayside.com
Finding the campground: From mile 148 of the Parks Highway in east Fairbanks, take the Airport exit east, continue for 1 mile, and turn left onto University Avenue. Drive 0.2 mile; the campground is on your right.
About the campground: A public campground with hookup sites, flush toilets, and WiFi? Yes, it does exist! This government campground seasonally contracts the management to a private company with excellent park hosts who provide luxuries like sparkling-clean toilets and Internet access. Chena River is also one of the most convenient places to camp, within walking distance of grocery stores, restaurants, and bus stops. Along with its urban location, the campground also has mature trees and fire pits. The wooded twenty-six-acre park nestles up to the banks of the

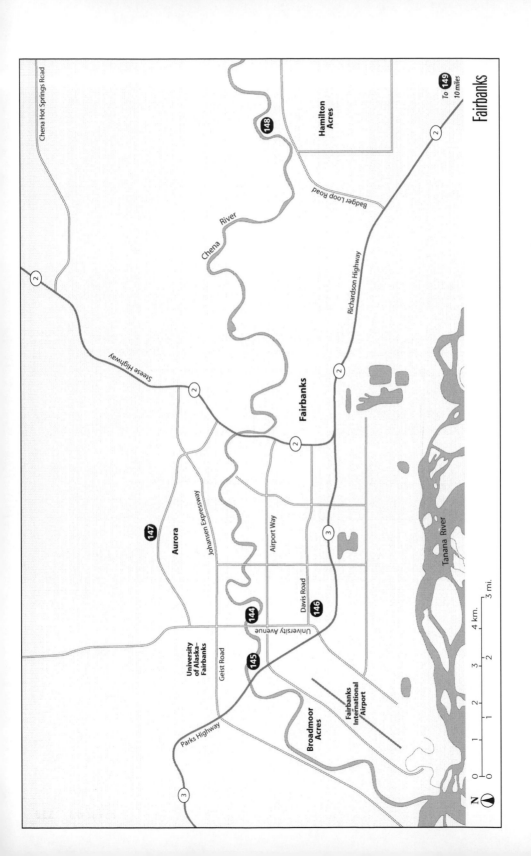

Fairbanks

Chena River, where a grassy day-use area with picnic sites is located. You probably wouldn't know you're camping in the city if it weren't for tent-rumbling aircraft noise. The campsites are spacious. For those traveling in RVs, there are eleven hookup sites with electricity, plus a dump station with water-fill. A large park area has a swing set and volleyball net.

145 River's Edge RV Park and Campground

Location: In Fairbanks
GPS: N 64° 50.367' / W 147° 50.026'
Season: Mid-May through mid-September
Sites: 114 full-hookup RV sites, 76 partial-hookup RV sites, 12 tent sites
Maximum length: 50 feet
Facilities: Tables, some grills, potable water, flush toilets, dump station, laundry, fishing/river access, WiFi, restaurant, gift shop
Fee per night: $$$–$$$$
Maximum stay: None
Management: Rivers Edge Resort, (907) 474-0286, (800) 770-3343, www.riversedge.net
Finding the campground: From mile 358 of the Parks Highway in east Fairbanks, exit onto Airport Way east, drive 0.4 mile, and turn left onto Sportsman's Way. Make an immediate left onto Boat Street and continue 0.4 mile to the resort on your right.
About the campground: This park is as luxurious as the resort it's attached to. Offering full-service amenities, more than fifty supersize deluxe full-hookup sites, and an unsurpassed riverfront location, the River's Edge is the premier location for many RVers. The park-like setting is home to a hotel, cottages, and restaurant, along with the campground. The sites are clean and basic; several directly on the river offer unobstructed views and access. You can fish for salmon and grayling from the park, and the staff can also organize many charters and tours beyond the Fairbanks area. Unfortunately, the airport is nearby, so noise is prominent.

146 Sven's Basecamp Hostel

Location: In Fairbanks
GPS: N 64° 49.627' / W 147° 48.451'
Season: Mid-May through mid-September
Sites: 10 tent sites
Maximum length: N/A
Facilities: Communal fire pit with benches, barbecue, kitchen, potable water, flush toilets, showers, volleyball, Internet access, canoe/vehicle rentals, charters
Fee per night: $$
Maximum stay: None
Management: Sven's Basecamp Hostel, www.svenshostel.com
Finding the campground: From mile 359 of the Parks Highway in Fairbanks, head north on University Avenue and drive 0.2 mile. Turn right onto Davis Road; the hostel is on your right after 0.1 mile.

About the campground: This hostel is much like a giant campground itself, with hostel beds in cabin tents and impressive woodsy communal areas including an open-air kitchen. The hostel hosts ten walk-in tent sites under mature trees. The shady campsites are small—just enough room for a tent on soft earthen patches of needles and grass. Gravel-ready vehicles as well as canoe and other gear rentals are available on site, and the incredibly helpful staff organize and lead a variety of wilderness adventures. This hostel is a gathering place for many group expeditions, so call in advance to be sure space is available.

147 Tanana Valley Campground

Location: In Fairbanks
GPS: N 64° 51.879' / W 147° 45.573'
Season: Mid-May through mid-September
Sites: 30 partial-hookup RV sites, 20 basic sites
Maximum length: 40 feet
Facilities: Tables, fire pits, potable water, showers, flush toilets, dump station, laundry, Internet access
Fee per night: $$
Maximum stay: None

One of the many big rigs along the Dalton Highway speeds past Sukapak Mountain.

Management: Tanana Valley Campground, (907) 456-7956, winter (907) 451-5557
Finding the campground: From mile 356.8 of the Parks Highway in Fairbanks, take the Geist/
Chena Pump Road exit and follow Geist Road east for 1.5 miles. Turn left onto University Avenue.
Drive 0.5 mile and turn right onto College Road. Continue 0.4 mile to the campground on your left.
About the campground: You'll find this cute wooded campground on the Tanana Valley Fair-
grounds, home to the Alaska State Fair the first week of August. Most sites are hidden from
the road. Sites aren't as spacious as the Chena River State Recreation sites, but they still offer
wooded atmosphere with a table and fire pit at each plus access to showers and laundry. RV sites
are electric-hookup-only, with two dump stations on site. Adjacent to the campground, visitors can
view the Creamers Wildlife Refuge and the Alaska Bird Observatory.

148 Riverview RV Park

Location: In Fairbanks
GPS: N 64° 49.985' / W 147° 30.927'
Season: May through September
Sites: 160 full-hookup RV sites, 6 tent sites
Maximum length: Any

Golden Heart Park in downtown Fairbanks.

Facilities: Tables, flush toilets, showers, laundry, WiFi, small store, horseshoes, fishing access, dump station, restaurant

Fee per night: $$$–$$$$$

Maximum stay: None

Management: Riverview RV Park, (907) 488-6392, (888) 488-6392, www.riverviewrvpark.net

Finding the campground: From mile 357 of the Richardson Highway, exit onto Badger Loop Road and head northeast for 2.5 miles to the campground on your left.

About the campground: Located between Fairbanks and North Pole, this campground's quiet riverside setting is a nice change. The well-maintained facilities include showers, laundry, a horseshoe pit, and a three-hole golf course. The campsites are in an open gravel lot with grass pads at each. There is also a tent-only area. Water access is a skip away, where you can fish for salmon and arctic grayling from the Chena River.

149 Chena Lake Recreation Area

Location: Near mile 346 of the Richardson Highway

GPS: N 64° 47.595' / W 147° 11.783'

Season: Late May through September

Swimming is popular at the Chena Lake Recreation Area.

Sites: 80 basic sites, 5 boat-in sites

Maximum length: Any

Facilities: Tables, fire pits, covered picnic area, potable water, flush and vault toilets, dump station, hiking/fishing/lake access, boat launch, playground, volleyball, basketball, horseshoes

Fee per night: $$

Maximum stay: 5 days

Management: Fairbanks North Star Borough, Chena Lake Recreation Area, (907) 488-1655, http://co.fairbanks.ak.us

Finding the campground: From mile 346.8 of the Richardson Highway, turn east onto Laurance Road and drive 2.5 miles to the entrance. Be sure to take a map at the kiosk to navigate your way through the large grounds.

About the campground: You might think you've stumbled upon the Venice Beach of Alaska when you catch a glimpse of the brave souls decked out in summer gear on the shore of the Chena Lake swimming beach. This recreation area is an ever-popular weekend getaway for local families. Lake activities include fishing, boating, swimming, volleyball, and cycling along the paved trails of Chena Lake. The waters are stocked, so anglers fit in as well.

Camping is divided into two areas. The first section you'll come upon is Lake Park, with a couple of loops of campsites. If you're in a large RV, you'll want to snag one of the pull-thrus in the second loop. All the basic sites include a table and fire pit. A few trees break up the sites. Lake Park is very busy on the weekends with three volleyball courts, two covered picnic areas, swimming beaches, and boat rentals (nonmotorized). If you're lucky enough to be camping with a boat, check out the five campsites located on the island in Chena Lake! The second camping area is at River Park. This attractive campground is less popular than its lakeside counterpart, although it, too, features a covered picnic area, volleyball court, and basic campsites. The area is a bit quieter, stretched along the river, and a bit closer to the wilderness with birch-shaded campsites and a 3-mile nature trail.

Chena Hot Springs Road

Chena Hot Springs Road

	Hookup Sites	Total Sites	Max. RV Length	Hookups	Toilets	Showers	Drinking Water	Fires	Dump Station	Recreation	Fee	Reservations
150 Rosehip Campground	0	37	Any	N	NF	N	Y	Y	N	HF	$$	N
151 Granite Tors Trail Campground	0	24	40	N	NF	N	Y	Y	N	HF	$$	N
152 Red Squirrel Campground	0	12	T	N	NF	N	Y	Y	N	HF	$$	N
153 Chena Hot Springs Resort	0	40	Any	N	F & NF	Y	Y	Y	Y	H	$$	N

The Ice Museum and Ice Bar at the Chena Hot Springs Resort.

150 Rosehip Campground

See map on page 129

Location: Mile 27 of Chena Hot Springs Road
GPS: N 64° 52.630' / W 146° 45.907'
Season: Mid-May through October
Sites: 33 basic sites, 4 walk-in tent sites
Maximum length: Any
Facilities: Tables, fire pits, potable water, vault toilets, hiking/fishing/river access
Fee per night: $$
Maximum stay: 15 days
Management: Alaska State Parks, Northern Area Office, (907) 451-2695, www.dnr.state.ak
.us/parks
Finding the campground: On the south side of Chena Hot Springs Road at mile 27.
About the campground: The shadowy birch and spruce forest makes this riverside campground a
real charmer. Rosehip Campground is also the take-out point for many who float the Chena River.
Campsites are a score as well, with huge back-in sites under lush trees. Some sites are deep
enough for large RVs, and all are located off a wide loop road. Four smaller tent sites are located
directly on the banks of the river. On site the small nature trail makes for a nice stroll. True to the
name of the grounds, wild roses bloom around May.

151 Granite Tors Trail Campground

See map on page 129

Location: Near mile 39 of Chena Hot Springs Road
GPS: N 64° 54.216' / W 146° 21.643'
Season: Mid-May through October
Sites: 24 basic sites
Maximum length: 40 feet
Facilities: Tables, fire pits, potable water, vault toilets, picnic area, hiking/river/fishing access
Fee per night: $$
Maximum stay: 15 days
Management: Alaska State Parks, Northern Area Office, (907) 451-2695, www.dnr.state.ak
.us/parks
Finding the campground: On the west side of Chena Hot Springs Road at mile 39.8.
About the campground: This campground is located close to the Granite Tors Trailhead. The highly
recommended 15-mile Granite Tors hike leads to granite pinnacle rock formations with a view of
the Tors, Alaska Range, and Chena River Valley. The campground encompasses twenty-four basic
sites, very large and located under the shade of birch, cottonwood, and spruce trees. The campground is also popular as the put-in point for relaxing Chena River float trips.

152 Red Squirrel Campground

See map on page 129

Location: Near mile 42 of Chena Hot Springs Road
GPS: N 64° 56.131' / W 146° 17.162'
Season: Mid-May through October
Sites: 12 tent sites
Maximum length: N/A
Facilities: Tables, fire pits, covered picnic area, potable water, vault toilets, hiking/fishing access
Fee per night: $$
Maximum stay: 15 days
Management: Alaska State Parks, Northern Area Office, (907) 451-2695, www.dnr.state.ak
.us/parks
Finding the campground: This campground is located on the north side of Chena Hot Springs
Road at mile 42.8.
About the campground: Red Squirrel is a great place to picnic, with two separate covered shelters
and tables on a pond. The facilities are clean and well maintained; one of the picnic shelters can
be reserved. The camping area is very basic, but there's plenty of grass for tenters.

153 Chena Hot Springs Resort

See map on page 129

Location: Near mile 56 of Chena Hot Springs Road
GPS: N 65° 03.224' / W 146° 03.520'
Season: Mid-April through October
Sites: 15 RV sites, 25 tent sites
Maximum length: Any
Facilities: Tables, fire pits, potable water, flush toilets, showers, dump station, laundry, hiking
access, hot springs pools, airstrip, restaurant, bar, WiFi, ice museum, charters
Fee per night: $$
Maximum stay: None
Management: Chena Hot Springs Resort, (907) 451-8104, www.chenahotsprings.com
Finding the campground: This campground is located at the end of Chena Hot Springs Road, at
mile 56.6.
About the campground: Alaskans have been soaking in the warmth of Chena Hot Springs for
more than a hundred years. Today the resort is one of the most popular destinations within the
state for Alaskans—and rightly so. This down-to-earth facility offers a variety of outdoor activities all
year long to go with the massive warm mineral water pool. The Ice Museum is created from better
than 1,000 tons of ice. The dog kennel has over fifty sled dogs if you'd like a chance at mushing.
During summer the dogs pull wheeled carts. "Chena" has a variety of outdoor activities accessible

from the resort year-round. The friendly staff can also organize outings and other more extravagant charters such as flight-seeing or rafting. The resort is also one of the more popular places to view the aurora borealis, generally viewable only in fall through spring when there is a chance of a clear dark sky. While most guests choose to stay at the moderately priced lodge, there is also an RV park and campground available on a first-come, first-served basis. There are fifteen RV sites (no hookups) along with twenty-five tent sites divided into two separate areas, plus a special pull-thru section for large RVs. Most of the campsites are located in a natural setting surrounded by trees. Of course, the real reason to stay here is to soak your limbs in the soothing mineral pools. The large rock pool is a real treat.

The Steese Highway

The Steese Highway

	Hookup Sites	Total Sites	Max. RV Length	Hookups	Toilets	Showers	Drinking Water	Fires	Dump Station	Recreation	Fee	Reservations
154 Upper Chatanika River State Recreation Site	0	25	25	N	NF	N	Y	Y	N	HF	$$	N
155 Mt. Prindle Campground	0	13	Any	N	NF	N	Y	Y	N	H	$	N
156 Ophir Creek Campground	0	19	25	N	NF	N	Y	Y	N	HF	$	N
157 Cripple Creek Campground	0	19	Any	N	NF	N	Y	Y	N	HF	$	N
158 Circle Park	0	10+	Any	N	N	N	N	Y	N	N	Free	N

154 Upper Chatanika River State Recreation Site

Location: Mile 39 of the Steese Highway
GPS: N 65° 11.528' / W 147° 15.420'
Season: May through October
Sites: 25 basic sites
Maximum length: 25 feet
Facilities: Tables, fire pits, picnic area, potable water, vault toilets, hiking/river/fishing access
Fee per night: $$
Maximum stay: 15 days
Management: Alaska State Parks, Northern Area Office (907) 451-2695, www.dnr.state.ak.us/parks
Finding the campground: On the west side of the Steese Highway at mile 39, just north of the river.
About the campground: Activities at Upper Chatanika are centered on the river. Locals seem to be lounging around the shores on most warm weekends during summer. A line and a lounge chair can add to the lure of the gravel bars, with fishing for grayling and sunbathing topping the preferred recreations. Along with the beautiful pebbled beach on site, this campground is a popular place to launch a canoe for a one- to two-day float trip down to the Lower Chatanika State Recreation Area. Camping is under tightly packed slender trees, which are delightfully dark on those never-ending sunny days. You can cool down in any of the twenty-five campsites. The small back-in sites are located off a short loop. They are best suited for small RVs, but offer more than enough space to make this a tenting hot spot.

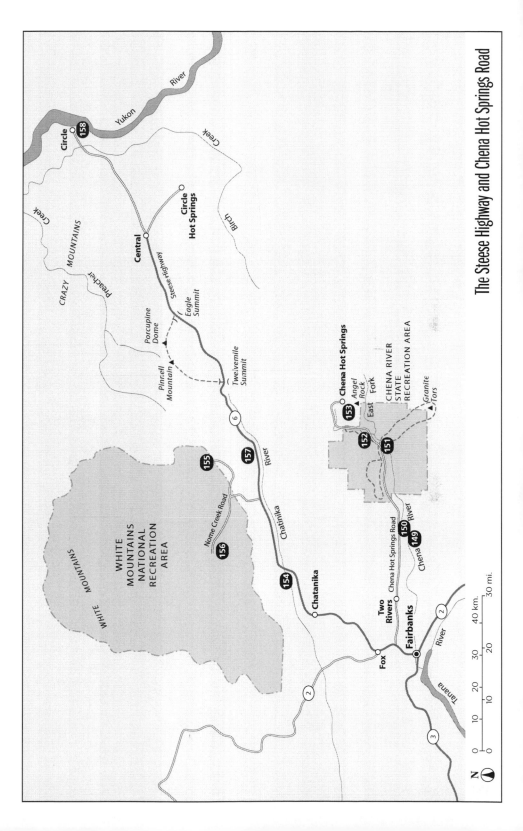

The Steese Highway and Chena Hot Springs Road

155 Mt. Prindle Campground

Location: Near mile 57 of the Steese Highway
GPS: N 65° 22.026' / W 146° 35.684'
Season: Late May through October
Sites: 13 basic sites
Maximum length: Any
Facilities: Tables, fire pits, potable water, vault toilets, hiking access
Fee per night: $
Maximum stay: 10 nights
Management: Bureau of Land Management, Fairbanks District Office, (907) 474-2200, (800) 437-7021, www.blm.gov/ak
Finding the campground: From mile 57.3 of the Steese Highway, turn west onto US Creek Road and drive 11 miles, passing through the Nome Creek Recreational Gold Panning Area at 6.9 miles and then following the signs to the Mt. Prindle Campground for another 4.1 miles.
About the campground: There are only thirteen sites in this rustic remote White Mountains campground. Aside from absorbing views of Mount Prindle, alpine tundra, and three outhouses, there

Fireweed blooms in a burn patch north of Fairbanks.

isn't much else around. Half of these deep back-in sites are separated by large shrubs and tiny trees. This campground isn't as well developed as neighboring Ophir Creek. The campground is, however, a preferred base for the beginning of a backcountry adventure off the only developed trail within the White Mountain National Recreation Area, the 16-mile Quartz Creek Trail. A variety of other backcountry options can launch from here as well.

156 Ophir Creek Campground

Location: Near mile 57 of the Steese Highway
GPS: N 65° 22.130' / W 147° 05.058'
Season: Late May through October
Sites: 19 basic sites
Maximum length: 25 feet
Facilities: Tables, fire pits, some grills, potable water, vault toilets, hiking/fishing/river access
Fee per night: $
Maximum stay: 10 nights
Management: Bureau of Land Management, Fairbanks District Office, (907) 474-2200, (800) 437-7021, www.blm.gov/ak
Finding the campground: From mile 57 of the Steese Highway, turn west onto US Creek Road. Drive 6.9 miles to the Nome Creek Recreational Gold Panning Area. Follow the signs toward Ophir Creek Campground by turning left onto a gravel road. Take the bumpy road for 12 miles to the campground on your left. Although it's not necessary, high-clearance vehicles are highly recommended for this road; otherwise you will want to take your sweet time getting to Ophir Creek.
About the campground: This campground is one of those rewards at the end of the bumpy road. The drive in—a high-rise journey through the White Mountains—offers the best of Alaskan scenery when mid- to late summer the burn areas support shockingly thick patches of magenta fireweed. Once you arrive here, you'll find a surprisingly nice and excellently kept campground. Ophir Creek is a well-used put-in point for float trips down the daring waters of the Beaver Creek National Wild River, and possibly a 360-mile float trip to the Yukon River. Rafting companies often set up base camps here. Campsites are well spaced off a wide gravel road and dispersed among spruce trees. Smaller sites are designed for tents, but small campers will also fit in.

157 Cripple Creek Campground

Location: Mile 60 of the Steese Highway
GPS: N 65° 16.584' / W 149° 39.021'
Season: Mid-May through October
Sites: 12 basic sites, 7 walk-in tent sites
Maximum length: Any
Facilities: Tables, fire pits, potable water, pit toilets, hiking/fishing/creek access
Fee per night: $
Maximum stay: 7 days

Management: Bureau of Land Management, Fairbanks District Office, (907) 474-2200, (800) 437-7021, www.blm.gov/ak

Finding the campground: The road is paved up to this campground, located on the north side of the Steese Highway at mile 60.

About the campground: This pleasant campground hosts large sites nestled in a spruce-and-birch forest. The well-maintained sites are an excellent deal. Along with the deep back-ins, walk-in tent sites are located directly on the river. All sites have a table and fire pit.

158 Circle Park

Location: In Circle
GPS: N 65° 49.509' / W 144° 03.686'
Season: Year-round
Sites: About 10 open sites
Maximum length: Any
Facilities: Some fire rings
Fee per night: Free

The trans-Alaska pipeline and Dalton Highway run parallel.

Wiseman is home to some real characters.

Maximum stay: None
Management: None
Contact: None
Finding the campground: This campground is located on the banks of the Yukon River at the end of the Steese Highway in the town of Circle at mile 161.3.
About the campground: This is the only official camping area in Circle, although it's not recommended. Camping is in a degraded trashed gravel lot with no services. Since the drive to Circle is so long, people often get stuck parking here, and some enjoy the riverfront bargain. There aren't official sites; campers tend to just park and set up anywhere in the very small lot. The facilities are not maintained and should be considered unusable, with deplorable pit toilets, an example of "you get what you pay for." The area is available for camping as long as snow permits. A couple of blocks away, the H. C. Company store has sometimes let people park overnight in their lot, but be sure to check for status within the store during business hours. Also try the Lower Creek Wayside, at mile 140.5. Although it's not an established campground, this clean, simple gravel lot with vault toilet allows overnight camping for tents and RVs.

The Elliott Highway

	Hookup Sites	Total Sites	Max. RV Length	Hookups	Toilets	Showers	Drinking Water	Fires	Dump Station	Recreation	Fee	Reservations
159 Northern-Moosed RV Park & Campground	20	35	50	WES	F	Y	Y	Y	Y	N	$$	Y
160 Olnes Pond Campground	0	10	Any	N	N	N	N	Y	N	HF	$$	N
161 Whitefish Campground	0	25	30	N	N	N	N	Y	N	F	$$	N
162 Manley City Park	0	20	25	N	NF	N	N	Y	N	N	$	N

159 Northern-Moosed RV Park & Campground

Location: In Fox
GPS: N 64° 57.736' / W 147° 37.252'
Season: Late May through September
Sites: 20 full hookup sites, 15 partial hookup sites, open tent camping
Maximum length: 50 feet
Facilities: Some tables, some firepits, dump station, potable water, flush toilets, showers, laundry, WiFi
Fee per night: $$
Maximum stay: None
Management: Northern-Moosed RV Park & Campground, (907) 451-0984, www.northern moosed.com
Finding the campground: From Fox take the Steese Highway north half a mile and turn right onto the Old Elliott Highway where the campground is on the left.
About the campground: This campground is still slowly being developed and includes some full and partial hookups. The wooded and grassy sites are a bit overgrown, but they are just far enough off the highway to be quiet.

160 Olnes Pond Campground

Location: Near mile 10 of the Elliott Highway
GPS: N 65° 04.669' / W 147° 44.672'
Season: May through October
Sites: About 10 primitive sites
Maximum length: Any

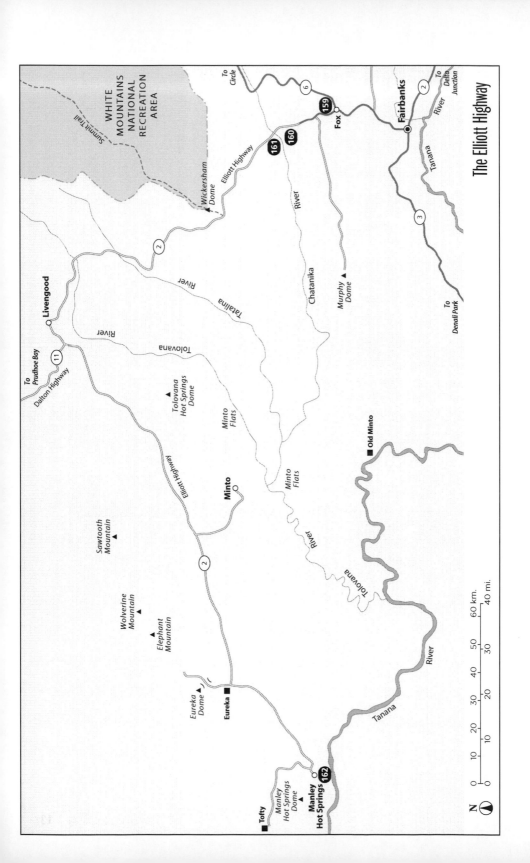

The Elliott Highway

Facilities: Some tables and fire pits, hiking/fishing/pond access
Fee per night: $$
Maximum stay: 15 days
Management: Alaska State Parks, Northern Area Office, (907) 451-2695, www.dnr.state.ak .us/parks
Finding the campground: From mile 10.6 of the Elliott Highway, turn south onto a gravel road at the sign for Olnes Pond. Drive 1 mile and turn right onto a small unlabeled dirt road that leads directly to the pond.
About the campground: Olnes Pond is not managed by State Parks and most of the facilities should be considered obsolete, but this doesn't seem to detour any campers. Rustic camping next to the small pond consists of about ten clearings among trees, a couple of open flat parking areas, and some primitive fire rings. Due to the limited camping areas on the Elliott, and fishing popularity, this run-down campground does have traffic and is open as long as the snow allows access.

161 Whitefish Campground

Location: Mile 11 of the Elliot Highway
GPS: N 65° 05.105' / W 147° 43.666'
Season: May through October
Sites: About 25 primitive sites
Maximum length: 30 feet
Facilities: Some tables and fire pits, fishing/river access
Fee per night: $$
Maximum stay: 15 days
Management: Alaska State Parks, Northern Area Office, (907) 451-2695, www.dnr.state.ak .us/parks
Finding the campground: Look for this campground on the south side of the Elliott Highway at mile 11, just west of Chatanika Bridge, on an unlabeled dirt road leading to river access.
About the campground: Much like Olnes Pond, Whitefish has unofficial campsites and unmaintained facilities. In fall angling for whitefish is a popular activity, but even then the grounds remain rather abandoned. The camping area consists of about ten formal-looking spots and a couple of large clearings where people tend to park larger campers and RVs. Some lucky tent sites are located directly on the riverfront. This campground is probably not suitable for substantial campers or RVs due to the narrow road and limited maneuvering room.

162 Manley City Park

Location: In Manley Hot Springs
GPS: N 65° 00.054' / W 150° 38.099'
Season: Year-round, weather permitting; not plowed in winter
Sites: 10 basic sites, 10 tent sites
Maximum length: 25 feet

Facilities: Tables, fire pits, pit toilets, river access
Fee per night: $
Maximum stay: 14 days
Management: Manley Hot Springs Association; contact Manley Roadhouse for payment and management information, (907) 672-3161
Finding the campground: This campground is just over the one-lane bridge as you enter Manley Hot Springs on the right side, across from the roadhouse at mile 152 of the Elliott Highway. Pay your fees at the Manley Roadhouse.
About the campground: Manley Hot Springs is a cute and interesting town worth visiting. The hot springs were never developed to their potential, but several tubs in a greenhouse owned by a local family can be visited. The center of activity and source for information on camping and the hot springs is the Manley Roadhouse. Here you'll find colorful locals, more than 200 kinds of liquor, and the place to pay your camping fees. The small basic campground is across the street from the roadhouse. There are ten tiny sites you can drive to and another ten walk-in sites along a slough. At a low cost a site, and within a stumble of the roadhouse, these shaded sites are a bargain.

The Dalton Highway

The Dalton Highway

	Hookup Sites	Total Sites	Max. RV Length	Hookups	Toilets	Showers	Drinking Water	Fires	Dump Station	Recreation	Fee	Reservations
163 Five Mile Camp	0	20	Any	N	NF	N	Y	Y	Y	N	Free	N
164 Arctic Circle Wayside	0	15	Any	N	NF	N	N	Y	N	N	Free	N
165 Coldfoot Camp	15	25	Any	WE	F	Y	Y	N	Y	N	$$–$$$$	N
166 Marion Creek Campground	0	27	Any	N	NF	N	Y	Y	N	H	$	N
167 Galbraith Lake	0	20	Any	N	NF	N	N	Y	N	F	Free	N

163 Five Mile Camp

Location: Near mile 60 of the Dalton Highway
GPS: N 65° 55.134' / W 149° 49.668'
Season: Year-round

The Dalton Highway stretches for 240 miles without services.

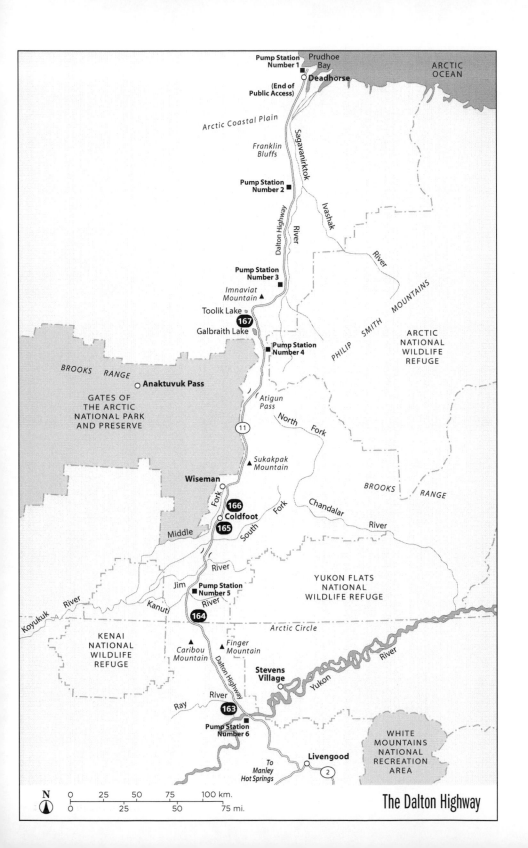

The Dalton Highway

Sites: About 20 primitive sites
Maximum length: Any
Facilities: Some fire rings, potable water, vault toilet, dump station
Fee per night: Free
Maximum stay: None
Management: Bureau of Land Management, Fairbanks District Office, (907) 474-2200, (800) 437-7021, www.blm.gov/ak
Finding the campground: From mile 60.4 of the Dalton Highway, take the second entrance road to the Hot Spot Café, but continue on the gravel road instead of turning left to the cafe parking lot. Drive 0.2 mile to the campground.
About the campground: This is the first of the three undeveloped campgrounds provided by the BLM along the Dalton. The open gravel lot sits on two bluffs, each with an outhouse and bear-proof garbage cans. Highway noise is relatively low from this point. A cafe is located just below the campground.

164 Arctic Circle Wayside

Location: Near mile 115 of the Dalton Highway
GPS: N 66° 33.522' / W 150° 47.702'
Season: Year-round
Sites: About 15 open sites
Maximum length: Any
Facilities: Day-use picnic area with tables, fire pits, vault toilet
Fee per night: Free
Maximum stay: None
Management: Bureau of Land Management, Fairbanks District Office, (907) 474-2200, (800) 437-7021, www.blm.gov/ak
Finding the campground: At mile 115.5 of the Dalton Highway, turn east at the BLM display sign for the Arctic Circle Wayside. Drive 0.3 mile to the hillside camping area.
About the campground: Located on a hillside of cottonwoods and willows above the Arctic Circle Wayside, this area has recently been redeveloped. Camping is open and seems to be based around a large open clearing and a couple of tables. The road can be muddy and narrow; be cautious with trailers and RVs.

165 Coldfoot Camp

Location: In Coldfoot
GPS: N 67° 15.075' / W 150° 10.642'
Season: May through September
Sites: 15 partial-hookup RV sites, 10 basic sites
Maximum length: Any
Facilities: Picnic area, flush toilets, showers, restaurant

Fee per night: $$–$$$$
Maximum stay: None
Management: Coldfoot Camp, (907) 474-3500, (866) 474-3400, www.coldfootcamp.com
Finding the campground: At mile 175 of the Dalton Highway, just past the Arctic Interagency Visitor Center, turn east at either turnoff for the loop road to Coldfoot. The cafe is in the center of the action 0.1 mile down the road.
About the campground: Here you will find the last gas until Deadhorse on your journey up the Dalton. This will also be the first sign of civilization on your journey back down. The rugged truck stop is the last hub for the long haul and is always busy. Run in conjunction with the cafe and gas station, the camping area has very basic RV parking, offering a combination of electric-only hookups, dry, and tent sites. All the campsites are in the open, but you likely won't spend much time here aside from trying to catch a few winks under the midnight sun. The nearby Arctic Interagency Visitor Center is a must-see with impressive natural history displays, delightfully helpful staff, trip-planning assistance, and the nicest restrooms on the North Slope.

166 Marion Creek Campground

Location: Mile 179 of the Dalton Highway
GPS: N 67° 18.955' / W 150° 09.565'
Season: May through September

The Arctic Circle Wayside.

Sites: 27 basic sites

Maximum length: Any

Facilities: Tables, some grills, fire pits, potable water, vault toilets, hiking access

Fee per night: $

Maximum stay: 14 days

Management: Bureau of Land Management, Fairbanks District Office, (907) 474-2200, (800) 437-7021, www.blm.gov/ak

Finding the campground: The campground is located on the east side of the Dalton Highway at mile 179, just south of Marion Creek.

About the campground: This is by far the nicest campground along the Dalton Highway. If you're planning to camp anywhere near Coldfoot and don't require a hookup, Marion Creek is the most comfortable and most aesthetically appealing choice. The campground is nestled in a droopy black spruce forest and has handsome mountain views. There are twenty-seven manicured sites located off two spacious gravel loop roads. About fourteen of the sites are oversize pull-thrus suitable for any size of rig. All have tables and fire rings (the last tables at camping areas to be seen on the Dalton as you head north); some have grills. No tents may be pitched on the tundra. Some sites have wooden tent platforms, but in others you will have to pitch in the gravel.

Camping along the Dalton is very basic and open with few, if any, services.

167 Galbraith Lake

Location: Near mile 275 of the Dalton Highway
GPS: N 68° 27.236' / W 149° 28.916'
Season: May through September
Sites: About 20 primitive sites
Maximum length: Any
Facilities: Fire rings, outhouse, fishing/lake access, airstrip
Fee per night: Free
Maximum stay: 14 days
Management: Bureau of Land Management, Fairbanks District Office, (907) 474-2200, (800) 437-7021, www.blm.gov/ak
Finding the campground: From mile 275 of the Dalton Highway, turn west onto the gravel road at the sign for Galbraith Lake. Drive 4.1 miles, passing directly through the parking lot of the Galbraith airstrip (2 miles in), to the dead end at the campground.
About the campground: The rolling tundra around Galbraith Lake, along with the last of the mountain views, lends some appeal to this undeveloped campground. The camping area is in a gravel lot past the airport near the placid lake, and is completely open with the exception of some low brush. The grounds also have bear-proof food lockers and garbage cans—a feature that says something about the local inhabitants. Sites are defined by fire rings, and some have views of the lake. You can search for fossils in the gravel along the shore or at the creek near the gravel pit opposite the airstrip.

The Glenn Highway

If you're heading to Anchorage, the odds are you will be driving along the Glenn Highway at some point. The road connects Anchorage to both the Richardson Highway and the Alaska Highway, stretching 328 miles to Tok. This National Scenic Byway passes through a landscape of rugged mountains, valley views, and glaciers receding into the carved peaks.

Beginning in downtown Anchorage, the highway leaves the city through the Chugach Mountains and half-million-acre Chugach State Park. The road then descends into the agricultural spread of the Matanuska Valley. In Palmer there are many full-service campgrounds popular with those visiting the Anchorage area. Also in Palmer, a side trip up Hatcher Pass Road leads to extravagant hiking and some primitive camps. At the Independence State Historical Park, you can wander the ruins of the old gold mine or camp at a trailhead to a glacier.

The Glenn stretches east out of the valley and past the Talkeetna Mountains, framed by peaks on both the north and south sides of the highway. The Matanuska Glacier peers at the road from the south. You can camp privately near this brilliant blue ice or book a tour to trek across the frozen beauty. Also keep an eye out for Dall sheep in the surrounding mountains, or take a hike up Sheep Mountain for a better view.

After the Matanuska Glacier area, amenities—along with campgrounds—become few and far between. Most services are run in conjunction with roadhouses, and restroom facilities fizzle out. This long stretch of road to Glennallen is known for spectacular displays of fall colors. Most RV parks and campgrounds are along the roadside, none straying far from the pavement. But they don't have to, with wilderness abounding along the sparsely populated road.

Outdoor opportunities along the Glenn Highway don't have the destination draw of those in the south. Calmer areas still offer good, but low-key, fishing for grayling and trout—but nothing near the Kenai's salmon insanity. Many trails fork away from the highway, but most of these are fall hunting trails or winter trails unlabeled in summer. With the transient environment of the Glenn Highway, you might think the campgrounds would be less apt to fill, but enough people pass through that the limited camping areas are often full. The Glenn Highway and Tok Cutoff receive thousands of visitors a year. Most are just in transit, but some will stop and take a hike or visit a glacier in this area of classic interior Alaska.

The highway hits Glennallen and junctions with the Richardson Highway, the gateway to Wrangell–St. Elias National Park. The glorious peaks of the Wrangell Mountains stretch to the east. Glennallen serves as the hub of the Glenn Highway, where you can get fast gas and a few snacks. After Glennallen the highway rolls northeast to another hub. This section of road is known as the Tok Cutoff and ends in Tok, the busy rest stop of the Alaska Highway.

The Glenn Highway: Anchorage to Glennallen

	Hookup Sites	Total Sites	Max. RV Length	Hookups	Toilets	Showers	Drinking Water	Fires	Dump Station	Recreation	Fee	Reservations
168 Bobby's RV Park	24	30	Any	WES	NF	N	Y	N	Y	N	$$-$$$$	Y
169 Fox Run RV Campground	30	36	Any	WES	F	Y	Y	Y	Y	HF	$$$-$$$$	Y
170 Matanuska Lake Campground	0	6	T	N	NF	N	Y	Y	N	HF	$	Y
171 Kepler Park	0	23	35	N	NF	N	Y	Y	N	N	$$	N
172 Matanuska River Park	35	80	35	E	F & NF	Y	Y	Y	Y	H	$$-$$$	N
173 Mountain View RV Park	103	103	Any	WES	F	Y	Y	Y	Y	Y	$$$-$$$$$	Y
174 Knik River Ranch	0	Open	Any	N	NF	N	Y	Y	N	HF	$-$$	N
175 Jim Creek Campground	0	20	Any	N	NF	N	Y	Y	N	HF	$	N
176 Moose Creek Campground	0	15	25	N	NF	N	N	Y	N	N	$	N
177 Pinnacle Mountain RV Park	28	42	Any	WE	F	Y	Y	Y	Y	N	$$-$$$	Y
178 King Mountain State Recreation Site	0	22	35	N	NF	N	Y	Y	N	N	$$	Y
179 Matanuska Glacier State Recreation Site	0	12	Any	N	NF	N	Y	Y	N	H	$-$$	N
180 Glacier Park	0	16	25	N	NF	N	Y	Y	N	H	$$-$$$$	N
181 Grand View RV Park	19	27	Any	WESC	F	Y	Y	Y	Y	N	$$$$	Y
182 Slide Mountain RV Park	14	14+	Any	E	F	Y	Y	N	N	N	$$-$$$$	Y
183 Mendeltna Creek Lodge	59	79	Any	WES	F	Y	Y	Y	Y	HF	$-$$	Y
184 Lake Louise State Recreation Area	0	58	Any	N	NF	N	Y	Y	N	HF	$-$$	N
185 Ranch House Lodge and RV Camping	50	60	60	WES	F	Y	Y	Y	Y	HF	$$-$$$$	Y
186 Tolsona Wilderness Campground	43	80	60	WE	F	Y	Y	Y	Y	HF	$$-$$$$	Y
187 Caribou Hotel and Restaurant	15	15	Any	WES	F	N	Y	N	N	N	$$$$	N
188 Northern Nights RV Park	23	26	Any	WES	F	Y	Y	Y	Y	N	$$-$$$	Y

168 Bobby's RV Park

Location: In Chugiak
GPS: N 61° 24.572' / W 149° 26.855'
Season: Mid-May through late September

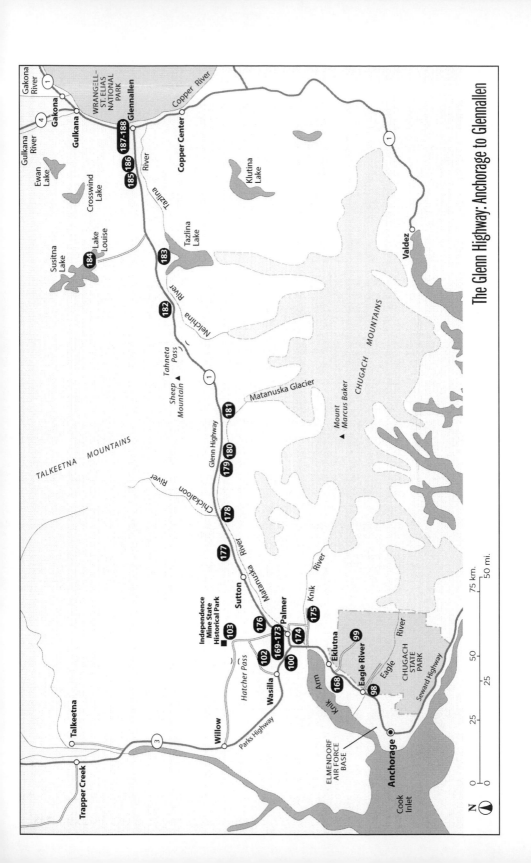

The Glenn Highway: Anchorage to Glennallen

Sites: 14 full-hookup RV sites, 10 partial-hookup RV sites, 6 tent sites
Maximum length: Any
Facilities: Some tables, potable water, portable toilets, dump station
Fee per night: $$–$$$$
Maximum stay: None
Management: Bobby's RV Park, (907) 688-2487, www.bobbys-rv-park.business.site
Finding the campground: From mile 21.5 of the Glenn Highway, take the Peters Creek exit west and turn left onto Bill Stephens Drive, to the campground on your right, at 20940 Bill Stephens Drive.
About the campground: This small RV park has fourteen side-by-side full-hookup and ten partial-hookup RV sites edged between a few trees and grass. With its desirable proximity to the Anchorage vicinity and nearby public transportation system, this little park gets a lot of visitors despite the limited facilities. On site there are a few tables and portable toilets.

169 Fox Run RV Campground

Location: In Palmer
GPS: N 61° 33.080' / W 149° 13.753'
Season: May through mid-September
Sites: 24 full-hookup RV sites, 6 partial-hookup RV sites, 6 tent sites
Maximum length: Any
Facilities: Tables, potable water, flush toilets, showers, dump station, laundry, WiFi, playground, boat rentals
Fee per night: $$$–$$$$
Maximum stay: None
Management: Fox Run RV Campground, (907) 745-6120, www.foxruncamp.com
Finding the campground: This campground is on the north side of the Glenn Highway at mile 36.3.
About the campground: Fox Run RV park is next door to the Kepler–Bradley Lakes State Recreation Area and therefore enjoys easy access to the lakes and hiking system. The facilities are older than the competition across the street at Homestead RV Park, and not as well developed. The waterfront is a draw for dedicated anglers or hikers. Sites are basic side-by-side spaces in an open gravel lot.

170 Matanuska Lake Campground

Location: In Palmer
GPS: N 61° 33.154' / W 149° 13.613'
Season: May through September
Sites: 6 tent sites, 4 basic sites
Maximum length: N/A
Facilities: Tables, fire pits, covered picnic area, potable water, vault toilets, hiking/fishing/lake access

Fee per night: $
Maximum stay: 7 days
Management: Alaska State Parks, Mat-Su/CB Area Office, (907) 745-3975, www.dnr.state.ak
.us/parks
Finding the campground: Look for the entrance to this campground next to the Fox Run RV Park
on the north side of the Glenn Highway at mile 36.4.
About the campground: Backpackers may prefer this small, rustic site if they are looking for
privacy—and there's a lot of it on sedate Matanuska Lake. This lesser-known campground seems
to be rarely inhabited, with the exception of anglers looking to benefit from the stocked waters.
Hiking within the Kepler–Bradley area is popular, but trails don't leave directly from the Matanuska
campground. Surprisingly, these six tent sites are available for reservation. The campsites are
located downhill past the day-use area, snugly fitted along a gravel cul-de-sac.

171 Kepler Park

Location: In Palmer
GPS: N 61° 33.140' / W 149° 11.946'
Season: May through mid-September
Sites: 23 basic sites
Maximum length: 35 feet
Facilities: Tables, fire pits, potable water, portable toilets
Fee per night: $$
Maximum stay: None
Management: Kepler Park, (907) 745-3043, www.keplerpark.us
Finding the campground: This campground is located on the north side of the Glenn Highway at
mile 37.4.
About the campground: One of the draws to this campground is trail access to recreate at Kepler-
Bradley lakes. They have basic sites with fire pits and picnic tables surrounded by woods.

172 Matanuska River Park

Location: In Palmer
GPS: N 61° 36.505' / W 149° 05.415'
Season: Early May through September
Sites: 35 RV partial-hookup RV sites, 45 basic sites
Maximum length: 35 feet
Facilities: Tables, fire pits, covered picnic area, potable water, flush toilets, showers, dump station,
soccer field, playground, hiking access
Fee per night: $$–$$$
Maximum stay: 14 days
Management: Matanuska-Susitna Borough, Parks and Outdoor Recreation, (907) 745-4801,
www.matsugov.us/RecServices/parks.cfm

Finding the campground: From mile 42.1 of the Glenn Highway, turn east onto Arctic Avenue/Old Glenn Highway. Drive 1.1 miles and turn left into the campground.

About the campground: This is by far the best deal in Palmer. The hundred-acre borough-run park has flush toilets, hot showers, and RV spots with electric hookups. Camping is divided into two sections. The upper paved RV loop has thirty-five side-by-side RV sites in grass, plus a cozy flower garden maintained by the hosts. Down the hill tenters and small RVs can set up in basic sites under old-growth cottonwood, birch, and spruce. The lower-level camping is a combination of back-ins and a few small pull-thrus. These wilderness-style sites are a bit overgrown with brush. Use caution around the thorny devil's club. Matanuska River Park is home to a soccer complex and a popular day-use area near the upper RV loop, so activity abounds. The lower grounds, however, are remote enough that traffic rarely wanders down. On site the Matanuska River Park Trail has about 1.5 miles of short strolls to ponds.

173 Mountain View RV Park

Location: In Palmer
GPS: N 61° 35.692' / W 149° 01.574'
Season: May through October
Sites: 77 full-hookup RV sites, 26 partial-hookup RV sites
Maximum length: Any
Facilities: Tables, covered picnic area with fire pit, potable water, flush toilets, showers, dump station, laundry, WiFi, boat charters
Fee per night: $$$–$$$$$
Maximum stay: None
Management: Mountain View RV Park, (907) 745-5747, (800) 264-4582, www.mtviewrv park.com
Finding the campground: From mile 42.1 of the Glenn Highway, turn east onto Arctic Avenue/Old Glenn Highway. Drive 2.8 miles and turn left onto Smith Drive; drive for 0.5 mile and turn right to continue on Smith Road. Drive 0.3 mile to the campground on your left.

About the campground: Nestled on the side of Lazy Mountain a few miles from Palmer, this RV park is the farthest off the highway and alluringly quiet. The camping area has plenty of grass and comfortable sites, a few of which are pull-thrus. There are also eight pleasing blocks of full private bathrooms. The park's specialty, however, is a three-hour boat tour out to nearby Knik Glacier and the backdrop for *Star Trek IV*. As with most river trips in Alaska, wildlife-viewing opportunities abound, from Dall sheep to migratory birds. Bring the binoculars!

174 Knik River Ranch Campground

Location: Near Palmer
GPS: N 61° 30.42' / W 149° 2.117'
Season: Late May through September
Sites: Open camping

Maximum length: Any
Facilities: Portable toilets
Fee per night: $–$$
Maximum stay: None
Management: Knik River Ranch, (907) 650-3588, www.knikriverranch.com
Finding the campground: This campground is located at the Knik River Bridge near Palmer at 16623 Parker Ranch Road.
About the campground: Knik River Ranch is being developed and may offer more services in the future. The large gravel lot allows campers the opportunity to set up along the water, and portable toilets are provided. The owners have many farm animals on site and breed dogs.

175 Jim Creek Campground

Location: Near Palmer
GPS: N 61° 31.525' / W 149° 0.146'
Season: Late May through September
Sites: 20 basic sites
Maximum length: Any
Facilities: Tables, fire rings, vault toilets
Fee per night: $
Maximum stay: 14 days
Management: Alaska Department of Natural Resources, Knik River Public Use Area, (907) 269-8400, www.dnr.alaska.gov/mlw/krpua/
Finding the campground: This campground is located near the Knik River Bridge south of Palmer. From the intersection of the Old Glenn Highway and Sullivan Ave, take Sullivan Ave east 1 mile to the campground.
About the campground: The Knik River Public Use Area now offers camping popular with ATV riders and others hoping to get on trails along the Knik River. The basic sites are mostly back-ins surrounded by woods and trails.

176 Moose Creek Campground

Location: Near Sutton
GPS: N 61° 40.9092' / W 149° 3.0420'
Season: Late May through September
Sites: 15 basic sites
Maximum length: 25 feet
Facilities: Tables, fire pits, vault toilets
Fee per night: $
Maximum stay: None
Management: Moose Creek Campground

Finding the campground: This campground is located on the north side of the Glenn Highway at mile 55 near Sutton.

About the campground: Moose Creek Campground is heavily wooded and rustic feeling while being close to the road. The basic sites don't have many amenities, but they offer a wilderness vibe.

177 Pinnacle Mountain RV Park

Location: Near mile 69 of the Glenn Highway
GPS: N 61° 44.637' / W 148° 39.634'
Season: Year-round
Sites: 14 full-hookup RV sites, 14 partial-hookup RV sites, 14 basic sites
Maximum length: Any
Facilities: Some tables and fire pits, water, showers, flush toilets, store, cafe, WiFi, electric-only in off-season
Fee per night: $$–$$$
Maximum stay: None
Management: Pinnacle Mountain RV Park, (907) 223-1952, www.pinnaclervandcafe.com
Finding the campground: On the north side of the Glenn Highway at mile 69.7.
About the campground: This pioneer-themed roadhouse-style RV park is located behind a cafe next to a pen of goats and other farm animals. The grounds are nicely kept with wagon wheels, old farm equipment, flower planters, and an antiques store on site. Campsites vary from large pull-thrus with water and electric hookups in the front lot to small tent spots in the woods.

178 King Mountain State Recreation Site

Location: Near mile 76 of the Glenn Highway
GPS: N 61° 46.541' / W 148° 29.692'
Season: Mid-May through mid-September
Sites: 22 basic sites
Maximum length: 35 feet
Facilities: Tables, fire pits, covered picnic shelter with fire pit, potable water, vault toilets
Fee per night: $$
Maximum stay: 14 days
Management: Alaska State Parks, Mat-Su/CB Area Office, (907) 745-3975, www.dnr.state.ak .us/parks; campground management privately contracted through Lifetime Adventures, (907) 746-4644, www.lifetimeadventures.net
Finding the campground: This state campground is located on the south side of the Glenn Highway at mile 76.1.
About the campground: This scenic campground is located between the Matanuska River and the mountains. Camping is divided into two loops, each with small sites best suited for tenters or small RVs. The sites near the river are not only larger but also nicer, a double joy combined with the sound of the glacial meltwaters streaming by.

179 Matanuska Glacier State Recreation Site

Location: Mile 101 of the Glenn Highway
GPS: N 61° 48.017' / W 147° 48.927'
Season: Mid-May through late September
Sites: 12 basic sites
Maximum length: Any
Facilities: Tables, fire pits, picnic area, potable water, vault toilets, hiking access
Fee per night: $–$$
Maximum stay: 15 days
Management: Alaska State Parks, Mat-Su/CB Area Office, (907) 745-3975, www.dnr.state.ak.us/parks
Finding the campground: On the south side of the Glenn Highway at mile 101.
About the campground: Alongside a glacier overlook, this camping area has twelve small, but nice, basic sites separated by forest. The campground is immediately uphill from the viewing area, which has vault toilets, tables, and killer views. The overlook lot doubles as an overnight parking place for large RVs and campers. From the overlook, Edge Nature Trail leads to glacier overlooks and is an easy twenty-minute stroll with rewarding backdrops.

180 Glacier Park

Location: Near mile 102 of the Glenn Highway
GPS: N 61° 47.578' / W 147° 47.854'
Season: May through late September
Sites: 16 basic sites
Maximum length: 25 feet
Facilities: Tables, potable water, portable toilets, hiking access, tours, small store, hiking access, gift shop
Fee per night: $$–$$$$
Maximum stay: None
Management: Glacier Park, (907) 745-2534, (888) 253-4480, www.matanuskaglacier.com
Finding the campground: From mile 102 of the Glenn Highway, turn right onto a gravel road at the sign for the park. Drive 0.9 mile to the campground office on your right.
About the campground: At Glacier Park you can drive almost all the way up to Matanuska Glacier, which is a short fifteen-minute walk from the parking area. The access is private, and an admission fee is charged to roll down the road. An up-close view of the glacier won't be had until you pay the price. Most campers stay at Glacier Park in accordance with their plans to explore the brilliant blue ice and some of the rustic sites perch along the road where you can see the glacier. The glacier is open for independent hikes, or you can book a tour or ice climbing with the staff on site. With the glacier as the main appeal, not much energy has been invested in developing the camping. There are sixteen basic sites scattered along the road after you pass through the gates.

181 Grand View RV Park

Location: Near mile 109 of the Glenn Highway
GPS: N 61° 47.908' / W 147° 36.423'
Season: Late May through mid-September
Sites: 10 full-hookup RV sites, 9 partial-hookup RV sites, 6 basic sites, 2 tent sites
Maximum length: Any
Facilities: Covered picnic area with tables and fire pit, potable water, flush toilets, showers, dump station, laundry, restaurant, WiFi, horseshoes
Fee per night: $$$$
Maximum stay: None
Management: Grand View Lodge Café and RV Park, (907) 746-4480, www.grandviewrv.com
Finding the campground: Look for the campground and cafe on the south side of the Glenn Highway at mile 109.7.
About the campground: This very clean gravel lot has unobstructed views of the surrounding mountains—and the highway. Sites are small but the packed pull-thrus are suitable for lengthy trailers. Camping here does reward you with a grand view of the surrounding range. You can watch for Dall sheep from the site and enjoy the down-home food.

182 Slide Mountain RV Park

Location: Near mile 135 of the Glenn Highway
GPS: N 61° 59.308' / W 147° 00.791'
Season: May through mid-September
Sites: 14 partial-hookup RV sites, open tent camping
Maximum length: Any
Facilities: Communal tables and grill, potable water, flush toilets, showers, WiFi
Fee per night: $$–$$$$
Maximum stay: None
Management: Slide Mountain Cabins and RV Park, (907) 822-3883, (907) 822-5864, www.rvparkalaska.com
Finding the campground: Look for the log-style buildings of the Slide Mountain RV Park on the north side of the Glenn Highway at mile 135.1.
About the campground: This new campground is popular year-round for log-cabin rentals. The tidy grounds have wide gravel pull-thrus with plenty of room for pop-outs. A few basic back-in sites with tables, fire pits, and grass are available as well. A nearby large clipped lawn with picnic table has open tent camping in the soft grass and a playground for the kids. Slide Mountain RV Park is connected to the Lake Louise trail system, a popular ATV and snowmobiling trail. A mile hike will take you to a fossil-hunting location.

183 Mendeltna Creek Lodge

Location: Mile 153 of the Glenn Highway
GPS: N 62° 02.930' / W 146° 32.360'
Season: May through mid-September
Sites: 50 full-hookup RV sites, 9 partial-hookup RV sites, 20 basic sites
Maximum length: Any
Facilities: Tables, fire rings, potable water, flush toilets, showers, dump station, laundry, restaurant, hiking/fishing/creek access
Fee per night: $–$$
Maximum stay: None
Management: Mendeltna Creek Lodge, (907) 822-3346
Finding the campground: This lodge is located on the south side of the Glenn Highway at mile 153 after the Mendeltna Creek Bridge.
About the campground: This campground is located on the "banks" of the charming Little Mendeltna, a humble creek that offers the soothing sounds of running water to many of the campsites located directly on it. The grounds are set off the road, separated from the roar of the advanced world by a thick forest of drunken spruce. If you're curious about Alaska's famous waterlogged tree, check out the free Museum of Alaska's Drunken Spruce on site—a penned-in area of the trees. Don't expect much more than a funny photo! The grounds feel rather earthy despite being a full-service RV park. About half the sites are pull-thrus, and many offer enough space for any size of RV or camper. The accommodating owners run an excellent restaurant on site. The owners have been making improvements so call ahead to make sure the campground is open.

184 Lake Louise State Recreation Area

Location: Near mile 160 of the Glenn Highway
GPS: N 62° 16.860' / W 146° 32.069'
Season: Late May through late September
Sites: 67 basic sites
Maximum length: Any
Facilities: Tables, fire pits, covered picnic area, potable water, vault toilets, hiking/fishing/lake access, boat launch
Fee per night: $–$$
Maximum stay: 15 days
Management: Alaska State Parks, Mat-Su/CB Area Office, (907) 745-3975, www.dnr.state.ak.us/parks
Finding the campground: From mile 159.8 of the Glenn Highway, take Lake Louise Road north for 17.2 miles to the state recreation area. The camping area is located at Lake Louise 0.4 mile farther down the road to your left, and at Army Point 0.7 mile down the road to your right.
About the campground: The Lake Louise State Recreation Area spans more than 500 acres and is home to two camping areas. This lake is popular year-round, stocked with fish and open to motors. The camping area is divided into two sections—Army Point and Lake Louise. Both have

basic sites covered in petite spruce and low-lying shrubs. The Lake Louise section has a few parking-lot-style sites that back up to fire pits and tables. About thirty more sites are located uphill from the boat launch; a few could hold a larger RV and have a view of the lake. The Army Point section has a string of waterfront sites in a simple gravel lot that could fit rigs of any size. The basic back-ins are the most wooded sites to be found in the park, offering privacy from neighbors.

185 Ranch House Lodge and RV Camping

Location: Mile 173 of the Glenn Highway
GPS: N 62° 6.120' / W 145° 58.078'
Season: Late May through September
Sites: 50 full-hookup RV sites, 10 tent sites
Maximum length: 60 feet
Facilities: Tables, fire pits, flush toilets, showers, dump station, laundry, hiking/creek/fishing access, WIFI, roadhouse
Fee per night: $$–$$$$
Maximum stay: None
Management: Ranch House Lodge and RV Camping, (907) 822-5634, www.ranchhouse lodge.com
Finding the campground: On the north side of the Glenn Highway at mile 173.
About the campground: This new RV park and restored historic roadhouse lines Tolsona Creek and offers nice tent sites nestled up to the water and large pull-thru RV sites. They also have cabins and appear to be pursuing more development. They may offer more amenities soon.

186 Tolsona Wilderness Campground

Location: Mile 173 of the Glenn Highway
GPS: N 62° 06.188' / W 145° 57.953'
Season: Late May through September
Sites: 43 partial-hookup RV sites, 37 basic sites
Maximum length: 60 feet
Facilities: Tables, fire pits, flush toilets, showers, dump station, laundry, hiking/creek/fishing access, WiFi
Fee per night: $$–$$$$
Maximum stay: None
Management: Tolsona Wilderness Campground, (907) 822-3865, http://tolsona.com
Finding the campground: On the north side of the Glenn Highway at mile 173.
About the campground: Tolsona Wilderness Campground is nicely removed from the highway. With clean RV park amenities and a woodsy wilderness environment, this campground offers the best in the Glennallen area for both tenters and those who travel in lengthy RV style. A snaking creek flows through the property, and eighty campsites are strategically placed along the waterfront. A few pull-thrus accommodate larger RVs, but the narrow road crosses one-lane bridges several times

and may limit maneuvering for large rigs; be sure to check in at the office with the hosts before driving through. Each wooded site has a table, fire pit, and fine creek views.

187 Caribou Hotel and Restaurant

Location: In Glennallen
GPS: N 62° 6.442' / W 145° 32.226'
Season: Late May through September
Sites: 10 full-hookup RV sites, 5 partial-hookup RV sites
Maximum length: Any
Facilities: Some tables, potable water, WiFi, restaurant
Fee per night: $$$$
Maximum stay: None
Management: Caribou Hotel and Restaurant, (907) 822-3302, www.caribouhotel.com
Finding the campground: This campground is located on the south side of the Glenn Highway at mile 186.5 in Glennallen.
About the campground: These no-frills side-by-sides offer hookups as you're passing through Glennallen.

188 Northern Nights RV Park

Location: In Glennallen
GPS: N 62° 06.460' / W 145° 29.178'
Season: May through October
Sites: 5 full-hookup RV sites, 18 partial-hookup RV sites, 3 tent sites
Maximum length: Any
Facilities: Tables, fire pits, flush and portable toilets, showers, dump station, WiFi
Fee per night: $$$–$$$$$
Maximum stay: None
Management: Northern Nights RV Park, (907) 822-3199, winter (928) 305-7933, www.northern nightscampground.com
Finding the campground: On the north side of the Glenn Highway at mile 188.7.
About the campground: This well-kept campground has some of the newest facilities in town and is set a little farther off the road than the other roadside RV parks in Glennallen. Most of the sites are pull-thrus suitable for large RVs; there is a small area for tents. This park is popular, and reservations are recommended from June through August. Due to the limited places to stay in Glennallen, show up on time or call in the morning if you will arrive later in the day; otherwise you might lose your reservation on the day of check-in. This campground was for sale and may change names.

The Glenn Highway: Glennallen to Tok (the Tok Cutoff)

	Hookup Sites	Total Sites	Max. RV Length	Hookups	Toilets	Showers	Drinking Water	Fires	Dump Station	Recreation	Fee	Reservations
189 Grizzly Lake Campground	0	23	35	N	F	Y	Y	Y	Y	F	$$-$$$$	Y
190 Hart D Ranch	40	60	40	WES	F	Y	Y	Y	Y	N	$$$$$	Y
191 Porcupine Creek State Recreation Site	0	12	60	N	NF	N	Y	Y	N	HF	$$	N
192 Eagle Trail State Recreation Site	0	35	35	N	NF	N	Y	Y	N	H	$$	N

189 Grizzly Lake Campground

Location: Mile 53 of the Tok Cutoff
GPS: N 62° 42.857' / W 144° 11.912'
Season: Mid-May through late September
Sites: 23 basic sites
Maximum length: 35 feet
Facilities: Tables, fire pits, potable water, flush toilets, showers, dump station, fishing/lake access
Fee per night: $$-$$$$
Maximum stay: None
Management: Grizzly Lake Campground LLC, (907) 822-5214
Finding the campground: On the south side of the Tok Cutoff at mile 53.
About the campground: If you can handle camping away from hookups, Grizzly Lake is a quiet and peaceful escape from the gravel lot campgrounds. There are just a few pull-thrus and back-in sites in the grass between a bed-and-breakfast and placid little Grizzly Lake. You can take out a boat rental and fish for grayling from the private lake or just enjoy the stunning views of the Wrangell Mountains.

190 Hart D Ranch

Location: Near mile 59 of the Tok Cutoff
GPS: N 62° 42.411' / W 143° 58.174'
Season: May through September
Sites: 30 full-hookup RV sites, 10 partial-hookup RV sites, 20 tent sites
Maximum length: 40 feet

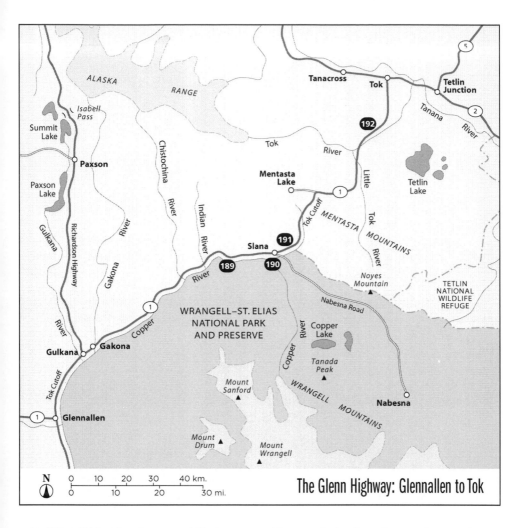

The Glenn Highway: Glennallen to Tok

Facilities: Tables, fire pits, covered picnic area, potable water, flush toilets, showers, dump station
Fee per night: $$$$$
Maximum stay: None
Management: Hart D Ranch, (907) 822-3973, www.hartd.com
Finding the campground: From mile 59.8 of the Tok Cutoff, turn east onto Nabesna Road and drive 0.5 mile to campground on your right.
About the campground: Hart D has very charming ranch-themed grounds with horse ties, wagon wheels, and a glowing heart out front. A wide gravel road leads to various sites spaced through trees; this campground is run in conjunction with a year-round lodge and bronze sculpture gallery.

191 Porcupine Creek State Recreation Site

Location: Near mile 64 of the Tok Cutoff
GPS: N 62° 43.662' / W 143° 52.258'
Season: Mid-May through mid-September
Sites: 12 basic sites
Maximum length: 60 feet
Facilities: Tables, fire pits, potable water, vault toilets, hiking/fishing/creek access
Fee per night: $$
Maximum stay: 15 days
Management: Alaska State Parks, Mat-Su/CB Area Office, (907) 745-3975, www.dnr.state.ak
.us/parks; management privately contracted to Hart D Ranch, (907) 822-3973
Finding the campground: Look for the Porcupine Creek campground on the north side of the Tok
Cutoff at mile 64.3.
About the campground: This campground consists of twelve basic campsites off a gravel circle.
The grounds are lush and forested with well-spaced sites. Three campsites located on the edge
of the gravel lot that could fit rigs of any length. The campground is full of pesky potholes—drivers
beware. An on-site lookout has excellent views of the ever-obvious volcanic Mount Sanford. Trails
from the campground lead to Porcupine Creek and Bear Valley.

192 Eagle Trail State Recreation Site

Location: Near mile 109 of the Tok Cutoff
GPS: N 63° 09.835' / W 143° 11.907'
Season: May through late September
Sites: 30 basic sites, 5 tent sites
Maximum length: 35 feet
Facilities: Tables, fire pits, covered picnic area with grills, potable water, vault toilets, hiking access
Fee per night: $$
Maximum stay: 15 days
Management: Alaska State Parks, Mat-Su/CB Area Office, (907) 745-3975, www.dnr.state.ak
.us/parks
Finding the campground: This campground is located on the north side of the Tok Cutoff at
mile 109.2.
About the campground: At Eagle Trail State Recreation Site, there are three loops of small basic
campsites. Each of the forested sites includes a table and fire pit. There are also four nice picnic
sites available for day use. You can hike and fish not far from the camping area. A 1-mile stroll
along a nature trail is a joy; serious hikers can head out to the old Valdez–Eagle Trail (which no
longer connects the two).

The Richardson Highway

The Richardson Highway begins in Valdez, an area often called Alaska's Little Switzerland. The land speaks for itself, with towering glaciated peaks spilling into the sea. Outside the city there are gorgeous canyons, rushing waterfalls, and summer wildflowers galore. Campers relish the high-alpine campgrounds and lush waterfront sites. Many nestle their nose to the sea at a downtown RV park or snuggle into a tent in thick woods.

Valdez is also known for another famous title. The trans-Alaska pipeline pumps oils to Port Valdez from the Arctic Ocean 800 miles away and often runs parallel to the Richardson Highway. The *Exxon Valdez* oil spill of 1989 was one of the most horrific in the nation's history and nearly devastated this once-productive fishing port. Slowly regaining grace from the spill, the area endures as some of the most beautiful, rugged country to be seen in the state.

The Richardson Highway heads north out of Valdez and stretches a total of 366 miles to Fairbanks. The highway traverses diverse landscape, from the Alaska Marine Highway of the sea to the Alaska Highway of the interior. This was the state's first road, the footpath for gold prospectors on their way to the Yukon on the Valdez–Eagle Trail. Today it offers campers options as diverse as the landscape it passes through.

As the highway heads north out of Valdez, it winds through the Chugach Mountains. Noteworthy Bridal Veil Falls and other sporadic waterfalls flow off the steep canyon walls. As the highway begins a straight leg north, Worthington Glacier nearly touches the road. At Worthington you can park your car not far from the ice, making it one of the most accessible glaciers in the state.

The Richardson Highway reaches its best-known fishing holes in the Copper Center. Here the Old Richardson Highway dips off to the side in a short loop accessing the Klutina River. This was the first non-native settlement in the area and remains home to historic buildings from pioneer times. It is also home to many fishing charters and fish camps. When the salmon are running, particularly the kings, the Copper Center Loop is a whirl of activity. At other times it may be as placid as the waters winding through it.

Not far north from the Copper Center, the Edgerton Highway forks off to the east. The road travels 33 paved miles to Chitina and the beginning of McCarthy Road. The drive down McCarthy Road is a wild 59-mile ride that climbs into a time capsule of early Alaska life at the city of McCarthy. You pass through the heart of Wrangell–St. Elias National Park and Preserve. At a gigantic 13.2 million acres, this park is the largest in the nation. It also has the largest population of glaciers on the continent, and the first you'll see will be the Kennicott Glacier directly at the road's end.

You'll have to walk the last 0.5 mile into McCarthy over the Kennicott River as it melts away from the glacier. Cars are not allowed in this funky little town. On the mountainside a few miles above McCarthy, the Kennicott Mine Town Site is complete with the ruins of many buildings and an old copper mill. These decaying structures are worth a wander around and are now a National Historic Landmark. Helpful park rangers on site can relay the history of copper mining in the area and lead you in the direction of supreme hiking trails. Or you can just enjoy the views

High-alpine views of Alaska's little Switzerland from the Blueberry Lake campground.

of the valley below. There are no established campgrounds within the park, but the backcountry is wide open. The former richest copper mine in America is a steep 5-mile hike up the mountain.

Running parallel with the pipeline, the Richardson Highway continues to Glenn-allen and its junction with the Glenn Highway. Campgrounds are spread around large flat open lakes. Farther down, the road also meets with Paxson and the Denali High-way, once the main route to Denali National Park (before the George Parks Highway was built). Today the Denali Highway is a scenic side trip along more than 100 miles of gravel.

The Richardson Highway follows the Delta River to Delta Junction, where it meets the Alaska Highway. From there the road curves northwest following the Tanana River and passes the Salcha River. Many campgrounds are located along these waterways. North of the junction, Quartz Lake State Recreation area gets people off the highway. From there it's a straight shot to Fairbanks.

Valdez

Valdez

	Hookup Sites	Total Sites	Max. RV Length	Hookups	Toilets	Showers	Drinking Water	Fires	Dump Station	Recreation	Fee	Reservations
193 Bear Paw RV Park and Bear Paw II	112	132	Any	WESC	F	Y	Y	Y	Y	N	$$$–$$$$$	Y
194 Bayside RV Park	104	113	Any	WESC	F	Y	Y	Y	Y	N	$$–$$$$	Y
195 Eagles Rest RV Park	300	300+	Any	WESC	F	Y	Y	Y	Y	N	$$$–$$$$$	Y
196 Chena RV Park	10	10	Any	WES	N	N	Y	N	N	N	$$$$$	N
197 Valdez Glacier Campground	0	101	50	N	NF	N	Y	Y	N	HF	$$$	N
198 Allison Point Access Site	0	60	Any	N	NF	N	Y	Y	N	F	$$	N
199 Valdez KOA Journey	65	85	75	WE	F	Y	Y	Y	Y	N	$$$–$$$$$	Y
200 Blueberry Lake State Recreation Site	0	25	35	N	NF	N	Y	Y	N	HF	$$	N
201 Tonsina River Lodge	10	Open	Any	WES	F	Y	Y	Y	N	N	$$$–$$$$	Y
202 Squirrel Creek State Recreation Site	0	25	Any	N	NF	N	Y	Y	N	F	$$	N

193 Bear Paw RV Park and Bear Paw II

See map on page 174

Location: In Valdez
GPS: N 61° 07.622' / W 146° 21.041'
Season: Early May through late September
Sites: 82 full-hookup RV sites, 30 partial-hookup RV sites, 20 tent sites
Maximum length: Any
Facilities: Tables, fire pits, potable water, flush toilets, showers, dump station, laundry, WiFi
Fee per night: $$$–$$$$$
Maximum stay: None
Management: Bear Paw RV Park, (907) 835-2530, www.bearpawrvpark.com
Finding the campground: To reach the main Bear Paw RV Park, follow the Richardson Highway as it becomes Egan Street in Valdez. Turn left onto Meals Avenue and drive 0.2 mile to the campground on your right. To find Bear Paw II, continue past the park on Meals Avenue and turn left onto Breakwater Street.
About the campground: The Bear Paw RV Park is divided into two sections. The main campground is in a well-groomed open gravel lot in downtown Valdez. From this location you can walk to the

ferry charters, just across the street from the downtown docks. Within the park, a variety of sites—from pull-thrus with full hookups to dry sites—can be booked. The second park, the Bear Paw II, is adults-only; no children allowed. This waterfront section is next to the harbor. The camping area includes wooded tent sites and thirty spacious full-hookup RV sites. They may be a bit more of a walk from town, but the more secluded camping atmosphere is inviting.

194 Bayside RV Park

See map on page 174

Location: In Valdez
GPS: N 61° 07.828' / W 146° 20.649'
Season: May through September
Sites: 75 full-hookup RV sites, 29 partial-hookup RV sites, 9 basic sites (no tents allowed)
Maximum length: Any
Facilities: Tables, potable water, flush toilets, showers, dump station, laundry, Internet access

Sea otters in Port Valdez.

Fee per night: $$-$$$$
Maximum stay: None
Management: Bayside RV Park, (907) 835-4425, (888) 835-4425, www.baysiderv.com
Finding the campground: This is the easiest campground to find in Valdez. Just follow the Richardson Highway into town as it becomes Egan Street; the Bayside RV Park is the first campground on your left before the road curves.
About the campground: On the edge of downtown, this open gravel lot has mountain and bay views, but it's not directly on the water. Bayside is a well-kept and popular park, within walking distance of almost everything. There are thirty-five oversize pull-thrus for large rigs. Any hookup site gets you free unmetered showers in clean restrooms. If you're looking to explore Valdez or catch a big one, Bayside staff can organize and give recommendations on just about every area activity. They've also been known to lure in bald eagles with treats, so the birds might accompany your stay. Reservations are recommended.

195 Eagles Rest RV Park

See map on page 174

Location: In Valdez
GPS: N 61° 07.856' / W 146° 20.821'
Season: Late April through mid-October
Sites: 278 full-hookup RV sites, 22 partial-hookup RV sites, open tent camping
Maximum length: Any
Facilities: Some tables, portable fire pits, potable water, flush toilets, showers, dump station, laundry, fish-cleaning facilities, WiFi
Fee per night: $$$-$$$$$
Maximum stay: None
Management: Eagles Rest RV Park, (907) 835-2373, (800) 553-7275, www.eaglesrestrv.com
Finding the campground: Eagles Rest RV Park is easy to find. Simply follow the Richardson Highway into town as it becomes Egan Street; the park is on your right across the street from the Bayside RV Park.
About the campground: This RV park at the base of the mountains is by far the biggest campground in Valdez, with around 300 campsites. The RV sites tend to be on the large side and grant easier access for those traveling in extra-large style. Many in RVs and campers are also pleased to find that you can wash your vehicles for free at Eagles Rest. The campground is primarily in a large, open gravel-and-grass lot. The grassy area has room for about fifty walk-in tent sites, a real score for tenters on a busy weekend. The grounds share a parking lot with a gas station and burger joint. It is also a quick walk to town. As fishing picks up in mid- to late summer, reservations are recommended. The staff can organize charters, and you can purchase your fishing license on site.

196 Chena RV Park

Location: In Valdez
GPS: N 61° 7.989' / W 146° 12.998'
Season: May through September
Sites: 10 full-hookup RV sites
Maximum length: Any
Facilities: Potable water, WiFi
Fee per night: $$$$$
Maximum stay: None
Management: Chena RV Park, (907) 378-6165
Finding the campground: In Valdez near the intersection of Chena Street and Meals Avenue.
About the campground: This basic full-hookup RV park has 10 sites for self-contained RVers.

197 Valdez Glacier Campground

See map on page 174

Location: In Valdez
GPS: N 61° 08.317' / W 146° 12.240'
Season: May through late September
Sites: 101 basic sites
Maximum length: 50 feet
Facilities: Tables, covered picnic area, fire pits, potable water, vault toilets, hiking/fishing access
Fee per night: $$$
Maximum stay: 15 days
Management: City of Valdez, (907) 835-4313, www.ci.valdez.ak.us; management privately contracted to Captain Jim's Charters, (907) 835-2282
Finding the campground: To find this campground, follow the Richardson Highway 3.5 miles out of Valdez (the mileage for the Richardson begins at the old town site, so this would be 0.6 mile before milepost 1) and turn north onto Airport Road. Drive 0.9 mile to the campground.
About the campground: The city operates this wooded Fort Greely campground a few miles out of town. The camping area is divided in two, with a newer front section. The new sites are the more popular place to stay, and rightly so. These sites are gravel back-ins about four times larger than the old earthen back section. The older half of the campground is less improved and more rustic, with small sites best suited for tents. These earthy sites are thickly wooded, some near the sweet sounds of a rushing waterfall. There is a reduced fee for military.

198 Allison Point Access Site

See map on page 174

Location: Near Valdez
GPS: N 61° 05.196' / W 146° 20.599'
Season: May through late September
Sites: 50 RV sites, 10 tent sites
Maximum length: Any
Facilities: Potable water, vault toilets
Fee per night: $$
Maximum stay: 15 days
Management: City of Valdez, (907) 835-4313, www.ci.valdez.ak.us; management privately contracted to Kimberlan's Water Taxi, (907) 835-2282

A fishing boat cruises by the RV park in Valdez.

Finding the campground: From mile 2.8 of the Richardson Highway, turn south onto Dayville Road and drive 3.5 miles to the beginning of the camping area. The campsites line the road for a little less than 0.5 mile. The road is labeled only on the direction heading toward Valdez.

About the campground: Allison Point is an authentic fish camp. Visit this campground when the pinks and the silver salmon are running and you can see and smell the experience. RVers and tenters alike pack in sardine-style to the 60 parking-lot-style sites here. If they're not throwing a line, camp guests are likely smoking or canning salmon on site or recounting the day's catch. Close to a salmon hatchery, this large campground is quite popular in mid-to-late summer despite being undeveloped and out of Valdez.

199 Valdez KOA Journey

Location: Near Valdez
GPS: N 61° 5.9868' / W 146° 12.9978'
Season: May through September
Sites: 65 partial-hookup sites, 20 basic sites
Maximum length: 75 feet
Facilities: Tables, communal fire pit, potable water, dump station, flush toilets, showers, WiFi, playground
Fee per night: $$$–$$$$$
Maximum stay: None
Management: Valdez KOA Journey
Finding the campground: This campground is located 5.7 miles southeast of Valdez on the Richardson Highway
About the campground: This KOA serves the needs of the booming summer camp season in Valdez. It is a few miles out of town. Most of the sites are partial hookups without sewage (dump station on site) in an open lot. The tent sites back up to a wooded area. You will find your standard KOA amenities and a bike path that leads to town.

200 Blueberry Lake State Recreation Site

See map on page 174

Location: Near mile 24 of the Richardson Highway
GPS: N 61° 07.267' / W 145° 41.343'
Season: Late May through September
Sites: 25 basic sites
Maximum length: 35 feet
Facilities: Tables, fire pits, covered picnic area, potable water, vault toilets, hiking/lake/fishing access
Fee per night: $$
Maximum stay: 15 days

Management: Alaska State Parks, Kenai/PWS Office, (907) 262-5581, www.dnr.state.ak
.us/parks; management privately contracted to Windfarm, (907) 255-2842

Finding the campground: From mile 24.2 of the Richardson Highway, turn south onto the road for Blueberry Lake State Recreation Site. Drive 0.4 mile to the campground. If you are pulling a trailer or driving an RV, you'll want to stick to the lower sites; follow the road to your right and scout the hillside sites on foot before attempting them.

About the campground: The area around Valdez is often referred to as Alaska's little Switzerland, and perhaps there is no better location to illustrate its Alp-like qualities than the Blueberry Lake campground. This high-alpine campground is located among rugged sharp peaks, with icy and snowy caps, and every campsite has a view. Camping is divided along two loops near small Summit and Blueberry lakes. The lower loop of sites sits on the edges of Blueberry Lake, and the upper loop sites rest on a spectacular ridge. The lakefront sites tend to be smaller but are in a more comfortable proximity to restroom facilities. Most are fairly open, with some brush and stout alders separating neighbors. The rather rustic facilities are not as new as in many state parks. Some sites do not have tables, but there are covered picnic areas along the lake. You can fish for grayling and rainbow trout in the tranquil lakes.

201 Tonsina River Lodge

Location: Mile 79 of the Richardson Highway
GPS: N 61° 39.721' W 145° 10.832'
Season: Late May through September
Sites: 6 full-hookup RV sites, 4 partial-hookup RV sites, open tent camping
Maximum length: Any
Facilities: Some tables and fire pits, potable water, flush toilets, showers, laundry, restaurant, WiFi
Fee per night: $$–$$$$
Maximum stay: None
Management: Tonsina River Lodge, (907) 822-3000, www.tonsinariverlodge.com
Finding the campground: The Tonsina River Lodge is located on the east side of the Richardson Highway at mile 79 just south of the river.
About the campground: This lodge offers a variety of services for campers including showers, laundry, and a popular Russian restaurant. Camping is in an open lot with some grassy areas. There are official RV sites and the rest is open.

202 Squirrel Creek State Recreation Site

See map on page 174

Location: Near mile 79 of the Richardson Highway
GPS: N 61° 40.001' / W 145° 10.561'
Season: May through October
Sites: 25 basic sites

Maximum length: Any
Facilities: Tables, fire pits, potable water, vault toilets, lake/fishing access
Fee per night: $$
Maximum stay: 15 days
Management: Alaska State Parks, Mat Su/CB Office, (907) 745-3975, www.dnr.state.ak
.us/parks; management privately contracted to Dog Song Enterprises (907) 822-5048
Finding the campground: Squirrel Creek is located on the east side of the Richardson Highway at
mile 79.6.
About the campground: These sites might not be manicured, but some of them perch above the
lake and offer picturesque views and direct access to the water. You'll find that the Squirrel Creek
campground fills even on weekdays. Anglers enjoy fishing for grayling and rainbow trout in the
creek. Individual campsites are very small, with a table, fire pit, and just enough room for a tent.
The sites off the lakefront are fairly desirable; others back up to the lovely lull of Squirrel Creek.
Some farther back just rest peacefully under the shade of the cottonwood-and-birch forest.

The Edgerton Highway and McCarthy Road

The Edgerton Highway and McCarthy Road	Hookup Sites	Total Sites	Max. RV Length	Hookups	Toilets	Showers	Drinking Water	Fires	Dump Station	Recreation	Fee	Reservations
203 Kenny Lake RV Park	10	19	Any	E	F	Y	Y	Y	Y	N	$$$	Y
204 Liberty Falls State Recreation Site	0	9	30	N	NF	N	Y	Y	N	N	$$	N
205 Copper River Campground	10		Any	N	NF	N	N	Y	N	F	Free	N
206 Glacier View Campground	0	20	30	N	NF	Y	Y	Y	N	H	$$	Y
207 Base Camp Glacier Camping	0	+	Any	N	NF	N	N	N	N	H	$$	N

203 Kenny Lake RV Park

Location: Mile 7 of the Edgerton Highway
GPS: N 61° 44.182' / W 144° 57.105'
Season: Year-round
Sites: 10 partial-hookup RV sites, 9 basic sites
Maximum length: Any
Facilities: Some tables, covered picnic area, potable water, flush toilets, showers, dump station, laundry, restaurant, gas station, small store, gift shop
Fee per night: $$$
Maximum stay: None
Management: Kenny Lake Mercantile and RV Park, (907) 822-3313, www.kennylake.com
Finding the campground: On the north side of the Edgerton Highway at mile 7.
About the campground: The Kenny Lake Mercantile and Campground is open year-round to serve out-of-season campers. You'll find electric-only RV parking in an open gravel lot as well as small wooded tent sites with tables tucked away in the trees. A few sites are pull-thrus. This is a nice base to pitch a tent, take a shower, do laundry, roast a marshmallow, and stock up on pricey gas!

204 Liberty Falls State Recreation Site

Location: Near mile 23 of the Edgerton Highway
GPS: N 61° 37.338' / W 144° 32.864'
Season: May through September
Sites: 3 basic sites, 6 tent sites
Maximum length: 30 feet

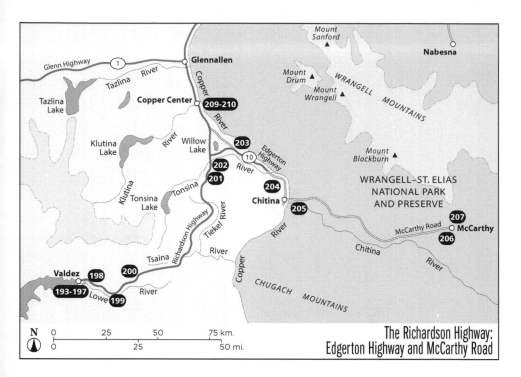

N
0   25   50   75 km.
0   25   50 mi.

The Richardson Highway:
Edgerton Highway and McCarthy Road

Facilities: Tables, fire pits, vault toilets
Fee per night: $$
Maximum stay: 15 days
Management: Alaska State Parks, Mat Su/CB Office, (907) 745-3975, www.dnr.state.ak.us/parks
Finding the campground: On the south side of the Edgerton Highway at mile 23.6, just west of Liberty Creek, turn south into the narrow, steep road (including a one-lane bridge) to the sites.
About the campground: This small campground is located next to cascading Liberty Falls. The peaceful, pleasing facilities are some of the most picturesque in the region.

205 Copper River Campground

Location: Near mile 1 of McCarthy Road
GPS: N 61° 31.728' / W 144° 24.251'
Season: May through October
Sites: 10 basic sites
Maximum length: Any
Facilities: Some tables and fire rings, vault toilets, fishing/river access
Fee per night: Free

Fireweed blooms at the Kennicott Mine Town Site. ▶

Maximum stay: None
Management: Alaska Department of Transportation, (907) 465-3900, www.dot.state.ak.us
Finding the campground: The Copper River Campground is at mile 1.4 of McCarthy Road, just north of the Copper River on your right. Drive slowly; it may be difficult to spot.
About the campground: This campground has about ten established sites with fire rings and tables under the shade of breezy cottonwoods. There are a few larger pull-thrus, but no official boundaries—just clearings in the trees where people make camp. On the opposite side of the road, informal camping is permitted in the sprawling gravel bars along the Copper River. When the salmon are running, this area is busy with activity. At most other times it is eerily quiet.

206 Glacier View Campground

Location: Near McCarthy
GPS: N 61° 26.129' / W 142° 57.528'
Season: Late May through September
Sites: 20 basic sites

The Kennicott glacier drains into the sprawling valley near the old mine ruins.

Maximum length: 30 feet
Facilities: Tables, fire pits, potable water, vault toilets, showers, hiking access, small store, outdoor cafe
Fee per night: $$
Maximum stay: None
Management: Glacier View Campground, (907) 554-4490, winter (907) 243-6677, www.glacierviewcampground.com
Finding the campground: You'll find the Glacier View on the south side of McCarthy Road at mile 58.7, less than a mile before the road's end.
About the campground: These inexpensive gravel campsites are located off a rugged, narrow gravel road. The sites are overgrown with brush and not too developed, suitable for tents and RVs of up to 30 feet. A short mile walk will take you to McCarthy. You can also rent a bike on site.

207 Base Camp Glacier Camping

Location: Near McCarthy
GPS: N 61° 26.032' / W 142° 56.646'
Season: Late May through September
Sites: Open camping
Maximum length: Any
Facilities: Pit toilet, hiking access
Fee per night: $$
Maximum stay: None
Management: Base Camp Root Glacier Camping, (907) 746-0606
Finding the campground: McCarthy Road dead-ends into this parking lot at mile 59.3.
About the campground: This gravel parking lot is at the entrance to the Kennicott River pedestrian bridge. Camping is allowed, but the facilities are extremely minimal. There is one pit-style out-house, a telephone, and an information kiosk. Some sites overlook the river. You can book a tour here or pay to park for a day if you decide not to overnight.

The Richardson Highway: Edgerton Cutoff to Delta Junction

The Richardson Highway: Edgerton Cutoff to Delta Junction

	Hookup Sites	Total Sites	Max. RV Length	Hookups	Toilets	Showers	Drinking Water	Fires	Dump Station	Recreation	Fee	Reservations
208 King for a Day	20	50	Any	WES	F	Y	Y	Y	Y	F	$$-$$$	Y
209 Salmon Grove Campground	35	35+	Any	E	F	Y	Y	Y	Y	F	$$-$$$$	N
210 Klutina Salmon Charters and Campgrounds	25	35	Any	E	NF	N	Y	Y	Y	F	$$-$$$$	Y
211 Dry Creek State Recreation Area	0	59	45	N	NF	N	Y	Y	N	N	$$	N
212 Sourdough Creek Campground	0	43	Any	N	NF	N	Y	Y	N	HFBL	$	N
213 Paxson Lake Campground	0	50	Any	N	NF	N	Y	Y	Y	FBL	$	N
214 Fielding Lake State Recreation Site	0	17	Any	N	NF	N	Y	Y	N	FBL	$	N
215 Donnelly Creek State Recreation Site	0	12	40	N	NF	N	Y	Y	N	N	$	N

208 King for a Day

Location: In Copper Center
GPS: N 61° 57.138' / W 145° 19.035'
Season: Late May through late August
Sites: 8 full-hookup RV sites, 12 partial-hookup RV sites, 30 basic sites
Maximum length: Any
Facilities: Tables, fire pits, potable water, vault toilets, showers, dump station, laundry, fishing access, fish-cleaning facilities, charters
Fee per night: $$-$$$
Maximum stay: None
Management: King for a Day Charters and Campground, (907) 822-3092, www.kingforaday charters.com
Finding the campground: From mile 100.5 of the Richardson Highway, take the gravel road located next to the sign KING FOR A DAY CAMPGROUND east for 0.2 mile to the campground.
About the campground: The three campgrounds around Copper Center are almost exclusively run as fishing camps and are likely to be closed if the fish aren't running. When the salmon show, however, it's quite a scene. King for a Day has a feeling of being tucked away—well, as tucked away as a busy fish camp can be. The sites are gravel and grass, some directly on the river with fishing access. The camping area is run in conjunction with the charter company for further exploration of hot fishing holes.

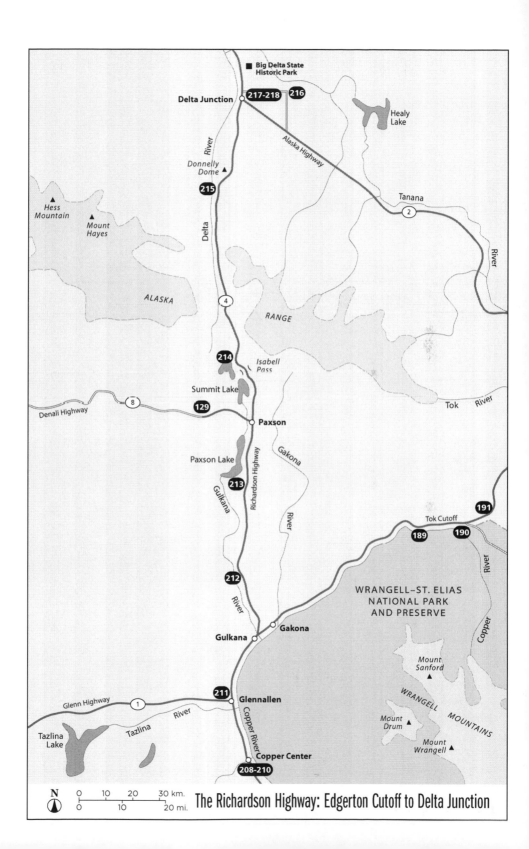

Big Delta State
Historic Park

Delta Junction 217-218 216

Healy
Lake

River

Alaska Highway

Donnelly
Dome

215

Tanana

2

Hess
Mountain

Mount
Hayes

Delta

River

ALASKA

4

RANGE

214

Isabell
Pass

Tok River

Summit Lake

Denali Highway 8 129

Paxson

Gakona

Paxson Lake

213

Richardson Highway

Gulkana

River

191

Tok Cutoff

189 190

River

212

WRANGELL–ST. ELIAS
NATIONAL PARK
AND PRESERVE

River

Gulkana Gakona

Copper

Mount
Sanford

Glenn Highway 1

211 Glennallen

Copper River

Mount
Drum

WRANGELL MOUNTAINS

Tazlina
Lake

Tazlina River

Mount
Wrangell

Copper Center

208-210

N

0   10   20   30 km.

0   10   20 mi.

The Richardson Highway: Edgerton Cutoff to Delta Junction

209 Salmon Grove Campground

Location: In Copper Center
GPS: N 61° 57.100' / W 145° 18.522'
Season: Mid-May through late August
Sites: 35 partial-hookup RV sites, open tent camping
Maximum length: 40 feet
Facilities: Tables, fire pits, flush toilets, potable water, vault toilets, showers, dump station, laundry, fishing access, fish cleaning facilities, charters
Fee per night: $$–$$$$
Maximum stay: None
Management: Salmon Grove's Campground, (907) 822-5822, www.klutinariver.com
Finding the campground: In Copper Center, from mile 106.1 of the Richardson Highway turn east on the road toward Copper Center, the north entrance to the Old Richardson Highway. Drive 5.2 miles to the park on the right, just after the Klutina River.
About the campground: Red salmon and kings up to fifty pounds can be snagged in the Klutina River and there is no doubt that in mid-July this fish camp will be packed. Charters are also available if you're looking to get away from the crowded banks of the campground. About half of the sites have electric hookups and there is a dump station on-site.

210 Klutina Salmon Charters and Campgrounds

Location: In Copper Center
GPS: N 61° 57.179' / W 145° 18.429'
Season: Late May through September
Sites: 25 partial-hookup RV sites, 10 dry sites
Maximum length: Any
Facilities: Some tables and fire pits, potable water, vault toilets, dump station, fishing access, fish cleaning facilities, charters
Fee per night: $$–$$$$
Maximum stay: None
Management: Klutina Salmon Charters and Campground, (907) 822-3991, www.klutinasalmon charters.com
Finding the campground: From mile 106.1 of the Richardson Highway, turn east on the road toward Copper Center, the north entrance to the Old Richardson Highway. Drive 5.1 miles to the park on your right, just before the Klutina River.
About the campground: Everyone here is fishing; it's the only reason to stop at the campgrounds in Copper Center. The Klutina Salmon's camping area has back-ins directly on the river. Most of the sites are small, but shaded pull-thrus are available for larger RVs, and some sites have electric

Worthington Glacier is accessible from the Richardson Highway.

hookups. There is a water and dump station as well. Tenters can find more secluded edge-of-the-lot pads to pitch their tent. Friday-night barbecues offer a drawing for a free charter.

211 Dry Creek State Recreation Area

Location: Mile 118 of the Richardson Highway
GPS: N 62° 09.136' / W 145° 28.475'
Season: Mid-May through mid-September
Sites: 50 basic sites, 9 tent sites
Maximum length: 45 feet
Facilities: Tables, fire pits, potable water, vault toilets, creek access
Fee per night: $$
Maximum stay: 15 days
Management: Alaska State Parks, Delta/Tok District, (907) 895-4599, www.dnr.state.ak
.us/parks; management privately contracted to Ancient Spruce, (907) 822-5208
Finding the campground: Dry Creek State Recreation Area is located on the west side of the Richardson Highway at mile 118, across from the airport.
About the campground: The campsites at Dry Creek are blanketed in trees. Tenters even have walk-in sites with tent pads. The sites are divided among three loops; there are a few large pull-thrus. With the management contracted out to a private company, the facilities are well kept with clean vault toilets. Dry Creek is also a popular picnic spot.

212 Sourdough Creek Campground

Location: Near mile 147 of the Richardson Highway
GPS: N 62° 31.642' / W 145° 31.085'
Season: Late May through October
Sites: 43 basic sites
Maximum length: Any
Facilities: Tables, fire pits, covered picnic area, potable water, vault toilets, hiking/fishing access, boat launch
Fee per night: $
Maximum stay: 7 days
Management: Bureau of Land Management, (907) 822-3217, www.blm.gov/ak
Finding the campground: On the west side of the Richardson Highway at mile 147.5, south of Sourdough Creek.
About the campground: Like most BLM campgrounds, Sourdough Creek is a bargain. The large gravel sites are located off a wide gravel road, with several good-size pull-thrus and elevated tent pads. Much of the grounds are broken up by low trees and brush, with views of the pipeline in the distance. Gulkana River float trips often end from here, with the launch a primary draw for water-loving campers. Anglers also flock to the waters of the Gulkana and Sourdough Creek in search of red or king salmon, grayling, or rainbow trout.

213 Paxson Lake Campground

Location: Near mile 175 of the Richardson Highway
GPS: N 62° 52.966' / W 145° 31.420'
Season: Late May through September
Sites: 40 basic sites, 10 tent sites
Maximum length: Any
Facilities: Tables, fire pits, potable water, vault toilets, dump station, boat launch, lake/fishing access
Fee per night: $
Maximum stay: 14 days
Management: Bureau of Land Management, Glennallen Field Office, (907) 822-3217, www.blm.gov/ak
Finding the campground: From mile 175 of the Richardson Highway, drive west onto the gravel road at the sign for Paxson Lake. The campground is in 1.3 miles.
About the campground: The camping area along Paxson Lake is divided into two loops; the lower is more popular with RVs thanks to its large pull-thrus and deep back-ins. The upper loop has a similar setup with more dwarf spruce and slightly smaller back-ins. The real treat on this loop are the ten spacious walk-in sites, some directly on the lake. These sites are a sheer pleasure for the backpacker or bicyclist, especially at the unbeatable price. Backpackers should be aware they do not have bear-proof food lockers. All sites have a table, fire pit, and some privacy through low-lying brush or trees from other sites. The few directly on the water can get a bit mucky, but the sounds of the crashing waves and unbeatable proximity to the lake make up for muddy boots. Paxson Lake has a popular boat launch and parking area with eighty spaces. This campground is often the put-in point for Gulkana River float trips. At the lake you can also fish for salmon, trout, and grayling.

214 Fielding Lake State Recreation Site

Location: Near mile 200 of the Richardson Highway
GPS: N 63° 11.674' / W 145° 38.932'
Season: June through mid-September
Sites: 17 basic sites
Maximum length: Any
Facilities: Tables, fire pits, potable water, vault toilets, fishing/lake access, boat launch
Fee per night: $
Maximum stay: 15 days
Management: Alaska State Parks, Northern Area Office, (907) 451-2695, www.dnr.state.ak.us/parks
Finding the campground: From mile 200.4 of the Richardson Highway, turn west, following the signs toward Fielding Lake for 1.5 miles to the campground on your right.
About the campground: Fielding Lake rests in a high basin dotted with numerous lakes and ponds. The campsites here are not well defined—more a conglomeration of snug side-by-side parking-lot-style spaces with a collection of tables and fire pits. Fielding Lake is a whopping

1,660 acres, all visible, because the area is treeless. The wind-whipped open bowl does have some benefits—the breathtaking panoramic view of the naked mountains may be worth the lack of privacy. The campground is up at about 3,000 feet and can get chilly. There's often ice on this lake until July, and the campground doesn't open until June when weather permits. You can fish for grayling, trout, and burbot.

215 Donnelly Creek State Recreation Site

Location: Mile 238 of the Richardson Highway
GPS: N 63° 40.416' / W 145° 53.040'
Season: Mid-May through mid-September
Sites: 12 basic sites
Maximum length: 40 feet
Facilities: Tables, fire pits, potable water, vault toilets
Fee per night: $
Maximum stay: 15 days
Management: Alaska State Parks, Northern Area Office, (907) 451-2695, www.dnr.state.ak us/parks
Finding the campground: On the west side of the Richardson Highway at mile 238.
About the campground: This rustic campground has views of some of Alaska's tallest peaks, with the Alaska Range poking up behind the thick, low spruce forest. The scenic campground is not well known and is almost always quiet. There are twelve basic sites, with tables, fire pits, and just enough room to pitch a tent.

Delta Junction

	Hookup Sites	Total Sites	Max. RV Length	Hookups	Toilets	Showers	Drinking Water	Fires	Dump Station	Recreation	Fee	Reservations
216 Clearwater State Recreation Site	0	17	Any	N	NF	N	Y	Y	N	HFBL	$	N
217 Snowed Inn RV Park	112	160	Any	WES	F	Y	Y	N	Y	N	$$-$$$$	Y
218 Delta State Recreation Site	0	25	35	N	NF	N	Y	Y	N	N	$	N

216 Clearwater State Recreation Site

See map on page 179

Location: Near Delta Junction
GPS: N 64° 03.158' / W 145° 25.969'
Season: Mid-May through mid-September
Sites: 17 basic sites
Maximum length: Any
Facilities: Tables, fire pits, picnic area, potable water, vault toilets, hiking/fishing/river access, boat launch
Fee per night: $
Maximum stay: 15 days
Management: Alaska State Parks, Northern Area Office, www.dnr.state.ak.us/parks
Finding the campground: You can reach this campground from either the Richardson or the Alaska Highway. From mile 268.3 of the Richardson Highway, turn east onto Jack Warren Road and follow the road as it changes names for 10.5 miles to the campground on your left. From mile 1414.8 of the Alaska Highway, turn north onto Clearwater Road, drive 5.3 miles, and turn right onto Remington Road. Continue 2.8 miles to the campground.
About the campground: The crystal-clear waters of this appropriately named campground lure anglers, rafters, and birders alike. If you're just passing through town, this small campground may seem a bit off the highway, but it is popular. A drive here will take you through agricultural fields you probably haven't seen since the lower 48. In spring and fall a pair of binoculars and a stroll down the well-structured boardwalk may reward you with views of the sandhill cranes and swans that flock to the area's barley fields and waterways. The boat launch usually sees moderate activity, with rafters heading toward the Tanana River and others looking for a quieter fishing hole. The camping area is shady and basic with well-organized gravel sites, including a couple of extra-large pull-thrus for rigs. Some smaller sites overlook the water.

217 Snowed Inn RV Park

See map on page 179

Location: In Delta Junction
GPS: N 64° 01.875' / W 145° 41.830'
Season: May through early September
Sites: 112 full-hookup RV sites, 48 tent sites
Maximum length: Any
Facilities: Tables, potable water, flush toilets, showers, dump station, laundry
Fee per night: $$–$$$$
Maximum stay: None
Management: Snowed Inn RV Park, (907) 895-4270
Finding the campground: Look for this campground on the north side of the Alaska Highway at mile 1421.
About the campground: Run in conjunction with a permanent mobile-home community, this older campground does little advertising for camping and, at a couple of miles out of town, almost always has open sites. Temporary sites are located in a weedy open lot with outdated decor and facilities. There are plenty of grassy spots for RVs of substantial length, along with wooded pockets for tents.

218 Delta State Recreation Site

See map on page 179

Location: In Delta Junction
GPS: N 64° 03.197' / W 145° 44.138'
Season: Mid-May through mid-September
Sites: 25 basic sites
Maximum length: 35 feet
Facilities: Tables, fire pits, covered picnic area, potable water, vault toilets
Fee per night: $
Maximum stay: 15 days
Management: Alaska State Parks, Northern Area Office, (907) 451-2695, www.dnr.state.ak .us/parks
Finding the campground: The Delta State Recreation Site is located a mile north of town, on the east side of the Richardson Highway at mile 267.1. It's adjacent to the airport.
About the campground: Because this campground is located next to a city-operated airstrip, don't be surprised to find your neighbors flew in for the night at the Delta State Recreation Site. Some sites offer views of takeoffs and landings. The camping area is located across the highway from the river among airy trees. There are twenty-five humble back-in sites best for campers and small RVs, along with a covered picnic area. Only a mile from Delta Junction services, you'll find these convenient public grounds and clean campsites an excellent choice if you're traveling by bike or foot.

The Richardson Highway: Delta Junction to Fairbanks

The Richardson Highway: Delta Junction to Fairbanks

	Hookup Sites	Total Sites	Max. RV Length	Hookups	Toilets	Showers	Drinking Water	Fires	Dump Station	Recreation	Fee	Reservations
219 Big Delta State Historical Park–Rika's Roadhouse	0	23	Any	N	NF	N	Y	Y	Y	N	$$	N
220 Quartz Lake State Recreation Area	0	117	Any	N	NF	N	Y	Y	N	HFBL	$	N
221 Birch Lake State Recreation Site	0	25	Any	N	NF	N	Y	Y	N	FBL	$$	N
222 "C" Lazy Moose RV Park	15	15+	Any	WES	F	Y	Y	Y	Y	N	$$–$$$$	Y
223 Harding Lake State Recreation Area	0	83	35	N	NF	N	Y	Y	Y	HFBL	$$	N
224 Salcha River State Recreation Site	0	48	Any	N	NF	N	Y	Y	N	FBL	$	N

219 Big Delta State Historical Park–Rika's Roadhouse

Location: Near Delta Junction
GPS: N 64° 09.277' / W 145° 50.576'
Season: Mid-May through mid-September
Sites: 23 RV sites
Maximum length: Any
Facilities: Picnic area with fire pits, potable water, vault toilets, dump station, restaurant, museum, gift shop
Fee per night: $$
Maximum stay: 15 days
Management: Alaska State Parks, Northern Area Office, (907) 451-2695, www.dnr.state.ak .us/parks
Finding the campground: From mile 275 of the Richardson Highway, turn north onto Rika Road and drive 0.1 mile to the campground on your left.
About the campground: Rika's Roadhouse and the area around Delta State Historical Park served as an important trading post during the early to mid-1900s, much as Delta Junction does today. Once a major stopping point on the Valdez–Fairbanks Trail, the roadhouse saw its share of Alaska's daring pioneers in the early days. Today you can catch a glimpse of life during Rika's heyday at a small museum operated by the local historical society. Camping is simply parking spaces in a characterless open gravel lot. Pull-thrus and numbered sites back up to an area with tables and fire pits. A concessionaire operates the touristy gift shop and restaurant.

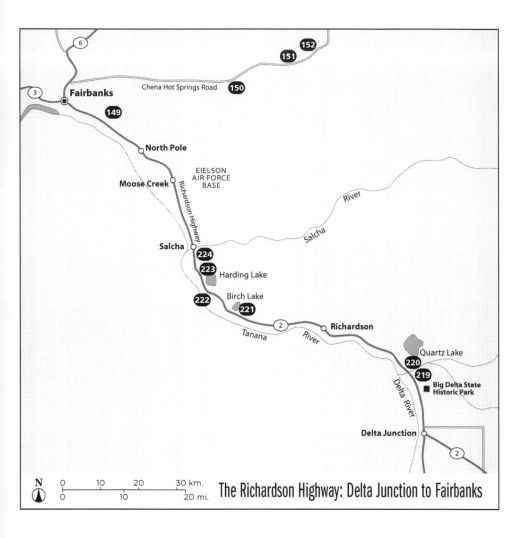

N
0   10   20   30 km.
0   10   20 mi.
The Richardson Highway: Delta Junction to Fairbanks

220 Quartz Lake State Recreation Area

Location: Near mile 277 of the Richardson Highway
GPS: N 64° 11.844' / W 145° 49.710'
Season: Early May through mid-September
Sites: 30 basic sites, 87 parking-lot-style spaces
Maximum length: Any
Facilities: Tables, fire pits, covered picnic area, vault toilets, hiking/fishing/lake access, boat launch, volleyball, boat rentals
Fee per night: $
Maximum stay: 15 days

Management: Alaska State Parks, Northern Area Office, (907) 451-2695, www.dnr.state.ak .us/parks

Finding the campground: From mile 277.9 of the Richardson Highway, turn north onto Quartz Lake Road and drive 2.4 miles to the Quartz Lake Campground. To reach Lost Lake, follow the signs to the left just before Quartz Lake.

About the campground: It may be called Quartz Lake, but you won't find any quartz around here. For most of the summer, the lake is more of a swamp; gravel for the campground and parking area had to be imported to harden the soil. The recreation area is always active, full of people and boats, with the primary draw being fish. Quartz Lake is stocked with trout and salmon. A fishing dock allows access to the weedy waters, but fishing from a boat is the most popular way to catch the trophy-size rainbows. There are two campgrounds located a short walk from each other.

The campground at Quartz Lake has sixteen basic sites along with about ninety overnight parking spaces available in an open parking lot. The basic sites are back-ins surrounded by woods and low brush up the hill from the lake. The open parking area can hold large RVs; the developed camping area is limited to vehicles of 50 feet or less. Several trails lead from the grounds, including the popular 1.8-mile Quartz Lake Loop connecting Lost and Quartz lakes. Lost Lake has a smaller campground with less activity. There are twelve basic sites. Here you'll find lakefront sites that are a little more dispersed than the neighboring grounds, yet very similar in setup. Both campgrounds have wooded earthen sites with tables and fire pits.

221 Birch Lake State Recreation Site

Location: Near mile 305 of the Richardson Highway
GPS: N 64° 18.866' / W 146° 38.708'
Season: Mid-May through late September
Sites: 20 basic sites, 5 tent sites
Maximum length: Any
Facilities: Tables, fire pits, picnic area, potable water, vault toilets, lake/fishing access, boat launch
Fee per night: $$
Maximum stay: 15 days
Management: Alaska State Parks, Northern Area Office, (907) 451-2695, www.dnr.state.ak .us/parks

Finding the campground: From mile 305.2 of the Richardson Highway, turn north onto the un-labeled road at the sign for the Birch Lake State Recreation Site. Drive 0.2 mile to the campground on your left.

About the campground: Stocked with trout, salmon, grayling, and arctic char, Birch Lake is popular with anglers year-round. In summer the lake buzzes with the sounds of motors as jet skiers and boaters rule the waters. The small campground has twenty basic sites, most of which are long enough for large RVs. Tenters get a shot at five walk-in lakeshore tent sites with trees and a view of the lake.

222 "C" Lazy Moose RV Park

Location: Near mile 314 of the Richardson Highway
GPS: N 64° 21.889' / W 146° 52.501'
Season: Late May to September
Sites: 10 full-hookup RV sites, 5 partial-hookup RV sites, open tent sites
Maximum length: Any
Facilities: Some tables and fire pits, potable water, flush toilets, showers, laundry, WiFi
Fee per night: $$–$$$$
Maximum stay: None
Management: Lazy Moose RV Park, (907) 488-8141
Finding the campground: On the west side of the Richardson Highway at mile 314.8.
About the campground: This new campground has sparkling facilities and plenty of room in an open gravel lot. The trees are young and yet large enough for shade. Each site has a table with a personal grass lawn. The camping area is nicely set in a gully below the bluff the highway is built on. There are some riverfront sites. Pull-thrus are available for large RVs, while tenters are nestled away in the woods.

223 Harding Lake State Recreation Area

Location: Near mile 321 of the Richardson Highway
GPS: N 64° 26.170' / W 146° 52.757'
Season: Mid-May through mid-September
Sites: 78 basic sites, 5 tent sites
Maximum length: 35 feet
Facilities: Tables, fire pits, covered picnic area, vault toilets, boil-first water, dump station, boat launch, hiking/fishing/lake access, volleyball net, baseball field
Fee per night: $$
Maximum stay: 15 days
Management: Alaska State Parks, Northern Area Office, (907) 451-2695, www.dnr.state.ak .us/parks
Finding the campground: From mile 321.5 of the Richardson Highway, head east on Harding Drive for 1.4 miles to the campground.
About the campground: This is a huge recreation area with the park headquarters on site. The lake is an epicenter of summer activity for the area—you might even catch some Alaskans swimming in the chilly waters. Fishing seems endless with salmon, trout, pike, arctic char, and burbot in the lake. Camping is in standard earthen back-ins separated by trees. Some are rather close together. The last few sites are the most spacious. The tent sites here are a decent-length walk away, which is great if you're looking to get away from the buzz. A separate open gravel lot with a few tables and fire pits can be used for large rigs with permission from the host. The open lot is available for parking between the hours of 8 p.m. and 9 a.m., so it should be considered a space to park for the night only.

224 Salcha River State Recreation Site

Location: Near mile 323 of the Richardson Highway
GPS: N 64° 28.242' / W 146° 55.529'
Season: Mid-May through late September
Sites: 45 side-by-side parking-lot-style spaces, 3 basic sites
Maximum length: Any
Facilities: Some tables and fire pits, potable water, vault toilet, fishing/river access, boat launch
Fee per night: $
Maximum stay: 15 days
Management: Alaska State Parks, Northern Area Office, (907) 451-2695, www.dnr.state.ak.us/parks
Finding the campground: From mile 323.1 of the Richardson Highway, turn northeast at the sign for Salcha River State Recreation Site. The campground is on your immediate left.
About the campground: The tangled grounds of Salcha River State Recreation Site are a popular area for ATV enthusiasts and boaters alike. The launch is located near two open lots at the farthest end of the road. Boaters are usually out to catch salmon, grayling, pike, burbot, or one of the many other kinds of fish the river offers. The camping area is rather dull. Most sites are parking-lot-style spaces in an open lot; there are only three basic sites.

For many the Alaska Highway is the ultimate road trip, passing through two countries, three states, and millions of acres of wilderness. At almost 1,500 miles long, the highway covers a significant stretch of the continent. It traverses glacial valleys, thick forests, lakes, rivers, wetlands, and tundra. The highway peaks over high mountain passes and plummets through low marshy wetlands. Outdoor enthusiasts have a plateful of options along the way. Hiking, fishing, birding, canoeing, and climbing trails abound. One recreational joy ties all the others in place—camping in this vast wilderness is nearly essential. There are excellent campgrounds along the way. Roadhouses usually offer RV parking, and the public campgrounds in both Canada and Alaska are superb.

The Alaska Highway hasn't always been so well developed. The route was built during World War II in response to a potential Japanese invasion. The Army Corps of Engineers quickly cut a rough road between southeastern British Columbia and interior Alaska. This created a link to the continuous road system and a route to carry ground supplies. The highway winds out of Dawson Creek, British Columbia, through the Rocky Mountains, then stretches northwest into Canada's rugged Yukon Territory. It finally reaches Alaska more than 1,000 miles from its start. Fewer than 300 miles are within the state. The highway was completed in less than a year, and was one of the roughest to exist in both countries. At this time the road was known as the Alaska–Canada Military Highway, which gave birth to its still-used nickname "the Alcan."

Since its completion in 1942, the road has been under a state of constant improvement. Today pavement covers most of the highway in a battle of nature versus construction. You'll likely pass over stretches of gravel in work zones that can go for miles. Preparation for this long haul is essential. Bring all the basics you would on any road trip through vast and remote places; just add mosquito repellent. There are up to 100 miles without services along the Alaska Highway in Canada. The weather varies; it can be as warm as ninety degrees Fahrenheit in the day and drop to freezing over snowy passes. The light can also be a surprise. Especially as you enter Alaska, the daylight can stretch nearly twenty-four hours with only short-lived twilight as the sun dips over the horizon for a couple of late-night hours.

Within Alaska the highway is completely paved—an easily traveled stretch with more frequent services than you'll find in Canada. Scenery endures regardless of borders. As you enter Alaska the highway passes through the Tetlin National Wildlife Refuge, home to hundreds of lakes and many species of migratory birds. A couple of delightful campgrounds nestle up to some of these small lakes. This is an excellent location for wildlife viewing, particularly waterfowl. Ducks, loons, and often trumpeter swans visit these water bodies and marshes every year to nest. Also keep an eye out for Dall sheep, bears, wolves, caribou, and moose on your lengthy journey.

As you leave the refuge behind, small black spruce groves give way to wide-open interior views. The first city you reach is Tok, originally built as a construction camp for World War II roadworkers. Today it is the junction of the Glenn Highway/Tok Cutoff. Whether you're entering or exiting the state, or driving a loop, you'll likely stop in Tok. The small town has been nicknamed Main Street Alaska thanks to its recurrent visitors. Here you'll find decent gas prices and good food along with reputable campgrounds. Not too far out of town, the Tok River State Recreation Area has a traditional government campground with wooded sites and fire pits along a pleasant river.

A little east of Tok, the Taylor Highway forks north from Tetlin Junction. This 150-mile mostly gravel road climbs to the historic town of Eagle and the mighty Yukon River. The Taylor connects via the "Top of the World Road" to Canada's Yukon Territory, a suitable name for the high ridge vistas of the area. The Fortymile River snakes in the valley below. This is a section of the largest designated National Wild, Scenic, and Recreational River in the country. In the 1880s miners flocked to the Fortymile Mining District and the various tributaries in search of gold. The precious metal can still be found in these rich gravels today. Follow the Taylor Highway into the Mosquito Fork Valley (bring your repellent) and descend into the raw town of Chicken for a chance at gold panning. This mysteriously named three-building ghost town and tourist trap is not to be missed!

From Tok and Tetlin Junction, the Alaska Highway leads northwest to another crossroads: The Alaska and Richardson highways meet in the city of Delta Junction. From there the Richardson leads to Fairbanks. Many campers will continue their drive north; some will have dipped south long ago. Either way, more adventures are to be had, even if the road isn't as rough or long as the ultimate "Alcan."

The Alaska Highway: Border City to Tetlin Junction

The Alaska Highway: Border City to Tetlin Junction

	Hookup Sites	Total Sites	Max. RV Length	Hookups	Toilets	Showers	Drinking Water	Fires	Dump Station	Recreation	Fee	Reservations
225 Deadman Lake Campground	0	15	35	N	NF	N	N	Y	N	F	Free	N
226 Lakeview Campground	0	11	25	N	NF	N	N	Y	N	F	Free	N
227 Naabia Niigh Campground	16	20	Any	WES	F	Y	Y	Y	Y	N	$-$$$	Y

225 Deadman Lake Campground

Location: Near mile 1249 of the Alaska Highway
GPS: N 62° 53.335' / W 141° 32.481'
Season: June through mid-September
Sites: 15 basic sites
Maximum length: 35 feet
Facilities: Tables, fire pits, picnic area, vault toilets, lake/fishing access
Fee per night: Free
Maximum stay: 14 days
Management: US Fish and Wildlife Service, Tetlin National Wildlife Refuge, (907) 883-5312, http://tetlin.fws.gov
Finding the campground: At mile 1249.3 of the Alaska Highway, turn south onto the unlabeled road at the sign for Deadman Lake Campground. Drive 1.2 miles to the campground.
About the campground: This small, free campground has a host and superb views of Deadman Lake. Campsites are located off a tight loop in a black spruce grove. A few by the boat launch are closer together but have direct water access; sites with a more secluded feeling sit in the trees. A short boardwalk trail meanders through the forest with interpretive displays on native plants and wildlife. Deadman Lake is also home to nightly ranger-led wildlife programs in summer. This is an excellent campground, along with its counterpart the Lakeview. Both have sparkling-clean facilities and fill quickly. It would not be surprising if they impose a fee in the future

226 Lakeview Campground

Location: Near mile 1256 of the Alaska Highway
GPS: N 62° 57.871' / W 141° 38.410'
Season: June through mid-September
Sites: 11 basic sites

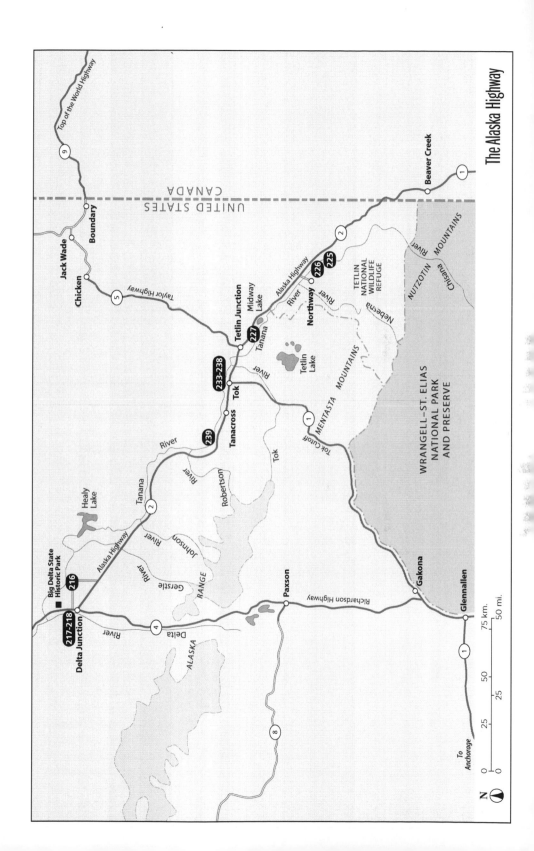

The Alaska Highway

Maximum length: 25 feet
Facilities: Tables, fire pits, vault toilets, lake/fishing access
Fee per night: Free
Maximum stay: 14 days
Management: US Fish and Wildlife Service, Tetlin National Wildlife Refuge, (907) 883-5312, http://tetlin.fws.gov
Finding the campground: From mile 1256.7 of the Alaska Highway, turn south at the sign for Lakeview Campground and drive 0.2 mile to the campground.
About the campground: Much like Deadman Lake, this pleasant little campground is a relief along the undeveloped roadsides of the Alaska Highway. Here you'll find eleven basic sites in a wooded area. The placid Yarger Lake offers fishing for pike and is known for birding opportunities—as is most of the refuge. Some lucky campers can spy the lake directly from their sites.

227 Naabia Niigh Campground

Location: Mile 1264 of the Alaska Highway
GPS: N 63° 00.557' / W 141° 48.172'
Season: May through September
Sites: 16 full-hookup RV sites, 4 tent sites
Maximum length: Any
Facilities: Tables, fire pits, flush and pit toilets, laundry, gas station, coffee shop, small grocery store, gift shop
Fee per night: $–$$$
Maximum stay: None
Management: Naabia Niigh Campground, (907) 778-2297
Finding the campground: This campground is located on the south side of the Alaska Highway at mile 1264.
About the campground: This typical Alaskan roadhouse operation has a unique name, Naabia Niigh, which means "by the muddy river" in the Native language. Camping here is behind a gas station with older facilities in an overgrown open lot with scattered trees. The very basic side-by-side sites include sixteen rugged back-ins with full hookups and four small tent sites. Also on site is a small store and gift shop with Native goods by local artists.

The Taylor Highway

228 West Fork Campground

Location: Mile 49 of the Taylor Highway
GPS: N 63° 53.217' / W 142° 14.116'
Season: Mid-May through mid-September
Sites: 25 basic sites
Maximum length: 60 feet
Facilities: Tables, fire pits, covered picnic area, potable water, vault toilets, lake access
Fee per night: $
Maximum stay: 7 days
Management: Bureau of Land Management, Fairbanks District Office, (907) 474-2200, www.blm.gov/ak
Finding the campground: On the west side of the Taylor Highway at mile 49.
About the campground: The BLM loosely maintains some surprisingly nice campgrounds along the Taylor Highway. The West Fork has two loops of informal campsites off a wide gravel road navigable by most rigs. These sites are narrow back-ins; a few overlook small Johna's Lake. Keep an eye out for trumpeter swans. Sites are small but private, with thick spruce and brush offering a relaxing shady retreat on those warm interior days. This campground serves as an access point for the Fortymile National Wild and Scenic River.

229 Chicken Gold Camp

Location: In Chicken
GPS: N 64° 04.014' / W 141° 56.448'
Season: Late May through September
Sites: 10 partial-hookup RV sites, open dry camping

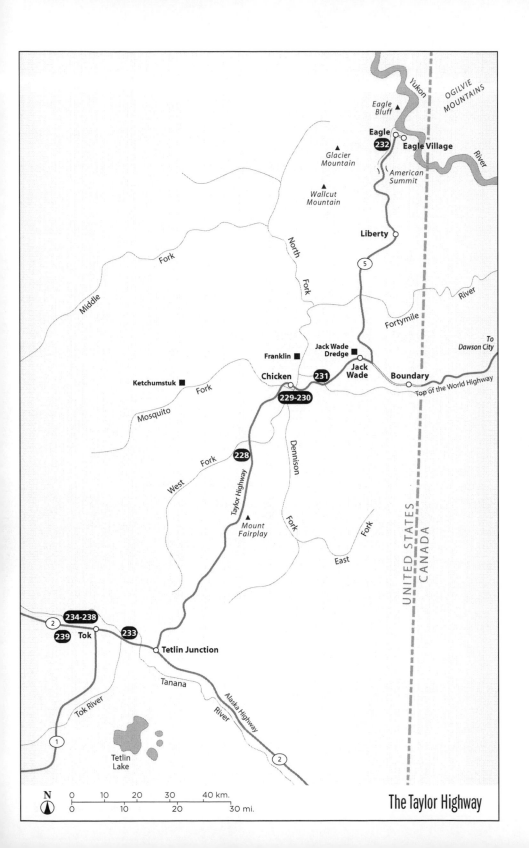

The Taylor Highway

Maximum length: Any

Facilities: Tables, fire pits, covered picnic area with grill, potable water, pit toilets, dump station, cafe, gift shop, WiFi

Fee per night: $$-$$$$

Maximum stay: None

Management: Chicken Gold Camp and Outpost, summer satellite phone (520) 413-1480, winter (907) 235-6396, www.chickengold.com

Finding the campground: From mile 66.4 of the Taylor Highway, turn onto the unlabeled gravel road toward the airport and Chicken. The park is on your immediate left.

About the campground: This campground is built on the original site of a 1930s gold camp along the rich gravels of Chicken Creek. You may expect Chicken to be rustic or even trashy, but this park, and the three-building town, are well maintained. The camping area at Chicken Gold Camp is landscaped with blooming flowerpots and crisp edges. The outbuildings and tables are all new and in pristine condition. Most sites are in a large open gravel lot. Some pull-thrus have electrical hookups. A gold panning area is in the center of the campground. The management has already shoveled in loose gravel for tourists to pan, and many are successful in finding color—even large flakes. What you find is yours to keep; gold panning is inexpensive. You can also rent kayaks or grab an espresso at the Chicken Creek Outpost on site.

Downtown Chicken.

230 The Goldpanner/Chicken Creek RV Park

Location: In Chicken
GPS: N 64° 04.268' / W 141° 56.070'
Season: Late May through September
Sites: 10 partial-hookup RV sites, open dry camping
Maximum length: Any
Facilities: Tables, fire pits, covered picnic area, potable water, pit toilets, dump station, WiFi, gift shop
Fee per night: $$–$$$$
Maximum stay: None
Management: Chicken Center/The Goldpanner, (907) 883-5081, www.chickenak.com
Finding the campground: From mile 66.6 of the Taylor Highway in Chicken, follow the signs to The Goldpanner/Chicken Creek RV Park just before the Chicken Creek bridge.
About the campground: The Chicken Creek RV Park offers camping in a basic open gravel lot. Most sites are back-ins, and some offer electric hookups. Specials for the campground are the best deals in town—often free dry camping if you fill up on gas. Gold panning and WiFi are also included with your stay here. RV sites with electricity are available for a small fee. A small on-site store has ice cream, coffee, gas, and a comical three-hole golf course.

The mighty Yukon River in Eagle. This river is up to a kilometer wide.

231 Walker Fork Campground

Location: Mile 82 of the Taylor Highway
GPS: N 64° 04.622' / W 141° 37.724'
Season: Late May through September
Sites: 19 basic sites
Maximum length: Any
Facilities: Tables, fire pits, covered picnic area with grill, potable water, vault toilets
Fee per night: $
Maximum stay: 10 days
Management: Bureau of Land Management, Fairbanks District Office, (907) 474-2200, www.blm.gov/ak
Finding the campground: The Walker Fork Campground is on the northwest side of the Taylor Highway at mile 82.
About the campground: This is the only place to stay between Chicken and Eagle. That said, it's surprisingly nice for being in such remote territory. The campground lies along the river with direct access, though you can't actually see the water from the sites. Half the sites are pull-thru separated by trees and brush. Each has a table and fire pit.

232 Eagle Campground

Location: In Eagle
GPS: N 64° 47.512' / W 141° 13.835'
Season: Late May through September
Sites: 16 basic sites
Maximum length: 35 feet
Facilities: Tables, fire pits, potable water, vault toilets
Fee per night: $
Maximum stay: 10 days
Management: Bureau of Land Management, Fairbanks District Office, (907) 822-3217, www.blm.gov/ak
Finding the campground: Follow the highway as you enter the town of Eagle and turn left onto the unlabeled road at the sign for the Eagle Campground/Fort Egbert Historic Site. Drive 0.9 mile, passing through Fort Egbert, to the campground on your left.
About the campground: You'll be surprised to find such a large developed campground in the small sparsely populated end-of-the-road town of Eagle. It even has a host. This earthy campground has extra-large sites, tall shady spruce, and nice new facilities. Large back-ins for any size of rig are distant enough from neighbors to create a tent-camping atmosphere. Potable water does not pump from the grounds. It is brought in and stored in plastic water tanks. The campground can fill up in the busy season, so arrive early. You can walk to historic Fort Ebert (a short-lived onetime government shot at subduing the wild gold-rush camps) from the grounds.

The Alaska Highway: Tok to Delta Junction

The Alaska Highway: Tok to Delta Junction

	Hookup Sites	Total Sites	Max. RV Length	Hookups	Toilets	Showers	Drinking Water	Fires	Dump Station	Recreation	Fee	Reservations
233 Tok River State Recreation Area	0	27	Any	N	NF	N	N	Y	N	HF	$$	N
234 Alaskan Stoves Campground	5	25	35	WES	F	Y	Y	Y	Y	N	$$-$$$$	Y
235 Three Bears Outpost	26	26	40	WES	F	N	Y	N	N	N	$$	N
236 Tok RV Village	166	177	70	WESC	F	Y	Y	Y	Y	N	$$$-$$$$	Y
237 Sourdough Campground	62	72	Any	WES	F	Y	Y	Y	Y	N	$$$-$$$$$	Y
238 Tundra Lodge and RV Park	54	132	Any	WES	F	Y	Y	Y	Y	N	$$$-$$$$$	Y
239 Moon Lake State Recreation Site	0	14	35	N	NF	N	Y	Y	N	HS	$$	N

233 Tok River State Recreation Area

See map on page 198

Location: Near mile 1309 of the Alaska Highway
GPS: N 63° 19.527' / W 142° 49.897'
Season: May through late September
Sites: 17 basic sites, 10 walk-in tent sites
Maximum length: Any
Facilities: Tables, fire pits, picnic area with fire pits, vault toilets, boat launch, hiking/fishing/ river access
Fee per night: $$
Maximum stay: 15 days
Management: Alaska State Parks, Northern Area Office, (907) 451-2695, www.dnr.state.ak .us/parks; management privately contracted to CWL Enterprises, (907) 883-5670
Finding the campground: Look for the turnoff for this campground on the north side of the Alaska Highway at mile 1309.2, just east of the Tok River.
About the campground: If you're planning on tenting anywhere near the Tok area, this camp- ground is an appealing alternative to the open gravel lots and roadhouse operations along the Alcan. The campsites at Tok River State Recreation Area are small back-ins located off a gravel loop road. The sites are small but earthy, with trees and high brush dividing the grounds. Ten lucky tenters can get a chance at shady walk-in sites on the waterfront. At the other end of the spec- trum, there are four pull-thrus in an open area at the entrance to the campground for large RVs.

These sites are not equipped with tables and fire pits like the smaller back-ins, but there is an inviting covered riverfront picnic area for day use.

234 Alaskan Stoves Campground

Location: In Tok
GPS: N 63° 19.967' / W 142° 56.995'
Season: May through September
Sites: 1 full-hookup RV sites, 4 partial hookups, 20 basic sites
Maximum length: 35 feet
Facilities: Tables, communal fire pit, potable water, flush toilets, showers, dump station, laundry
Fee per night: $$–$$$$
Maximum stay: None
Management: Alaskan Stoves Campground, (907) 590-7363, www.alaskanstoves campground.com
Finding the campground: This campground is located on the south side of the Alaskan Highway at mile 1313.
About the campground: This awesome hostel and campground has a clean shower house, laundry, and unique tent accommodations. The campground has a funky hostel and communal vibe that is absent along much of the Alaskan Highway. Sites are mostly in an open gravel lot with trees on the edges.

235 Three Bears Outpost

Location: In Tok
GPS: N 63° 20.093' / W 142° 57.745'
Season: Late May through September
Sites: 8 full-hookup RV sites, 18 partial-hookup RV sites
Maximum length: 40 feet
Facilities: Potable water, flush toilets, showers, dump station
Fee per night: $$
Maximum stay: None
Management: Three Bears Outpost, (907) 883-5195, www.threebearsalaska.com
Finding the campground: This campground is located on the south side of the Alaskan Highway at mile 1313.
About the campground: This basic place to park an RV or take a shower is run in conjunction with the outpost and hardware store.

236 Tok RV Village

See map on page 198

Location: In Tok
GPS: N 63° 20.084' / W 142° 57.971'
Season: Mid-May through mid-September
Sites: 104 full-hookup RV sites, 62 partial-hookup RV sites, 11 tent sites
Maximum length: 70 feet
Facilities: Tables, some fire pits, potable water, flush toilets, showers, dump station, laundry, WiFi, gift shop
Fee per night: $$$–$$$$$
Maximum stay: None
Management: Tok RV Village, (907) 883-5877, www.tokrv.net
Finding the campground: You can't miss the large international flag display along the Alaska Highway outside the Tok RV Village at mile 1313.4.
About the campground: This full-service RV park is the largest and most developed campground in the area, with almost 200 sites that fill regularly. Campsites are a combination of back-ins and pull-thrus in side-by-side spaces. Most are in an open gravel lot, but a few are enclosed by mature trees and vegetation. The campground is broken up by plenty of grass. Showers are included with RV sites. The up-to-date facilities are well maintained.

237 Sourdough Campground

See map on page 198

Location: In Tok
GPS: N 63° 18.687' / W 143° 00.257'
Season: Year-round
Sites: 22 full-hookup RV sites, 40 partial-hookup RV sites, 10 tent sites
Maximum length: Any
Facilities: Tables, covered picnic area, communal fire pit, potable water, flush toilets, dump station, showers, laundry, restaurant, WiFi
Fee per night: $$$–$$$$$
Maximum stay: None
Management: Sourdough Campground, (907) 883-5543, www.sourdoughcampground.com
Finding the campground: This campground is located about 1.5 miles outside Tok headed toward Anchorage, at mile 123.3 of the Tok Cutoff. It's on the northwest side of the road.
About the campground: Between the all-you-can-eat pancake breakfasts and nightly "pancake toss," the Sourdough Campground must go through a lot of pancakes. If you're staying in the Tok area and have a sense of adventure, this one-of-a-kind campground should be your first stop. The comical hosts enliven the crowds with nightly shows, a twist between humor and traditional Alaskan themes, often with bluegrass music. Local artists will sometimes join the show. Camping is in

a wooded area; some sites are separated by spruce and vegetation. There aren't a lot of spaces for very large RVs, so reservations are recommended. A short paved trail leads to town.

238 Tundra Lodge and RV Park

See map on page 198

Location: In Tok
GPS: N 63° 20.320' / W 143° 00.992'
Season: Mid-May through mid-September
Sites: 30 RV full-hookup RV sites, 24 partial-hookup RV sites, 78 dry sites
Maximum length: Any
Facilities: Some tables and fire pits, potables water, flush toilets, showers, dump station, laundry, lounge, WiFi
Fee per night: $$$–$$$$$
Maximum stay: None
Management: Tundra Lodge and RV Park, (907) 883-7875
Finding the campground: You'll find this campground about a mile west of Tok on the north side of the Alaska Highway at mile 1314.8.
About the campground: The Tundra RV Park has the best prices in the Tok area and includes hot showers with your stay. The large campground is in need of a face-lift compared with some of the crisply manicured parks with more modern facilities, but there is plenty of room for weary travelers. Along with full hookups, and water and electric hookups, there are eighty dry sites in an overgrown lot. Some have aging picnic tables and fire pits.

239 Moon Lake State Recreation Site

See map on page 198

Location: Near mile 1331 of the Alaska Highway
GPS: N 63° 22.562' / W 143° 32.667'
Season: May through late September
Sites: 14 basic sites
Maximum length: 35 feet
Facilities: Tables, fire pits, potable water, vault toilets, hiking/swimming/lake access
Fee per night: $$
Maximum stay: 7 days
Management: Alaska State Parks, Northern Area Office, (907) 451-2695, www.dnr.state.ak .us/parks
Finding the campground: From mile 1331.9 of the Alaska Highway, turn northeast at the sign for the Moon Lake State Recreation Site and drive 0.2 mile to the campground.

About the campground: Given the crowds that flock to Moon Lake on weekends, it looks as if every local is enjoying this swimming hole. A sandy beach is roped off as a swim area. The recreation area also includes a boat launch popular with motorboats and a beachside picnic area with grills. You can even land your floatplane on this popular little lake. Camping consists of fourteen basic back-in sites in two loops. They're fairly close together, but most folks here are out on the water.

Southeast Alaska

Southeast Alaska is distinct from its mainland counterpart. This splice of the coast is something of a water-soaked dreamland blanketed by rain forest, glaciers, and the sea. It is a land with misty ocean ports where fishing ships pass by humpback whales, where black bears roam seashores and petroglyphs wash up on rocky tidal beaches. Ancient trees dripping with moss and mushrooms soak up raindrops. The southeast encompasses thousands of islands stretching from the shores of lower British Columbia up the coast to mainland Alaska. Water is the livelihood of the people, the economy, and the ecology. Here the survival and beauty of the area relies on the drenching precipitation. It is no surprise, then, that locals refer to the constant showers as their "liquid sunshine."

Traveling to the southeast is either by boat or plane. The islands are connected to the continuous road system by private boats and the Alaska Marine Highway, a state-operated public ferry system. You can drive your car onto these ferries, transport your kayak or pet, and even camp on the solarium decks. Camping on the Alaska Marine Highway is free with your cost of passage. You can sleep in the open air under heat lamps or pitch your tent right on the deck (don't forget duct tape to secure the corners!).

Large ferries and cruise ships sail from Washington State to British Columbia and twenty-eight Alaskan ports. Referred to as the Inside Passage, this area has calm protected waters shielded by the mountainous islands. Mild climate is moderated by warm ocean currents. This topography was carved by glaciers and ice fields. Side trips to Misty Fjords National Monument and Glacier Bay National Park enhance geologic understanding if you're new to the area.

Southeast Alaska offers some of the most beautiful campgrounds in the state. Many are within the Tongass National Forest. At seventeen million acres the forest is the largest unit in the nation; it covers nearly every island in the southeast and offers both wilderness retreat and subsistence. The Tlingit and Haida tribes have lived here and thrived for thousands of years, and today many still do. Fishing and logging support many local economies. Tourism carves its own place into the system; some islands cater to the industry, while others rarely see tourists.

When you're deciding which islands to visit, do your research. Each is unique, with different cultural and camping opportunities. The islands are even wildlife-specific. One island may have grizzly bears and moose, while another only has deer and black bears. Certain coves are renowned for whale-watching. Some islands are known for thick eagle populations. Take into account the geological features, parks, and sights you hope to see. Then check the ferry and schedules. Some islands are only serviced once or twice a week. Consider the timetables and make your reservations in advance. Ships do fill up, especially for vehicles.

Each island offers a host of activities and campgrounds. Some are more developed than others. Ketchikan is the first stop on the Marine Highway as you travel north and is a favorite for whirlwind cruise ship tours. Almost a million tourists pass through annually, and the liners have nearly bought up downtown to accommodate the knickknack shoppers. On the other side of the sphere, an island away, Prince of Wales is home to the road less traveled, and there are 2,000 miles of it! This island was extensively logged and had roads (along with jaw-dropping clear-cut logging) carved into the landscape. POW, as the locals call the island, is becoming increasingly popular with outdoor enthusiasts who wish to explore its hundreds of miles of pavement as well as more than 1,000 miles of rough road leading to kayaking coves, limestone caves, and public lands galore.

Wrangell doesn't cater to cruise ships, either. The island has an economy largely dependent on fishing and logging. This is a piece of the southeast that tourists often pass by—which is unfortunate since some of the most exclusive campsites within the Tongass National Forest and beautiful trails await the adventurer. John Muir once called Wrangell's Stikine River "the Yosemite of Alaska."

The Alaska Marine Highway barely escapes through the Wrangell narrows north of the island. The ferry then docks in Petersburg, a Norwegian-flavored cannery town and serious fishing port on Mitkof Island. This authentic southeastern community has a picturesque downtown framed by jagged snowcapped peaks. Lush government campgrounds sit outside the city. Another fishing island, Sitka, was once the capital of Russian America, known as the Paris of the Pacific. Beautiful Russian Orthodox churches still grace the city lines. Juneau, the capital of Alaska, is the third largest city in the state and home to about 30,000 people—along with more than half that number in bald eagles. Downtown is stocked full of cosmopolitan delights, yet the wilderness surrounding it is one of a kind. Not far from the city line, you can pitch your tent beneath the backdrop of stunning Mendenhall Glacier.

The southeast ends in Haines and Skagway, where you can exit the Marine Highway and drive the path the Klondike stampeders once trekked in snow. Following the Haines or the Klondike Highway north through Canada's British Columbia and Yukon Territory, you can meet the Alaska Highway and enter the state once again through the interior. Or you could continue on the Marine Highway, which sails west from here. A tour through southeast Alaska can go in many directions, but wherever you sail or land, good campgrounds are easy to come by. So pack your rain gear and lots of socks!

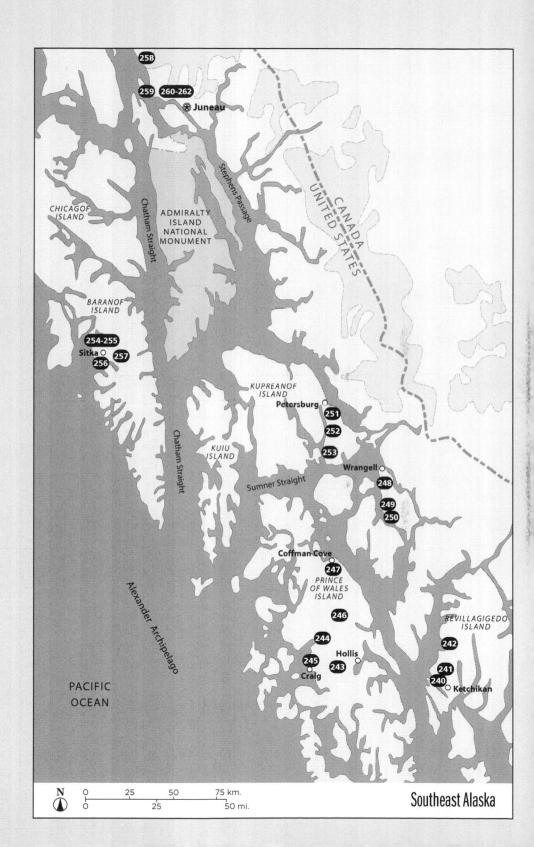

Southeast Alaska

Ketchikan

	Hookup Sites	Total Sites	Max. RV Length	Hookups	Toilets	Showers	Drinking Water	Fires	Dump Station	Recreation	Fee	Reservations
240 Signal Creek	0	24	35	N	NF	N	Y	Y	N	HF	$	Y
241 Last Chance Campground	0	19	35	N	NF	N	Y	Y	N	HF	$	Y
242 Settler's Cove State Recreation Site	0	14	35	N	NF	N	Y	Y	N	HF	$$	N

240 Signal Creek

Location: Near mile 7 of the North Tongass Highway
GPS: N 55° 24.476' / W 131° 41.982'
Season: Late April through late March
Sites: 24 basic sites
Maximum length: 35 feet
Facilities: Tables, fire pits, potable water, vault toilets, hiking/fishing/creek access
Fee per night: $
Maximum stay: 14 days
Management: USDA Forest Service, Tongass National Forest, Ketchikan–Misty Fiords Ranger District, (907) 225-2148, www.fs.fed.us/r10/tongass
Finding the campground: From downtown Ketchikan, drive north on North Tongass Highway to mile 7 and turn right onto Revilla Road. Drive 1.3 miles to the campground on your right.
About the campground: If Ketchikan is your first stop in southeastern Alaska, head out for a drive to the Signal Creek campground to view an old-growth forest characteristic of the region. The beauty of the mature towering hemlock and spruce trees can enliven even the weariest traveler. Several forested hiking trails disperse from the area, including a popular stroll around picturesque Ward Lake. Signal Creek also has a well-developed camping area adjacent to the lake's popular sportfishing hole. There are twenty-four basic sites spaciously dispersed through the large trunks of the big trees, with a few snugger, more exposed sites along the small lake. During the high season this popular, yet quiet, campground often fills. A separate camping area opens for overflow during the busiest times; inquire with your hosts. The majority of the campground shuts down after Labor Day, but a few sites remain open and free of charge for off-season campers until March 30.

241 Last Chance Campground

Location: Near mile 7 of the North Tongass Highway
GPS: N 55° 25.972' / W 131° 41.180'
Season: Late May through September
Sites: 19 basic sites
Maximum length: 35 feet
Facilities: Tables, fire pits, potable water, vault toilets, hiking/fishing/lake access
Fee per night: $
Maximum stay: 14 days
Management: USDA Forest Service, Tongass National Forest, Ketchikan–Misty Fiords Ranger District, (907) 225-2148, www.fs.fed.us/r10/tongass
Finding the campground: From downtown Ketchikan, head north on the North Tongass Highway to mile 7 and turn right onto Revilla Road. Drive 2.3 miles to the campground on your right.
About the campground: Adjacent to Ward Creek, this campground has nineteen thickly wooded campsites. Each has a table and fire pit and plenty of room for tents. They are located off a wide paved road through a stately forest much like that at Signal Creek. The facilities are clean and

Creek Street in downtown Ketchikan.

well developed. There is a little less activity than at the lakeside camp down the road. As with any Ketchikan-area campground, if you're tenting bring a tarp for extra protection from the often drenched grounds.

242 Settler's Cove State Recreation Site

Location: Near mile 18 of North Tongass Highway
GPS: N 55° 30.639' / W 131° 43.554'
Season: Mid-April through mid-October
Sites: 14 basic sites
Maximum length: 35 feet
Facilities: Tables, fire pits, covered picnic area, potable water, vault toilets, hiking/fishing/ beach access
Fee per night: $$
Maximum stay: 7 days
Management: Alaska State Parks, Ketchikan Ranger Station, (907) 247-8574, www.dnr.state .ak.us/parks
Finding the campground: Settlers Cove State Recreation Site is located before the end of the North Tongass Highway at mile 18.2 on the west side of road.
About the campground: Nestled next to the rocky shores of Settlers Cove, this cozy campground has a small loop of campsites popular with kayakers and a cove popular with whales. The forested campsites are in sets of two, putting neighbors fairly close to each other, with a shared driveway but separate tables and fire pits. A couple of lucky campers can line the placid shores of the beach and sleep with the sweet sound of the sea. This secluded end-of-the-road campground is likely to fill up quickly at any time through the summer. If you are just passing through, be sure not to miss the 0.25-mile wheelchair-accessible stroll from the campground to a waterfall.

Prince of Wales

243 Harris River Campground

See map on page 209
Location: 11 miles west of Hollis
GPS: N 55° 28.028' / W 132° 51.406'
Season: Year-round
Sites: 14 basic sites
Maximum length: Any
Facilities: Tables, fire pits, covered picnic area, potable water, vault toilets, hiking access
Fee per night: $
Maximum stay: 30 days
Management: USDA Forest Service, Tongass National Forest, Craig Ranger District, (907) 826-3271, www.fs.fed.us/r10/tongass
Finding the campground: This newer campground is located roughly halfway between Craig and Hollis on the Craig–Klawock–Hollis Highway. You'll find it 11.3 miles from Hollis and 19.7 miles from Craig on the south side of the road.
About the campground: These spacious campsites are just off the highway along a wide gravel road, allowing accessibility for big rigs. Tenters will also enjoy this campground since about half the sites have tent pads. As with most campgrounds in southeast Alaska, the soggy grounds can get very wet. The campsites are dispersed through a small grove of Alaskan yellow cedar and the ever-present muskeg. A few sites connect by a boardwalk trail through the middle of the grounds. The highlight of the campground is a walk-in picnic area about 300 feet from the parking area across a footbridge. Directly beside the roar of the creek, the covered picnic area has dry tables, grills, a fire pit, potable water, a vault toilet, and the feeling of forested seclusion. This is an excellent place for anyone to stop and enjoy lunch! These grounds are open to campers year-round, and camping is free from October through April.

244 Log Cabin RV Park

See map on page 209

Location: In Klawock
GPS: N 55° 33.433' / W 133° 05.092'
Season: Mid-April through December
Sites: 14 full-hookup RV sites, 6 basic sites
Maximum length: 35 feet
Facilities: Some tables, potable water, flush toilets, showers, laundry, marina, fishing access, boat launch, boat rentals, charters
Fee per night: $$–$$$$
Maximum stay: None
Management: Log Cabin Resort and RV Park, (907) 755-2205, (800) 544-2205, www.logcabin resortandrvpark.com
Finding the campground: From the north end of Klawock, turn north onto Big Salt Road, just east of the state troopers' office, and drive 0.4 mile to the park on your right.
About the campground: Snugly placed on a strip of land between the small resort and shores of Saltwater Beach, the Log Cabin RV Park is popular and often booked. Anglers prefer this quiet RV park tucked back into a residential neighborhood; it looks like something of a fishing camp—minus the noise. The very small campground has waterfront charm with boats slowly sailing in and out through the day. Mature hemlock and spruce trees surround the sites, much to the pride of the owners. A sign as you enter cautions QUIET—TREES GROWING. There are a couple of pull-thrus, but room to maneuver is limited; call ahead if you're in a large RV.

245 Rain Country RV Park

See map on page 209

Location: In Craig
GPS: N 55° 28.522' / W 133° 08.041'
Season: Mid-May
Sites: 10 full-hookup RV sites
Maximum length: Any
Facilities: Some tables, flush toilets, showers, laundry
Fee per night: $$–$$$$
Maximum stay: None
Management: JS True Value Hardware/Rain Country RV, (907) 826-3632

Many hiking trails in southeastern Alaska have wooden boardwalks due to the muskeg.

Finding the campground: The park is located in the north end of Craig. Head from Klawock to Craig on the Craig–Klawock Highway, turning south onto JS Drive just as you enter town. Drive 0.1 mile to the gravel lot next door to the True Value hardware store.

About the campground: Rain Country is the only RV park in Craig, and the new grounds have minimal facilities so far. Camping is in an open gravel lot next to a residential neighborhood and hardware store. The back-in sites are bland and open, with a few tables scattered around. Most people will find this is a good place to park the rig and then go explore Craig on foot. The park is managed by the hardware store and you must coordinate with the folks there; call ahead for reservations.

246 Eagle's Nest Campground

See map on page 209

Location: Between Klawock and Thorne Bay
GPS: N 55° 42.159' / W 132° 50.265'
Season: May through September
Sites: 9 basic sites, 2 tent sites
Maximum length: 40 feet
Facilities: Tables, fire pits with grill, covered picnic area, potable water, vault toilets, hiking/fishing/creek access, canoe launch
Fee per night: $
Maximum stay: 14 days
Management: USDA Forest Service, Tongass National Forest, Craig Ranger District, (907) 826-3271, www.fs.fed.us/r10/tongass
Finding the campground: From the intersection of Big Salt Road (Thorne Bay Road) and Prince of Wales Road halfway between Thorne Bay and Klawock, head east on Thorne Bay Road for 1.7 miles to the campground on the north side of road.

About the campground: The uniquely designed sites at Eagle's Nest allow you to camp above the squishy soils of the muskeg, with wooden tent platforms and boardwalks throughout the grounds. The easily accessible grounds include nine basic gravel sites off a paved road and a couple of walk-in tent sites right on the water of Balls Lake. Shaded in hemlock and spruce, they all offer a lot of privacy and charm. Each has a fire pit and table. A small 0.5-mile trail traverses the grounds, leading to a salmon platform and a short 300-foot jog down to the canoe launch. As the name implies, this is a popular spot for viewing bald eagles; when you're not looking out for the ever-present deer, keep an eye up for Alaska's favorite winged creature. If you're just passing through the area, don't miss the Balls Lake Picnic Area, 0.5 mile west of this campground, a walk-in covered picnic area with two tables, fire pit with grill, and sweeping views overlooking the lake and surrounding mountains.

247 Oceanview RV Park

See map on page 209

Location: In Coffman Cove
GPS: N 56° 00.938' / W 132° 49.560'
Season: May through late September
Sites: 14 full-hookup RV sites
Maximum length: Any
Facilities: Tables, fire pits, potable water, flush toilets, showers, laundry, beach access
Fee per night: $$-$$$$
Maximum stay: None
Management: Oceanview RV Park, (907) 329-2032, www.coffmancove.org/rvpark
Finding the campground: From Coffman Cove on Bay View Road, turn north onto Zarembo Drive (at the edge of the small city park). Drive 0.1 mile to the campground on your right.
About the campground: This small pleasant park is located downhill from the road along the waterfront and has a secluded feel. This is also the only place to stay in this often abandoned-looking town and inner-island ferry stop. The side-by-side campsites are cozy and basic, with a small line of trees beside them. Many are right on the water. The Oceanview also takes tents and has a low-cost bunkhouse available. The facilities are well maintained with clean restrooms, hot showers, and laundry. The bunkhouse even has a communal kitchen.

Wrangell

	Hookup Sites	Total Sites	Max. RV Length	Hookups	Toilets	Showers	Drinking Water	Fires	Dump Station	Recreation	Fee	Reservations
248 City Park	0	6	T	N	F	N	Y	Y	N	H	Free	N
249 Shoemaker Bay Recreation Area	16	21	Any	E	F & NF	N	Y	Y	Y	N	Free–$$$	N
250 Nemo Point Recreation Site	0	15	25	N	NF	N	N	Y	N	H	Free	N

248 City Park

See map on page 209
Location: In Wrangell
GPS: N 56° 27.094' / W 132° 22.903'
Season: Year-round
Sites: 6 tent sites
Maximum length: N/A
Facilities: Tables, fire pits, covered picnic area with fireplace, potable water, flush toilets, baseball field, playground, hiking/beach access
Fee per night: Free
Maximum stay: 24 hours
Management: Wrangell Parks and Recreation Department, (907) 874-2444
Finding the campground: From the ferry terminal in downtown Wrangell, head south on the Zimovia Highway for 2.7 miles to the campground on your right. This park is not well labeled, so look for the historic cemetery on your right as you leave town; after the last grave, turn right into the park.
About the campground: This free city campground offers walk-in tent sites under a dark canopy of old-growth trees on a blanket of moss and pine needles. The basic sites include a table and fire pit and are only a few feet from the parking area. The park stretches along the shores of Zimovia Strait with scenic seaside campsites and sounds of the sea. A 4.5-mile bike path leads along the waterfront and is popular with cyclists and morning joggers. Next to the tenting area, a large covered picnic pavilion includes a fireplace and several tables. Watch out for devil's club (the commonly encountered thorny shrub of Alaska) as you explore the grounds. The park has a playground and block of flush toilets. The maximum stay here is twenty-four hours, but once you catch a glimpse of the toilet facilities, it may not seem too short a stay.

249 Shoemaker Bay Recreation Area

See map on page 209

Location: Near mile 4 of the Zimovia Highway
GPS: N 56° 25.037' / W 132° 20.830'
Season: Year-round
Sites: 16 partial-hookup RV sites, 5 tent sites
Maximum length: Any
Facilities: Tables, fire pits, grills, potable water, vault and flush toilets, dump station, playground, horseshoes, volleyball, tennis court
Fee per night: Free–$$$
Maximum stay: 10 days in RV park, 5 days in tent campground
Management: Wrangell Parks and Recreation Department, (907) 874-2444
Finding the campground: From the ferry terminal in downtown Wrangell, head south on the Zimovia Highway for 4.5 miles to the harbor and Shoemaker Bay Recreation Area on your right.
About the campground: The Shoemaker Bay Recreation Area has camping in two sections. From Wrangell heading south on the Zimovia Highway, you will reach the RV section first directly along the road. These electric-hookup-only sites are a combination of back-ins and large pull-thrus set between the water and highway. Situated next to the harbor, you can watch the boats glide by and soak up the views of Zimovia Strait. Vault toilets are located near the dump station in the busy harbor parking lot that centers the grounds. Just east of the harbor parking is the day-use and tent camping area across from the Rainbow Falls Trailhead. Here you will find a similar setup to City Park, including a covered picnic area with a fireplace, flush toilets, horseshoes, and volleyball court. Camping here is not only free, but available for up to five days. Overall this is a relaxing campground even with all the highway and human activity.

250 Nemo Point Recreation Site

See map on page 209

Location: Near mile 13 of the Zimovia Highway
GPS: N 56° 18.337' / W 132° 20.392'
Season: Mid-May through September
Sites: 15 basic sites
Maximum length: 25 feet
Facilities: Tables, fire pits, vault and pit toilets, hiking/beach access
Fee per night: Free
Maximum stay: 10 days
Management: USDA Forest Service, Tongass National Forest, Wrangell Ranger District, (907) 874-2323, www.fs.fed.us/r10/tongass
Finding the campground: The best way to begin your stay at the Nemo set of campsites is to stop at the Forest Service office in Wrangell to get a map. From there you should probably visit

the Nemo hosts and discuss road conditions and directions. To reach the hosts from the ferry, drive 13.5 miles south on the Zimovia Highway; at the sign for the Nemo Point State Recreation Site, turn right onto FR 6267. The hosts will be on your left. You will also find the first few camping areas, and the most popular and accessible sites, along this road. Just past the camp hosts at 0.6 mile on your right is the Yunshookuh Loop campsite; 1 mile past that the Three Sisters Overlook Campsite is also on your right. From Three Sisters, go 0.5 mile and veer right onto another gravel forest road, then drive 0.3 mile to the dead end at the Anita Bay campground.

About the campground: The Forest Service campsites on Wrangell are set up like no others in Alaska. In all there are about fifteen campsites scattered across the island, sometimes dozens of miles apart. The campsites are in clusters of up to three, and as few as one. These camping areas are unique, combining outstanding overlooks, rustic isolation, and clean, well-developed facilities. The most popular sites peer out at Zimovia Strait from a high bluff. You can watch for whales and ships passing by. The oversize campsites include tables, fire pits, and clean vault or pit toilets. You can't find a better-maintained secluded campground in the state. Much of the credit belongs to the recurrent hosts, who spend time and heart on keeping sites clean—along with the "sst's" or "sweet smelling toilets," as they'll boast. They also keep free firewood stocked at the sites as much as possible.

Nemo Point Recreation Site campsites have spectacular views of Zimovia Strait.

Petersburg

251 Frog's RV Park

See map on page 209

Location: In Petersburg
GPS: N 56° 46.738' / W 132° 58.043'

Petersburg shows its Norwegian influence.

Season: Year-round
Sites: 10 full-hookup RV sites
Maximum length: Any
Facilities: Potable water, flush toilets, showers, laundry
Fee per night: $$$
Maximum stay: None
Management: Frog's RV Park, (360) 482-8589
Finding the campground: From mile 3 of the Mitkof Highway, turn west onto Scow Bay Loop Road and drive 2.1 miles to the campground on your right.
About the campground: Frog's RV Park is a real Petersburg experience, embodying the cannery-town atmosphere in an open cluttered waterfront gravel lot overlooking the fish-processing plants. There is a horde of permanent residents living in small trailers and camper shells. Most sites are side-by-side gravel spaces in a combination of back-ins and pull-thrus. The views beyond the campground are impressive, but the older facilities deter most RV-park-goers.

252 The Trees RV Park

See map on page 209

Location: Near mile 10 of the Mitkof Highway
GPS: N 56° 41.164' / W 132° 55.672'
Season: May through late September
Sites: 7 full-hookup RV sites, 8 partial-hookup RV sites, open tent camping
Maximum length: 40 feet
Facilities: Tables, potable water, flush toilets, showers, dump station, laundry, small store
Fee per night: $$–$$$$
Maximum stay: None
Management: The Trees RV Park and General Store, (907) 772-2502
Finding the campground: From the ferry terminal in Petersburg, drive south on the Mitkof Highway for 9.5 miles (to mile 10.5); the campground is on your left.
About the campground: It probably won't be surprising that this small campground is nestled in a thick grove of trees just off the highway. The classic old-growth forest of the southeast lends a lot of beauty to this small loop of tiny back-in sites. There may be little privacy, with your neighbors close by and the road just across the way, but the forested grounds still maintain a cozy mountain feel. A small general store and coffee shop on site carries basic toiletries and groceries.

253 Ohmer Creek Campground

See map on page 209

Location: Near mile 21 of the Mitkof Highway
GPS: N 56° 34.692' / W 132° 44.508'

Ohmer Creek offers lush wooded sites

Season: May through November
Sites: 11 basic sites
Maximum length: 35 feet
Facilities: Tables, fire pits, potable water, vault toilets, hiking/fishing/river access
Fee per night: Free
Maximum stay: 14 days
Management: USDA Forest Service, Tongass National Forest, Petersburg Ranger Distinct, (907) 772-3871, www.fs.fed.us/r10/tongass
Finding the campground: From the ferry terminal in Petersburg, head south on the Mitkof Highway for 21 miles (the road becomes gravel after milepost 17) to the campground on your right.
About the campground: You'll know you're in a temperate rain forest when you visit the Ohmer Creek Campground. The lush grounds are home to memorable old-growth trees dripping in moss and wet mushrooms. A boardwalk trail wanders through the enchanting forest. There are small and large sites with nice tables and fire pits. A few are along the creek, but due to the thickness of the brush you'd never know the water was there. Camping here is a bargain from May through September and free the rest of the year. The campground is hosted during the high months and well maintained. Toward fall campers may thin out, but fishing for salmon has just begun.

Sitka

Sitka	Hookup Sites	Total Sites	Max. RV Length	Hookups	Toilets	Showers	Drinking Water	Fires	Dump Station	Recreation	Fee	Reservations
254 Starrigavan Bay Campground	0	33	35	N	NF	N	Y	Y	N	HF	$$	Y
255 Sitka Sportsman's Association RV Park	16	16	Any	WES	F	Y	Y	N	Y	N	$$$$	Y
256 Sealing Cove RV Parking	26	26	Any	WE	F	N	Y	N	Y	N	$$$	N
257 Sawmill Creek Campground	0	11	Any	N	NF	N	N	Y	N	H	Free	N

254 Starrigavan Bay Campground

See map on page 209

Location: Near mile 7 of Halibut Point Road
GPS: N 57° 7.967' / W 135° 22.002'
Season: Year-round
Sites: 19 basic sites, 14 walk-in tent sites
Maximum length: 35 feet
Facilities: Tables, fire pits, covered picnic area, potable water, vault toilets, hiking/beach/fishing access
Fee per night: $$
Maximum stay: 14 days
Management: USDA Forest Service, Tongass National Forest, Sitka Ranger District, (907) 747-6671, www.fs.fed.us/r10/tongass; reservations at (877) 444-6777, www.recreation.gov
Finding the campground: From downtown Sitka, head north on Halibut Point Road for 7.1 miles to the campground on your left, 0.5 mile past the ferry terminal.
About the campground: With the trails alone you could spend a good day exploring the area around this campground. On site there are boardwalks leading to wildlife- and salmon-viewing decks, as well as the nearby Old Sitka State Historical Site. Camping is divided into three loops: two drive-in and one backpacker. These are recently remodeled campsites that are well spaced and well developed. The backpacker loop has particularly nice hike-in sites, thanks to both the seclusion and the hilltop location. They have all the same facilities as drive-in sites with spacious pads, new vault toilets, and potable water. Backpackers may also be pleased to find a large communal covered cooking area. No parking is provided for these campsites. Three more secluded hike-in campsites located off the Bayside Loop include one parking space each and overlook Starrigavan Bay.

The drive-in sites are large with deep back-ins. All sites have mountain views and plenty of foliage and trees. The Estuary Loop has more basic sites as well as a nice easy-grade hiking trail for a closer peek at the forest. To maintain the quiet camping atmosphere of this forest campground, the gates are locked between 10 p.m. and 7 a.m. from Labor Day through September 15. Be sure to arrive within the proper time frame. Camping is a bit more expensive at these grounds, and fees continue year-round. Fees for basic sites go down from September 15 through April 1, and continue at a fair cost year-round for walk-in sites.

255 Sitka Sportsman's Association RV Park

See map on page 209

Location: Near mile 6 of Halibut Point Road
GPS: N 57° 07.621' / W 135° 22.952'
Season: Year-round
Sites: 8 full hook-up RV sites, 8 partial hook-up RV sites
Maximum length: Any
Facilities: Some tables, potable water, flush toilets, showers, dump station
Fee per night: $$$$
Maximum stay: None
Management: Sitka Sportsman's Association, (907) 623-7740, www.rvsitka.com
Finding the campground: You'll find this camping area a little over a block from the ferry terminal. As you exit the ferry, turn right onto Halibut Point Road; the park is on your right. From downtown Sitka, head north on Halibut Point Road for 6.3 miles to the campground on your left.
About the campground: A hop and skip away from the ferry, this campground has room for RVs in sixteen side-by-side spaces in an open gravel lot. Half of the spaces have full hookups, and the others include water and electric. Although the grounds are very basic, there is a city-style building with a block of restrooms and showers. As with most places in Sitka, you'll find great views of the water and mountains.

256 Sealing Cove RV Parking

See map on page 209

Location: In Sitka
GPS: N 57° 02.943' / W 135° 20.909'
Season: April through October
Sites: 26 partial-hookup RV sites
Maximum length: Any
Facilities: Potable water, flush toilets
Fee per night: $$$
Maximum stay: 30 days

Management: City and Borough of Sitka, (907) 747-3439, www.cityofsitka.com

Finding the campground: From the intersection of Lake Street and Sawmill Creek Road in Sitka, follow the signs to Japonski Island south down Lake Street. Pass over the bridge to the overnight parking area on the left side of the road for a total of 0.9 mile. The paved parking lot is a bit hard to identify. Look for it on your immediate left as you cross the bridge. There aren't a lot of signs.

About the campground: This harborside parking area is located outside of downtown at the base of O'Connell Bridge on Japonski Island. The "RV park" is little more than a paved parking area with water and electric hookups and wide-open views of Sealing Cove. Sites are paved side-by-side stalls with rules against additions or extensions on your RV. Essentially this a parking lot without services aside from a block of flush toilets and one table under a covered picnic area. A dump station is available for campers free of charge at the wastewater treatment facility a few blocks away on Kruzov Avenue.

257 Sawmill Creek Campground

See map on page 209

Location: Near mile 5 of Sawmill Creek Road
GPS: N 57° 03.718' / W 135° 12.570'
Season: April through December
Sites: 11 basic sites
Maximum length: Any
Facilities: Tables, fire pits, pit toilets, hiking/fishing/creek access
Fee per night: Free
Maximum stay: 14 days
Management: USDA Forest Service, Tongass National Forest, Sitka Ranger District, (907) 747-6671, www.fs.fed.us/r10/tongass

Finding the campground: This campground is about 9 miles southeast of town. From the ferry terminal, head south on Halibut Point Road for 7.1 miles to town, then turn south onto Sawmill Creek Road. Drive 8 miles and turn left onto Blue Lake Road. A sign notes that this road "is not maintained for passenger cars," though the gravel is in fairly good condition. Drive 1.4 miles up the road and turn right at the sign for the campground. This road is not maintained for RVs.

About the campground: Down a bumpy road, this rustic campground has basic sites and primitive facilities, but the price is right. Campsites are small and loosely maintained with rickety tables and older fire pits. Sawmill Creek might lack the brand-new facilities of Starrigavan, but it also lacks the traffic. The camping area is rather quiet and has good vistas of rugged surrounding peaks. At this site you'll have to pack in your own firewood and water, and pack out your own garbage. A short trail leading over a small footbridge is a 2.5-mile loop popular with local hikers and families.

Juneau

Juneau	Hookup Sites	Total Sites	Max. RV Length	Hookups	Toilets	Showers	Drinking Water	Fires	Dump Station	Recreation	Fee	Reservations
258 Eagle Beach State Recreation Area	0	16+	Any	N	NF	N	Y	Y	N	HF	$$	N
259 Auke Village Recreation Area	0	11	25	N	NF	N	Y	Y	N	HF	$	N
260 Auke Bay RV Park	31	31	45	WES	F	Y	Y	N	Y	N	$$-$$$$	Y
261 Glacier Nalu Campground Resort	47	57	40	WESC	F	Y	Y	N	Y	N	$$-$$$$	Y
262 Mendenhall Campground	18	76	45	WES	F	Y	Y	Y	Y	H	$-$$$	Y

258 Eagle Beach State Recreation Area

See map on page 209

Location: Near mile 27 of the Glacier Highway
GPS: N 58° 31.672' / W 134° 48.916'
Season: Mid-May through late September
Sites: 16 basic sites, open RV camping
Maximum length: Any
Facilities: Picnic area, fire pits, potable water, vault toilets, hiking/beach/fishing/river access
Fee per night: $$
Maximum stay: 15 days
Management: Alaska State Parks, Southeast Area Office, (907) 465-4563, www.dnr.state.ak .us/parks
Finding the campground: From the ferry terminal, turn left (west) onto the Glacier Highway and drive 14 miles to the campground on your left (mile 27.6).
About the campground: These primitive sites are almost 30 miles from downtown Juneau, and half that from the ferry terminal. The grounds overlook Lynn Canal and the surrounding ranges and are less popular with tourists; they host more day-hiking traffic than overnight visitors. Camping includes sixteen wooded sites designed with tenters in mind. These are primitive clearings with fire pits. A large open gravel area allows overnight parking for RVs, but this lot does not have specified camp spaces, fire pits, or tables.

259 Auke Village Recreation Area

See map on page 209

Location: Near mile 14 of the Glacier Highway
GPS: N 58° 22.542' / W 134° 43.712'
Season: Mid-May through late September
Sites: 11 basic sites
Maximum length: 25 feet
Facilities: Tables, fire pits, potable water, vault toilets, hiking/fishing/beach access
Fee per night: $
Maximum stay: 14 days
Management: Forest Service, Tongass National Forest, Juneau Ranger District, (907) 586-8800, www.fs.fed.us/r10/tongass
Finding the campground: From the ferry terminal, turn left (west) onto the Glacier Highway and drive 1 mile to the campground entrance on your left (mile 14.7).
About the campground: This campground was recently revamped and now hosts eleven well-developed and leveled basic campsites. The sites are large and lush under towering coastal trees. Each has a table and fire pit, and many boast excellent views. On weekends and any sunny summer evening, the day use at this campground can get heavy. Most people are out enjoying the surplus of trails in the area as well as the desirable hike-in picnic shelters along the beachfront of Auke Bay.

260 Auke Bay RV Park

See map on page 209

Location: Near mile 12 of the Glacier Highway
GPS: N 58° 23.255' / W 134° 39.044'
Season: May through September
Sites: 23 full-hookup RV sites, 8 partial-hookup RV sites
Maximum length: 45 feet
Facilities: Some tables, potable water, flush toilets, showers, dump station, laundry
Fee per night: $$–$$$$
Maximum stay: None
Management: Auke Bay RV Park, (907) 789-9467
Finding the campground: From the ferry terminal, turn right (east) onto the Glacier Highway and drive 1.4 miles to the campground on your left (mile 12.4).
About the campground: This RV park has two small lots of spaces mostly occupied by permanent residents. Set aside are about thirty back-in sites for campers. Most of the sites have full hookups. The proximity to the ferry can't be beat, but this plain camping area has a hard time standing up to some of the beauties around Juneau.

261 Glacier Nalu Campground Resort

See map on page 209

Location: In Juneau
GPS: N 58° 24.208' / W 134° 36.261'
Season: Year-round
Sites: 47 full-hookup RV sites, 10 tent sites
Maximum length: 40 feet
Facilities: Some tables, communal tables and fire pit, covered picnic area, potable water, flush toilets, showers, dump station, laundry, WiFi
Fee per night: $$–$$$$
Maximum stay: 21 days
Management: Glacier Nalu Campground Resort, (907) 789-1990, www.glaciernalu.com
Finding the campground: From the ferry terminal, turn right (east) onto the Glacier Highway and drive 1.7 miles. Turn left onto Mendenhall Loop Road. The campground is on your left after 2.2 miles.
About the campground: Suitably located in a grove of mature spruce, this charming spot isn't far from Mendenhall Glacier and the ferry terminal. The full-service RV park includes tent sites and is near a bus stop, convenient for backpackers if the government campground is full. The large forested sites and groomed grounds—combined with up-to-date and sparkling-clean facilities—make this RV park popular. Reservations are highly recommended. The RV sites are large back-ins off a wide gravel loop. A soft earthen tent area is available along a footpath. The tent sites do not have tables or fire pits, but there is a communal picnic area.

262 Mendenhall Campground

See map on page 209

Location: Near mile 12 of the Glacier Highway
GPS: N 58° 24.747' / W 134° 35.468'
Season: Mid-May through mid-September
Sites: 9 full-hookup RV sites, 9 partial-hookup RV sites, 51 basic sites, 7 tent sites
Maximum length: 45 feet
Facilities: Tables, fire pits, potable water, flush and vault toilets, showers, dump station, hiking access
Fee per night: $–$$$
Maximum stay: 14 days
Management: USDA Forest Service, Tongass National Forest, Juneau Ranger District, (907) 586-8800, www.fs.fed.us/r10/tongass; reservations at (877) 444-6777, www.recreation.gov
Finding the campground: From the ferry terminal, turn right (east) onto the Glacier Highway and drive 1.7 miles. Turn left onto Mendenhall Loop Road, continue for 2.5 miles, and turn left onto

A cruise ship docks up in Juneau.

Montana Creek. Drive 0.7 mile to the campground on your left. It's adjacent to the Forest Service visitor center, a highly recommended stop with interactive exhibits.

About the campground: Overlooking Mendenhall Lake and Glacier, this four-star government campground is worth visiting for the views alone. Receding from an icefield high above Juneau, Mendenhall Glacier melts slowly into the small lake at the campground center. Noted by John Muir as "one of the most beautiful of all coastal glaciers," Mendenhall is a must-see on your trip in southeastern Alaska.

The camping area is sprawled between small ponds in a mature forest. The large and well-developed campsites are located in the moist mossy woods. Some have views of the lake and the brilliant blue glacier. Most sites are gravel back-ins with wooden tent pads to keep campers off the soggy soils. Many sites are wheelchair-accessible. Set farther back from the lake, a few large pull-thrus with hookups could fit long rigs. Enhancing the comfort of this lovely campground, hookups are offered for RVs, and hot showers are available in the clean restroom buildings. Despite all the services and crisp facilities, this campground does not lose its wilderness charm. A trip to Juneau would not be complete without a meander around one of Alaska's king campgrounds.

Skagway

Skagway	Hookup Sites	Total Sites	Max. RV Length	Hookups	Toilets	Showers	Drinking Water	Fires	Dump Station	Recreation	Fee	Reservations
263 Pullen Creek RV Park	46	51	Any	WE	F	Y	Y	Y	Y	N	$$$–$$$$	Y
264 Garden City RV Park	86	91	Any	WESC	F	Y	Y	N	Y	N	$$$$	Y
265 Dyea Campground	0	22	25	N	NF	N	N	Y	N	H	$	N

263 Pullen Creek RV Park

See map on page 235

Location: In Skagway
GPS: N 59° 27.082' / W 135° 18.969'

Camping is free on the decks of the solarium on the Alaska Marine Highway.

Season: May through September
Sites: 46 partial-hookup RV sites, 5 walk-in tent sites
Maximum length: Any
Facilities: Some tables and fire pits, potable water, flush toilets, showers, dump station
Fee per night: $$$–$$$$
Maximum stay: None
Management: Pullen Creek RV Park, (907) 983-2768, www.skagwayrvparks.com
Finding the campground: This campground is literally right around the corner from the ferry. Exit the ferry and turn right (east) onto 2nd Street. Follow 2nd as it goes over the train tracks; the park is on your right.
About the campground: The humorous decor of this homespun campground includes an empty toilet and golf cart in the gazebo, and a few more restroom lawn ornaments. The grounds are one of the few places to park an RV in town, but there isn't a whole lot of room. There are forty-six partial-hookup RV sites with water and electric, or electric only, and a few walk-in tent sites. A string of narrow RV sites lines the waterfront. You can walk to most shops from here.

264 Garden City RV Park

See map on page 235

Location: In Skagway
GPS: N 59° 27.710' / W 135° 18.345'
Season: May through September
Sites: 86 full-hookup RV sites, 5 tent sites
Maximum length: Any
Facilities: Potable water, flush toilets, showers, dump station, laundry, WiFi, gift shop
Fee per night: $$$$
Maximum stay: None
Management: Garden City RV Park, (907) 983-2378, (844) 983-2378, www.skagwayrvparks.com
Finding the campground: From the ferry terminal, head left for 1 block over to State Street. Drive 15 blocks to the campground on the corner of State Street and 15th Avenue.
About the campground: In the center of downtown, this large RV park is popular and fills throughout the summer. The up-to-date grounds have very clean facilities. Campsites are in an open lot with plenty of pull-thrus. There isn't much for greenery, but some grass breaks up the lot.

265 Dyea Campground

See map on page 235

Location: Mile 6.5 of Dyea Road
GPS: N 59° 30.330' / W 135° 20.897'
Season: May through late September

Sites: 22 basic sites
Maximum length: 25 feet
Facilities: Tables, picnic area, fire pits, vault toilets, hiking access
Fee per night: $
Maximum stay: 14 days
Management: Klondike Goldrush National and Historic Park, (907) 983-2921, www.nps.gov/klgo
Finding the campground: This campground is about 10 miles west of Skagway. To get there from downtown Skagway, follow State Street as it becomes the south Klondike Highway. At mile 2.3 turn west onto Dyea Road. Drive 6.5 miles to campground on your left. The road out to Dyea is not recommended for large RVs. The campground itself may hold larger rigs, but the road is probably best suited for those 25 feet or under.

About the campground: If you're visiting Skagway and have some time to tour, a trip out to the backwoods of Dyea Road is a great choice. This campground is located within the Klondike Goldrush National and Historic Park near the original townsite of the short-lived gold-rush boomtown of Dyea, an excellent historical stop to brush up on your Klondike history. The camping area is primitive with wooded sites located off a bumpy earthen road. With only a small fee per night, camping is a bargain. Backpackers should feel right at home here. Just don't forget to bring your water purifier or to haul some water in. Same goes for firewood. If you're stopping by for a scenic drive, there are some wonderful riverfront picnic sites on the banks of the Taiya River. The tables may be a bit rusty, but the scenery is fantastic. The campground is a short walk from the Chilkoot Trailhead, the beginning of the historic trail that once was traversed by stampeders all the way to the Yukon.

Haines and the Haines Highway

Haines and the Haines Highway

	Hookup Sites	Total Sites	Max. RV Length	Hookups	Toilets	Showers	Drinking Water	Fires	Dump Station	Recreation	Fee	Reservations
266 Chilkoot Lake State Recreation Site	0	34	Any	N	NF	N	Y	Y	N	FBL	$$	N
267 Salmon Run Campground and Cabins	0	25	50	N	F	Y	Y	Y	N	N	$$	Y
268 Chilkat State Park	0	32	30	N	NF	N	Y	Y	N	HFBL	$$	N
269 Haines Hitch-up RV Park	92	92	Any	WESC	F	Y	Y	N	Y	N	$$$$–$$$$$	Y
270 Oceanside RV Park	23	30	45	WESC	F	Y	Y	Y	N	N	$$$–$$$$	Y
271 Portage Cove State Recreation Site	0	8	T	N	NF	N	Y	Y	N	N	$	N
272 Mosquito Lake State Recreation Site	0	5	20	N	NF	N	N	Y	N	FBL	$	N

266 Chilkoot Lake State Recreation Site

Location: Near Haines
GPS: N 59° 20.168' / W 135° 33.748'
Season: June through mid-October
Sites: 34 basic sites
Maximum length: Any
Facilities: Tables, covered picnic area, fire pits, potable water, vault toilets, boat launch, fishing/lake access
Fee per night: $$
Maximum stay: 7 days
Management: Alaska State Parks, Haines Ranger Station, (907) 766-2292, www.dnr.state.ak.us/parks
Finding the campground: From Main Street in downtown Haines, head north on 2nd Street for 0.2 mile, then turn right onto Lutak Road. Drive 8.8 miles along the windy waterfront and turn left at the sign. Continue on the paved road for 1 mile to dead-end at the campground.
About the campground: This stunning all-Alaskan campground is on the edge of beautiful Chilkoot Lake and surrounded by steep mountains. Seaplanes often land here, and local families pop out of the cabins with camping gear in hand. Kayaking classes meet at the campground while fishermen cast lines into the lake. There may be a lot of activity, but it is a tranquil crowd. Chilkoot River teems with salmon, and the fish pass near the campground entrance is a great area for spotting grizzlies. The camping area is located on a ridge beside the lake. The large sites are under

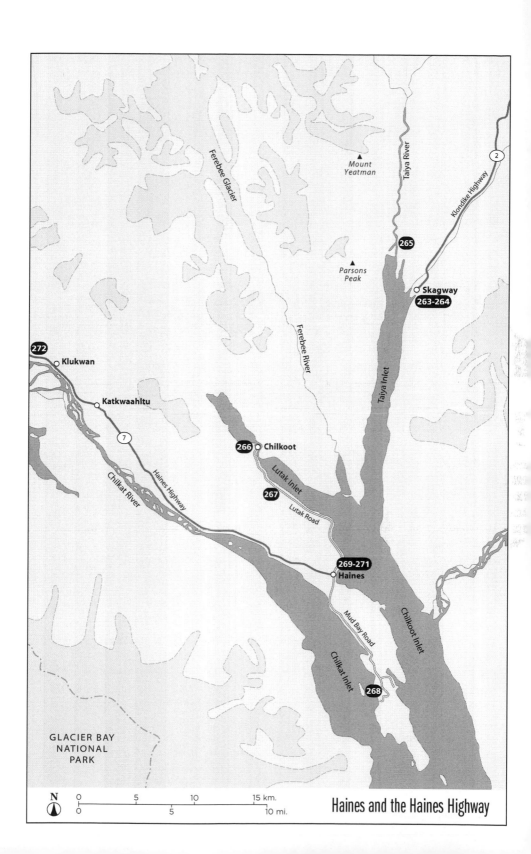

old-growth spruce off a wide connecting road. Each has a table and fire pit, and on rainy days you can take advantage of the covered day-use picnic areas.

267　Salmon Run Campground and Cabins

Location: Near Haines
GPS: N 59° 17.952' / W 135° 30.963'
Season: May through mid-October
Sites: 25 basic sites
Maximum length: 50 feet
Facilities: Some tables and fire pits, flush toilets, potable water, showers
Fee per night: $$$-$$$$
Maximum stay: None
Management: Salmon Run Campground and Cabins, (907) 766-3240, www.salmonrunrv campground.com
Finding the campground: From Haines, head north on Front Street and turn right onto Lutak Road. Drive 7 miles to the campground on your left (just 2.1 miles past the ferry terminal).
About the campground: This is an excellent campground if you're looking to get out of town but still enjoy a bit of comfort. The campsites are located on a ridge above the highway with a bird's-eye view of Lutak Inlet and the surrounding peaks. You can take advantage of these sites if you'd like a gorgeous backdrop and a basic open side-by-side space is sufficient. Farther up the hill, back-in sites are located in a stand of tall spruce. The facilities are fairly minimal, with some tables and fire pits as well as showers. The campground also has a private beach across the road for guests.

268　Chilkat State Park

Location: 7 miles south of Haines
GPS: N 59° 08.395' / W 135° 22.209'
Season: Mid-May through mid-September
Sites: 29 basic sites, 3 tent sites
Maximum length: 30 feet
Facilities: Tables, picnic area, fire pits, potable water, vault toilets, boat launch, hiking/fishing/lake access
Fee per night: $$
Maximum stay:
Management: Alaska State Parks, Haines Ranger Station, (907) 766-2292, www.dnr.state.ak .us/parks
Finding the campground: From the Haines Highway at the southern end of Haines, turn south onto Mud Bay Road. Follow the road as it makes frequent turns, driving a total of 6.6 miles. Turn right at the sign for the park; the campground is 1.5 miles down the road.

About the campground: "Haines is for hikers," the saying goes, and with its excellent hiking and camping Chilkat State Park justifies it. Dotted through an evergreen forest, these basic sites are located off a gravel loop on the edge of the Chilkat Inlet. Most sites don't overlook the water, but a small patch of walk-in tent sites do. As you head down the hill, look for the tent camping sign, easy to miss just before boat launch. From there a short walk leads to three magnificent sites, perfect for those looking to be away from the bustle of the car-camping loop. These beauties are under towering trees and thick foliage. Watch out for the pesky plant known as devil's club; it's easily masked by other green bushes, and its festering thorns are a real annoyance. Several trails lead from the area, including two pleasant and easy walks along the beach. On site you can also stop by the visitor center, which has stunning views of Rainbow and Davidson Glaciers and free spotting scopes.

269 Haines Hitch-up RV Park

Location: In Haines
GPS: N 59° 14.134' / W 135° 27.579'
Season: Mid-May through mid-September
Sites: 92 full-hookup RV sites
Maximum length: Any
Facilities: Tables, potable water, flush toilets, showers, dump station, laundry, WiFi, gift shop
Fee per night: $$$$–$$$$$
Maximum stay: None
Management: Haines Hitch-up RV Park, (907) 766-2882, www.hitchuprv.com
Finding the campground: You'll find Haines Hitch-up RV Park on the south side of Main Street just east of the junction with Haines Highway.
About the campground: This is probably the best-kept campground in Haines. This park is blanketed in clean-cut grass with groomed edges. Campsites are a combination of back-ins and pull-thrus directly on the flawless lawn. The facilities are all polished to the max. Unmetered showers are included with the cost of camping for two people. Note that the grounds are highly regulated, with restrictions on just about everything—probably why everything looks so perfect.

270 Oceanside RV Park

Location: In Haines
GPS: N 59° 14.113' / W 135° 26.524'
Season: Year-round
Sites: 23 full-hookup RV sites, 7 tent sites
Maximum length: 45 feet
Facilities: Some tables and fire pits, picnic area with tables and fire pit, barbecue, potable water, flush toilets, shower, laundry, WiFi, gift shop
Fee per night: $$$–$$$$
Maximum stay: 30 days
Management: Oceanside RV Park, (907) 766-2437, www.oceansiderv.com

The Chilkoot Lake State Recreation Site.

Finding the campground: This campground lies along the waterfront at the edge of downtown Haines. From Haines, drive east on Main Street until it dead-ends into Front Street. Turn left onto Front Street; the park is on your immediate right.

About the campground: Almost everyone has an ocean view at this RV park. You really can't get closer to the water's edge in Haines than the Oceanside—in fact, you'll want to be careful when you back that big rig in! Seven tent sites, along with a string of RV sites, nose up to the shore. The park has great proximity to both town and the harbor, so it is no surprise that it fills regularly. Many walk straight to a fishing charter, sea excursion, museum, or the downtown shops a block away.

271 Portage Cove State Recreation Site

Location: In Haines
GPS: N 59° 13.574' / W 135° 25.549'
Season: Early May through mid-September
Sites: 9 tent sites
Maximum length: N/A
Facilities: Tables, fire pits, potable water, vault toilets
Fee per night: $
Maximum stay: 7 days

Management: Alaska State Parks, Haines Ranger Station, (907) 766-2292, www.dnr.state.ak .us/parks

Finding the campground: To reach this campground from downtown Haines, head east until you hit the waterfront, then turn right onto Front Street/Beach Road. Follow this street for 2 miles to the Portage Cove State Recreation Site on your left, just past the Port Chilkoot Docks.

About the campground: These eight walk-in tent sites are located on a knoll overlooking the inlet a couple of miles from downtown. Follow the wooden steps down to a large open grassy pad. The sites are not identified by spaces or numbers; access to fire pits and tables is shared. It rains a lot in Haines, and there's nothing to secure a tarp with here. This campground is limited to hikers and cyclists, with no motorists allowed.

272 Mosquito Lake State Recreation Site

Location: Near mile 27 of the Haines Highway
GPS: N 59° 27.250' / W 136° 01.687'
Season: May through late September
Sites: 5 basic sites

Mosquito Lake.

Maximum length: 20 feet
Facilities: Tables, fire pits, pit toilets, fishing/lake access, boat launch
Fee per night: $
Maximum stay: 7 days
Management: Alaska State Parks, Haines Ranger Station, (907) 766-2292, www.dnr.state.ak
.us/parks
Finding the campground: From mile 27 of the Haines Highway, turn north onto Mosquito Lake
Road. Follow the very small signs down the gravel road for 2.2 miles and veer right at the fork.
Continue 0.3 mile beyond the fork to a narrow gravel road on your right that leads down to the
campground. The signs are very poor here, and this last turn is hard to see. Drive slowly and watch
your odometer.
About the campground: Seaplanes dock at the petite shore of this campground. The camping
area is very primitive—just a few clearings and fire pits and tables along a tiny narrow dirt road.
With the exception of the very first site, there is limited space here, and the grounds are best
suited for tents. If you're going to bring any RV or camper in here, it's wise to walk in first and
check out the maneuverability. This is a good place for seclusion; the trade-off is less developed
grounds and older toilet facilities.

Kodiak Island
and the Bush

Most remote camping in Alaska is reached by plane or boat, and it doesn't involve developed campsites. In a state where roads access only a small portion of the public land, many campers venture off to explore "the bush." In these remote areas there are very few established trails, creating opportunities for backcountry travelers and backpackers. However, there are a few places on Alaska's edges that offer both a trip out of the ordinary and established campgrounds accessible via local roads.

One such area is Kodiak Island. Known as Alaska's Emerald Isle for its brilliantly green peaks, Kodiak is the largest island in the state and second in the nation only to Hawaii's Big Island. The seaside port also has a gorgeous waterfront, an attractive town with fun people, good coffee shops, and some of the best camping around.

Access to Kodiak is becoming increasingly easier and less expensive. The island is on the Alaska Marine Highway system. You can pick up the ferry from Homer at the southern tip of the Kenai Peninsula. A fast ship will get you there in around ten hours. You can pitch your tent on the ferry deck for free if you sail on an overnight. Others will choose to take a more expensive plane ride to the island. Even though increasing numbers of tourists visit each year, Kodiak is a hardworking fishing town with one of the most productive ports in Alaska.

You won't find any RV parks or private campgrounds on Kodiak Island. But you will find three natural campgrounds run by Alaska State Parks. They are located between 4 and 50 miles out of town in various directions. Of the trio, Fort Abercrombie has the most breathtaking views and handsome trees. Buskin River is known for unparalleled roadside fishing and small, accommodating sites. Pasagshak is the remote and primitive seaside beauty where buffalo are known to roam the shores.

From one of the southernmost locations to one of the northernmost, Nome, Alaska, also has an established campground for its visitors. Located on the south side of the Seward Peninsula, Nome was once the Wild West of the Arctic, where thousands of gold prospectors in the early 1900s flocked to pan the rich sands of the beach. Nome is a friendly town to tour. The Iditarod Trail Sled Dog Race ends here in March, and at that time the city caters to a mass of tourists. You'll find that these people know their business. Nome is a terrific place to experience the Arctic and

Camping on the deck of the Kodiak Ferry

the bush. Just bring lots of layers and a good-time attitude for this boomtown. The Bureau of Land Management runs one very nice campground 40 miles east of Nome along beautiful Salmon Lake. Renting a car may be a challenge since there are limited vehicles in the area, so make reservations ahead of time.

Kodiak Island

Kodiak Island

	Hookup Sites	Total Sites	Max. RV Length	Hookups	Toilets	Showers	Drinking Water	Fires	Dump Station	Recreation	Fee	Reservations
273 Fort Ambercrombie State Historical Park	0	13	35	N	NF	N	Y	Y	N	H	$$	N
274 Buskin River State Recreation Site	0	15	35	N	NF	N	Y	Y	N	HF	$$	N
275 Pasagshak River State Recreation Site	0	12	40	N	NF	N	Y	Y	N	F	$$	N

273 Fort Ambercrombie State Historical Park

Location: Near Kodiak
GPS: N 57° 50.073' / W 152° 21.393'
Season: May through October
Sites: 13 basic sites
Maximum length: 35 feet
Facilities: Tables, fire pits, potable water, vault toilets, hiking access, museum
Fee per night: $$
Maximum stay: 7 days
Management: Alaska State Parks, Kodiak Area Office, (907) 486-6339, www.dnr.state.ak .us/parks
Finding the campground: From downtown Kodiak, head west on Center Street and turn right onto Rezanof–Monashka Bay Road. Go 3.6 miles and make a right at the sign for Fort Ambercrombie State Historical Park. Drive 0.2 mile to the campground on your right.
About the campground: This beautiful campground has the best location on Kodiak Island. The camping area sits high on a coastal bluff in a grove of gigantic old-growth spruce. The spacious campsites are scattered through the ruins of a World War II installation. You can climb around the bunkers and visit the Military History Museum. Each earthen campsite has a table, a fire pit, and plenty of room for tents on soft pine-needle beds. There are two loops of spacious shady back-in sites along with an open area for RV overflow. Keep an eye and an ear out for whales below. If you're lucky enough to stay here on a Saturday night, don't miss the ranger programs.

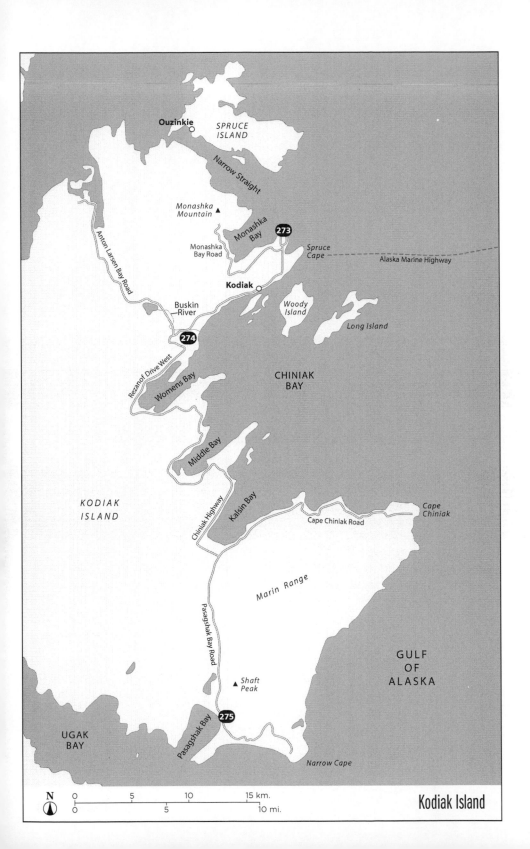

Kodiak Island

274 Buskin River State Recreation Site

Location: Near Kodiak
GPS: N 57° 45.372' / W 152° 29.876'
Season: May through October
Sites: 15 basic sites
Maximum length: 35 feet
Facilities: Tables, fire pits, covered picnic area, potable water, hiking/fishing/river/beach access
Fee per night: $$
Maximum stay: 14 days
Management: Alaska State Parks, Kodiak Area Office, (907) 486-6339, www.dnr.state.ak
.us/parks
Finding the campground: From downtown Kodiak, drive west on Center Street and turn left onto the Chiniak Highway. Go 4.1 miles and turn left at the sign for the park onto a gravel road. Drive 0.4 mile to the campground on your left.
About the campground: This huge 168-acre recreation site borders the Buskin River near the airport. Inside the park is the most popular sportfishery on the island. It's also the most accessible.

Kodiak Island brown bears.

The camping area has small sites located along two similar loops separated by high brush and a few trees. The basic sites have tables and fire pits; there's a covered picnic area. The campground is designed with tenters in mind, but small campers and RVs can swing a few sites. An open gravel RV overflow area is available for larger rigs.

275 Pasagshak River State Recreation Site

Location: 40 miles south of Kodiak
GPS: N 57° 27.498' / W 152° 26.990'
Season: Late May through October
Sites: 12 basic sites
Maximum length: 40 feet
Facilities: Some tables and fire pits, picnic area, potable water, vault toilets, fishing/beach access
Fee per night: $$
Maximum stay: 14 days
Management: Alaska State Parks, Kodiak Area Office, (907) 486-6339, www.dnr.state.ak
.us/parks
Finding the campground: Head west out of Kodiak on Rezanof Drive. Follow the road for 42.6 miles to its junction with Pasagshak Bay Road. Head south on Pasagshak Bay Road for 8.8 miles to the campground.
About the campground: Located at the mouth of Pasagshak River, this is a popular area for salmon fishing. It's also the most primitive campground on Kodiak Island. Camping is on the edge of the beach, with four-star bay views and smells of the sea. The area is listed by Alaska State Parks as having twelve basic sites, but they aren't well defined. Various walk-in campsites are scattered around the grounds and difficult to identify; a few are found near the host and along the shore where the river meets the bay. Some have fire pits and tables. RVs and campers can park in a small gravel lot next to the river. You can't beat the price of this campground—it's free. Buffalo are known to roam the area. If you're interested in exploring, a drive up the coast leads to a surfing beach (yes, surfing!) and one for hunting fossils.

Nome

Nome	Hookup Sites	Total Sites	Max. RV Length	Hookups	Toilets	Showers	Drinking Water	Fires	Dump Station	Recreation	Fee	Reservations
276 Salmon Lake Campground	0	6	30	N	NF	N	N	Y	N	F	Free	N

276 Salmon Lake Campground

Location: 40 miles north of Nome
GPS: N 64° 55.028' / W 164° 57.683'
Season: May through October
Sites: 6 basic sites

Nome traffic.

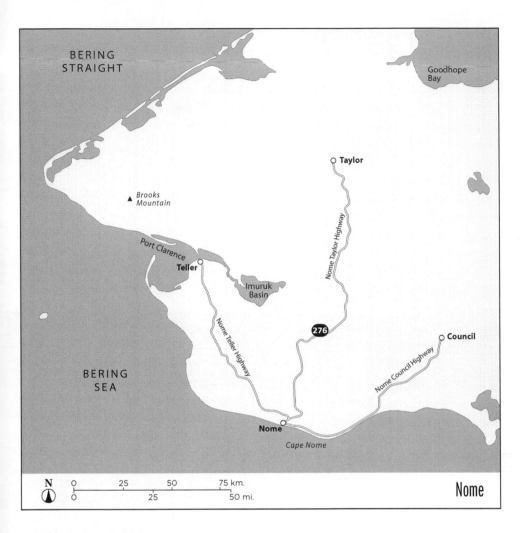

Maximum length: 30 feet

Facilities: Tables, picnic area, fire pits, pit toilet

Fee per night: Free

Maximum stay: 14 days

Management: Bureau of Land Management, Nome Field Station, (907) 443-2177, www.blm.gov/ak

Finding the campground: From Nome, head north on Nome Taylor Highway (also referred to as Beam Road and Taylor Road). Drive 40 miles down this pothole-ridden gravel road and turn right at the sign for the Salmon Lake Campground. Follow the narrow one-lane road for 0.7 mile to its dead end at the lakefront campground.

About the campground: This is the best place to camp in the Nome area and the only one with facilities. The catch is, you have to find a way to get there. This can be a problem since car rentals often cost more than a hotel in Nome, but if you're determined to see the wilds of Alaska's bush, a

Much of the Alaskan backcountry is accessed by plane.

drive out to Salmon Lake is worth it. A journey to Nome is not complete without a trip through the wind-whipped tundra, berry fields, and abandoned gold dredges of the area.

The Salmon Lake Campground is small and remote but very well maintained. There are six basic campsites neatly placed between high bushes beside the large lake. Each has a newer table and fire pit. There is one very clean pit toilet and bear-proof lockers. A couple of extra picnic tables and fire pits sit along the beach for day use. Keep in mind that this campground is sited in an area of sprawling open tundra; there's no place to collect firewood nearby. Your best bet is to collect driftwood along the beach before you head out here or purchase some in town. If you can't round up transport to this beautiful lake, you can explore Nome's other camping option—free camping on Golden Sands Beach. The beach tends to be extremely windy, with rough roaring waves and a high tide. Of course, this does not deter a few semi-permanent characters camped out along the shore waiting to strike it rich in Nome's golden gravels.

Index